Circular Narratives in Modern European Literature

Circular Narratives in Modern European Literature

Juan Luis Toribio Vazquez

BLOOMSBURY ACADEMIC
NEW YORK • LONDON • OXFORD • NEW DELHI • SYDNEY

BLOOMSBURY ACADEMIC
Bloomsbury Publishing Inc
1385 Broadway, New York, NY 10018, USA
50 Bedford Square, London, WC1B 3DP, UK
29 Earlsfort Terrace, Dublin 2, Ireland

BLOOMSBURY, BLOOMSBURY ACADEMIC and the Diana logo are trademarks of
Bloomsbury Publishing Plc

First published in the United States of America 2022
This paperback edition published 2024

Copyright © Juan Luis Toribio Vazquez, 2022

For legal purposes the Acknowledgements on p. x constitute an extension
of this copyright page.

Cover design by Eleanor Rose
Cover image © Getty Images

All rights reserved. No part of this publication may be reproduced or transmitted
in any form or by any means, electronic or mechanical, including photocopying,
recording, or any information storage or retrieval system, without prior
permission in writing from the publishers.

Bloomsbury Publishing Inc does not have any control over, or responsibility for, any third-party websites referred to or in this book. All internet addresses given in this book were correct at the time of going to press. The author and publisher regret any inconvenience caused if addresses have changed or sites have ceased to exist, but can accept no responsibility for any such changes.

Library of Congress Cataloging-in-Publication Data

ISBN: HB: 978-1-5013-8487-5
PB: 978-1-5013-8491-2
ePDF: 978-1-5013-8489-9
eBook: 978-1-5013-8488-2

Typeset by Deanta Global Publishing Services, Chennai, India

To find out more about our authors and books visit www.bloomsbury.com and
sign up for our newsletters.

Contents

Foreword   vi
Acknowledgements   x

1   Introduction: The genealogy of linearity   1
2   Nietzsche's bequest: Buddha's shadow and the 'greatest burden'   35
3   The birth of circularity: Strindberg, Stein and Azorín   75
4   '*Vivir es volver*': Queneau, Nabokov and Kharms   103
5   Circulus vitiosus litterae: Joyce, Borges and the Theatre of the Absurd   135
6   Circular echoes: Robbe-Grillet, Calvino, Cortázar and Blanchot   167
7   Conclusion: Circular narratives in modern European literature   203

References   215
Index   226

Foreword

At first glance, it might seem that the dominant model for thinking time, history and the life of the individual in Western cultures has long been a rectilinear one and that this model has become all the more pervasive since the European Enlightenment. For at the heart of the Enlightenment project lay the idea of progress, and more precisely of human progress, from barbarism to ever greater levels of civilization, from ignorance to an ever more comprehensive knowledge, reflected above all in the many remarkable advances of science and technology. According to this linear, and even teleological, way of thinking, humanity becomes ever more human, realizing its species potential, understanding increases, and technologies become ever more advanced, efficient and effective. To take just one example among many, it seems self-evident that modes of communication and transportation have improved in a more or less linear fashion over the past two centuries. From the letter to the telegraph to email and today's social media platforms, communications technologies have surely been on a linear track towards the ideal of almost instantaneous contact. Whereas one formerly had to wait days, weeks or even months for a letter to reach its destination, today one can communicate with others around the world with only a millisecond's delay. As for major advances in medical science, these have included antibiotics, anaesthetic, the eradication of certain diseases, effective treatments for many others and the significant lengthening of lifespans, at least in parts of the world. The development of a Covid-19 vaccine in a matter of months, rather than years, has been among the most recent examples of dramatic progress in medical science.

This linear model is reflected not only in conceptions of human history and science but also in the increasingly widespread idea of the self as something that can be improved, the primary aim of the individual becoming the realization of their potential. Many of us now tend to think of our lives in a linear way, as an accumulation of knowledge and experience, a process of maturation. Accordingly, one of the dominant metaphors for the life of the individual is that of the journey. And yet, as one of the founding works of Western literature, Homer's *Odyssey*, demonstrates, some of the most important and meaningful journeys can in fact be cyclical in nature. The story of Odysseus is a *nostos*, a return home.

The epic poem named after him charts the completion of a simultaneously linear and circular movement initiated when he joined the Achaean forces mustered to besiege Troy in order to return Helen to her husband and punish the Trojans for having harboured her and her lover, Paris. While much of the *Odyssey* focuses on what hinders Odysseus' return home, including the time he spends with Calypso and Circe, experiences that retard or even threaten the achievement of that movement, the overall trajectory of the narrative also remains distinctly circular. And of course, however inclined we might be to think of our lives in a linear fashion, we are likely to find ourselves at some point thinking of the lifecycle as precisely that, a circular movement that will return us to a form of infancy.

As Juan Luis Toribio Vazquez demonstrates with considerable skill, circular narratives can take many forms, and they also have a history. Indeed, while the long history of Western literature may have been dominated by linear narratives that have tended to endorse and even embody a teleological conception of history, civilization, society and the individual, particularly during the Christian era, the modern era, and more precisely the twentieth century, witnessed the remarkable emergence of various forms of circular narrative. Why should this have happened when it did, and what are we to make of it? Toribio Vazquez highlights the importance of Friedrich Nietzsche in this prevalence of circular narratives in the twentieth century and above all the philosopher's challenging of teleological and, as he maintained, essentially Christian thought. At the heart of Nietzsche's later philosophy is a championing of circularity in the form of eternal recurrence, as both a pre- and a post-Christian way of conceiving human experience. While commentators have long debated whether Nietzsche's idea of eternal recurrence was merely a thought experiment, designed to test our ability to overcome nihilism by embracing the endless repetition of the same or as a model for Being as such, the key point here is that the notion of circularity undoubtedly played a central role in his later thought, and impacted powerfully on thinkers and, perhaps above all, writers who wrote in his wake.

Nietzsche's influence on twentieth-century philosophy and culture more generally was profound, and this was reflected in no small part in a remarkable flourishing of circular narratives, in works by a wide range of writers across cultures and continents, including, as Toribio Vazquez reveals, household names such as James Joyce, Jorge Luis Borges and Vladimir Nabokov, alongside other less well-known writers such as José Martínez Ruiz, Daniil Kharms and Maurice Blanchot. While there were certainly other thinkers of circularity whose influence was evident in the twentieth century – not least that of the Italian philosopher Giambattista Vico on Joyce – it was Nietzsche's notion of eternal recurrence that exerted the greatest impact, often in subterranean ways.

What emerges from Toribio Vazquez's extended study, with its many close readings framed within a broader philosophical and literary-historical context, is that the literature of the twentieth century was marked by a flourishing of circular narratives that tells us a great deal about how thinkers during that period challenged the way in which human history and the life of the individual had long been thought. In some respects, this turn to models of circularity constituted a counter-Enlightenment move, insofar as its critique of teleological thinking included in its line of fire ideas of progress that were firmly rooted in the Enlightenment. As Toribio Vazquez acknowledges, it would be a mistake to put all of this down to Nietzsche's influence in any direct way, not least because that influence was bound up with profound historical currents, most notably two world wars and the Holocaust, as well as scientific insights into the origin of the universe and, in particular, the possibility that an expanding universe would one day start to contract, returning everything to its point of origin. Such events and insights inevitably led many to question any unproblematic idea of human progress and were the context in which ideas of nihilism became unavoidable.

It would also be a mistake to assume that circular narratives are always necessarily nihilistic or that they must in all cases suggest entrapment, failure or meaninglessness. Toribio Vazquez offers a persuasively nuanced typology of circular narratives in the modern period, and this helps to show that any simple conclusions as to their nature or meaning would be unduly limiting. Nietzsche's call for the embracing of the idea of eternal recurrence was, after all, an attempt to overcome nihilism rather than to submit to it. As the literary examples reveal, circular narratives can in fact be as liberating as they can be imprisoning. Circularity is no less viable a mode of being than linearity. Everything depends, as Nietzsche would be the first to insist, on the interpretation. Interpretations generally entail values, and to understand both the nature and the meaning of circular narratives in the twentieth century involves a reflection on the moral or ethical impact of those narratives. The matter is never purely abstract or conceptual. As that great early narratologist Aristotle observes, narrative impacts on our emotions as much as it does upon our cognitive faculties. It can teach us, often in complex ways, about what it means to be human and how we might best live our lives. The reader's experience of circular narratives may not always be an explicitly didactic one, but it is as likely to change the way in which we feel as that in which we think.

Having undertaken the first in-depth study of circular narratives in literature, Toribio Vazquez concludes his work by observing a movement away from such circularity in recent decades. He rightly observes that this should not be taken as any kind of proof that circular narratives will not themselves return, for literary history is certainly not characterized by any simple linear progression, having been marked by numerous recurrences – one need only think of the neo-classical or the neo-gothic. That said, it would seem that there was a particular historical moment, one that is now passing, in which such circular narratives played a particularly important role in literary composition. Those forms are themselves a key, if but one among others, to the understanding of that historical era when so many seeming certainties began to fall away, and Western culture had to face the chastening prospect that any reassuringly teleological sense of history, and indeed of humanity, was an illusion. If this insight found its first full articulation in philosophy, it was soon being expressed in literature, across cultures and languages. So it is that Toribio Vazquez's study has implications well beyond the aesthetic. For to think in a circular manner, or what Joyce in *Finnegans Wake* terms a 'commodious vicus of recirculation', is not only to challenge linear, teleological conceptions of history, society and the individual; it is also to offer an alternative, potentially enriching way of thinking experience and the world as such.

Shane Weller

Acknowledgements

I wish to thank Professor Shane Weller, for his encouragement and guidance throughout the entire project; Thirthankar Chakraborty, for his invaluable friendship and inspiring conversations during our time at the University of Kent; Ursula Paggetta, for her patience, kindness and reassurance in the early stages of this project; and, especially, Sofia Vazquez Navarrete, for her unconditional love and support.

1

Introduction
The genealogy of linearity

Despite their innumerable differences, most literary narratives have an underlying linear structure that comes to light either throughout the course of the story or at its resolution. Even many of those texts that do not follow a chronological sequence, or where the protagonists undertake a seemingly circular journey leading them back to the starting point, usually exhibit a core linear development that becomes apparent at the story's closing. Nevertheless, narrative itself (like time) is not inherently linear.[1] The historical predilection for this structural model is actually contingent on the way in which literature has traditionally been understood and conceptualized.

The reason for linearity's prevalence lies in the original conception of narrative as serving primarily a moral or didactic purpose, rather than an aesthetic one. The optimum structure for such an end is one where the entire text works (albeit subliminally) towards presenting a certain value, theme or teaching in a gradual, coherent and unified manner. The linear form thus became the paradigmatic structure of literary narratives, not because of its ostensible adherence to the natural sequence of language but because it is inherently *teleological*: it presents a situation that is either subverted or reaffirmed in the text's ending, endowing the entire sequence of events with a specific meaning. The pervasiveness of narrative linearity is therefore a direct result of the fact that literature has traditionally been understood as having a specific *telos*. Aristotle's definition of literature as *mimesis*, Kant's delineation of the concept into two types of 'arts of speech' (2007: 59)[2] or the Romantic equation of the literary art with a certain kind of personal

---

[1] Time was not always perceived as linear. Many ancient civilizations had a circular conception of time (see Chapter 2), and it is only with the rise of the Judaeo-Christian tradition that linear time becomes a prevalent conception in the West.

[2] The arts of speech are rhetoric and poetry. 'Rhetoric is the art of carrying on a serious business of the understanding as if it were a free play of the imagination; poetry, is the art of conducting a free play of the imagination as if it were serious business of the understanding' (Kant 2007: 59).

expression all reveal how deeply teleology is engraved in the understanding (and therefore also in the production) of literary narrative.

However, while linear narratives pervade most of Western literary history, be they in the form of monomyths,[3] Aristotelian three-part dramas or naturalist novels, throughout the course of the twentieth century an unprecedented process of formal experimentation led to the appearance of a range of alternatives to the linear model. This book will present one possible history of the developments of narrative, focusing on one alternative to linearity: circular forms. The central aim of the study will be to highlight the emergence of a tendency to adopt circular structures in the European literature of this time, in order to showcase and discuss the significance of this phenomenon. Although this 'trend' was neither a unified nor a conscious movement, but rather a series of works arising sporadically in different countries and times, the works in question all express similar concerns and ideas through the use of a variety of circular forms. Furthermore, this book will also show that the renewed understanding of narrative leading to the emergence of this circular trend was anticipated by Friedrich Nietzsche's critiques of truth, knowledge, language and metaphysics, and especially by his related discussions of nihilism and the idea of eternal recurrence.[4]

This is not to suggest that the authors considered in this study were necessarily influenced by Nietzsche's ideas, that this influence was either direct or conscious or even that they read his work (although most of them did), but that there is a clear connection between the kind of thinking motivating the use of circular narrative forms and his philosophy. The reason for focusing purely on Nietzsche's work as a potential catalyst for the kind of narrative structures analysed in this

---

[3] See Joseph Campbell's *The Hero of a Thousand Faces* (1949).
[4] Although *The Will to Power* (1901) is not, strictly speaking, one of Nietzsche's works at all, having been put together from his notes after his death, and while it will be *Thus Spoke Zarathustra* (1883), as well as the works leading to it, that will be considered in most detail when examining Nietzsche's discussion of these notions (since these texts already contain the essence of his thought and were among the most influential of his oeuvre, both to the general public and on the literature of the period under scrutiny), this book includes references to Walter Kaufmann's edition of *The Will to Power* (1968) rather than the *Nachlass* for the sake of convenience, since this text is far more readily available than the unpublished notes.
  It is also important to emphasize at this point that while Nietzsche was not the father of these notions (Schopenhauer, for instance, was his precursor in many respects), nor the only thinker engaged in reflecting upon these questions during this period, he stands as an iconic figure, the accepted founder of the discourse (as Michel Foucault would define it) on the concept of nihilism. Nietzsche was one of the first to examine this complex question in such detail and at the same time to render it in such a beautifully clear way. He is one of the most original, and certainly the most significant, thinker to foresee and analyse a concept that would shortly, after his death, become a central concern of Western society.

book, rather than on other late-nineteenth-century philosophers such as Henri Bergson,[5] is that Nietzsche's analysis of nihilism and its subsequent deliberations were particularly influential on the European literary scene of the twentieth century, perhaps owing to his poetic style. His announcement of an incipient crisis of values permeated all areas of artistic expression, haunting not only the European intelligentsia of the time but also the culture more widely. Yet, said catalyst might have also been violence and horror witnessed by the European continent during this time, owing to events such as (but not limited to) the Franco-Prussian conflict, the Russian Revolution, two world wars, Nazi and Soviet totalitarianism, and the Holocaust.

These events elicited a thorough questioning of the existing *Weltanschauung*, since the changes they brought about rendered many of its core values and assumptions senseless. It is this context alone that made the ideas that Nietzsche articulated in the 1880s particularly relevant, especially his conception of nihilism. Consequently, this book will not simply argue in favour of a direct line of influence between Nietzsche and the authors of the literary works to be examined. While the emphasis placed upon discussing this relationship might suggest an oversimplification of this impact, seemingly converted into a question of sources and direct influence, it is important to underscore from the outset that this is clearly not the case, and other factors (historical, political and social, as well as philosophical) are unquestionably determinative of the emergence of the 'circular trend'. That said, irrespective of whether Nietzsche's work was indeed key in prompting certain writers to employ circular narrative structures, the literary texts considered in this book warrant a reading from within the framework of his philosophy, since such a reading brings to light the significance implicit in these experimental forms of narrative configuration.

The impact of Nietzsche's thought in the twentieth century is no great mystery, and both critical and literary works that attempt to come to terms with his thinking of nihilism are plentiful. However, even in a field that might seem somewhat oversaturated, not all the effects of this impact have been accounted for. It is remarkable to note that Nietzsche's disquieting analysis of nihilism and his shattering idea of eternal return are perceptible in a wide array of literary works and not merely as thematic motifs (a topic that has been amply discussed by literary

---

[5] Bergson argued for a more ramified model of time, which Gilles Deleuze would eventually build on with his notion of rhizomes.

scholars) but, crucially, as a structuring principle. Indeed, the idea of eternal return has arguably had its greatest impact in certain new forms of narratives.

In order to prepare the ground for the study of the different circular narratives, this chapter will examine Nietzsche's early critiques and related discussions of the concept of nihilism and the idea of eternal recurrence, so that we may subsequently determine the importance of these notions in triggering the process of formal experimentation leading to the emergence of a circular narrative trend. First, however, this Introduction will provide the necessary context for the ensuing analyses by working towards two specific ends. It will start by considering the meaning of the term 'narrative', because, although ostensibly self-explanatory, its definitions (and their fluctuations) are key in shedding some light on the reasons why narrative form was conceptualized as it has been throughout Western history; and it will then move on to examine how linearity was established as the paradigmatic narrative structure in Western literature, by looking at a range of historical theorizations of literature and the linear model.

On narrative and form: From myth to story

Even if the term 'narrative' might not seem in need of elucidation, it is important to begin by considering its significance. Not only because, as Gérard Genette remarks, we normally use it 'without paying attention to, even at times without noticing, its ambiguity' (1983: 25) but because its definition provides us with decisive insights into the ways in which it has been understood throughout history, and this, in turn, will allow us to comprehend how the nature and function of its structure have been conceptualized over time too.

The definition of narrative has been a matter of much and very intense debate in recent times, principally owing to the fact that it attracted considerable critical interest during the second half of the twentieth century (especially from the French structuralists),[6] experiencing a radical inflation that culminated in the notorious poststructuralist view that sees most communicative acts as narratives.[7] Recent analyses tend to begin with the rather totalizing and tautological definition ('everything is narrative') that identifies it as being both 'everywhere' (Bennet and Royle 2016: 52) and, as Rolland Barthes famously

---

[6] See Herrnstein Smith (1980).
[7] Nietzsche's problematizing of the notion of 'truth' makes the distinction between knowledge and narrative collapse, so the inflation of the signifier is potentially a result of this idea.

claimed in his 'Introduction to the Structural Analysis of Narrative', 'simply *there*, like life itself' (1988: 95). Despite the ambiguity of Barthes' remark, most scholars seem to agree that this assertion is an appropriate starting point for this discussion, for it reveals that 'To raise the question of narrative is to invite reflection on the very nature of culture, and possibly, even on the nature of humanity itself' (White 1999: 1) – given that if narrative is, and always has been, everywhere, it is also necessarily an intrinsic part of what makes us human: our basic drive to make sense of the world that surrounds us.

However, since claiming that narrative has always been everywhere does not tell us much about what it actually is, in order to clarify the term further let us turn to the analysis of its etymology. Hayden White tells us:

> The words *narrative*, *narration*, to *narrate*, etc., derive via the Latin *gnarus* ('knowing', 'acquainted with', 'expert', 'skilful', etc.) and *narrb* ('relate', 'tell') from the Sanskrit root *gnâ* ('know'), with the same root yielding γνώριμος ('knowable', 'known'). (White 1999: 215)[8]

This etymological description shows the double logic underlying the concept: not only signifying but emerging, at the same time, from the opposing notions of narration as an action (to narrate) and as an object (a narration). This twofold nature is not a mere instance of polysemy or lexical derivation, given that the loss of one of these two aspects entails a loss of the overall significance of the concept too. Narration is not just the act of recounting a certain 'knowledge', since not all acts of reciting 'facts' constitute narratives. Neither does the term merely signify the material object, that is, the 'text' (be it oral, written, visual, etc.) that is recounted in a narrative act, given that not all texts, in the sense of 'pieces of knowledge', are narratives (at least in the traditional, pre-postmodern sense). The term thus arises from the necessary combination of the two concepts of 'knowing' and 'telling',[9] and it is in fact the presence of the second term within

---

[8] The definition derived from its etymology again falls into the tautological game which seems to characterize narrative, in that it appears to be definable only through the circular referential play of its constituents: a narrative being either 'that which is narrated' or the act of narrating a 'narrative' (which is, again, 'that which is narrated').

[9] Yet, there is an in-built inequality between the two notions from which the term derives: since one (narration as noun) appears to prevail over the other, given that one can only narrate something if there is something to narrate. The term's definition thus implies that the narrative act is irremediably secondary to the narrative text, obliquely determining that although the way a narrative is presented or organized is important, it is less so than the actual content narrated or that one works in the service of the other. However, critics such as Jonathan Culler do not see an inequality but a 'double logic', whereby the story seems paradoxically to both precede and ensue narrative discourse (see Culler 1981). In any case, since prior to the twentieth century narrative was seen as a means towards a specific *telos* (be it mimetic, expressive, didactic, etc.), a text's form inevitably lost its intrinsic

the definition that points towards one of its essential attributes (explicitly absent yet implicit in the etymological description of the word): its form.

The 'verbal' or 'productive' facet of the term not only echoes the specific historical (or rather pre-historical) situation in which narrative arises, where literary texts were transmitted orally by an expert (the narrator) who had the role of sharing his knowledge (*mythos*) through the narrative act. This lexical root also suggests, as Martin McQuillan points out, that narratives were a 'communal method by which knowledge is stored and exchanged' (2000: 2) – both 'a form of knowledge' and the act of transmitting said 'knowledge', hence implicitly establishing that there is a specific manner in which such knowledge must be transmitted. The relationship between narrative and knowledge revealed by the term's etymology points to the importance of its structure, suggesting that if the function of narrative is didactic, its internal organization must also be aimed at such an end. The key point is therefore that narrative organizes events (changes of state) in a specific way, one that works towards the transmission of knowledge through the establishment of cause and effect relations.

Yet, while this embryonic relationship, manifest at the time in which the earliest surviving narratives originated (*c.* 2000 BCE), deteriorated to the point where one could no longer describe narrative as the 'transmission of knowledge', the particular structure conceived to work towards such an aim, the linear form, was preserved. The reasons for this are many and complex. The 'transcendentalization' of the concept of knowledge, resulting from the transition from *mythos* to *logos* in ancient Greek thought,[10] and instigated further by the ensuing rise of Christianity, made the division between fact and fiction (which had very little to do with literature initially) acquire tremendous importance in the understanding of the concept of 'knowledge', resulting in a gradual distancing of the two notions (given that knowledge was increasingly equated, or at least strongly linked, with the concept of 'truth', empiricism and reason, while literature in general and narrative in particular became gradually associated with the concept of 'fiction'). The use of 'knowledge' as a criterion determining 'narrativity' became increasingly problematized and was soon dismissed, leading to a progressive shift from the perception of narrative as the 'transmission of knowledge' to the act of reciting a 'story'. Indeed, as McQuillan

(aesthetic) value in favour of such a purpose (the positing of a certain teaching, emotion, theme, etc.). This devaluation also displays a paradox: that form is an absolute prerequisite for a certain linguistic expression to be considered as a narrative, yet a minor aspect of the narrative object (its value residing purely in the degree to which it conveys content).

[10] See Buxton (2001).

observes, in everyday speech we rarely distinguish between the terms 'story' and 'narrative' (2000: 3), and most dictionaries of the English language (*OED, Merriam-Webster, Cambridge*, etc.), as well as many of the leading narratologists of recent times, also agree in establishing narrative as a synonym of story or at least are very emphatic on this relationship.[11] What is at stake in these designations is an implicit foregrounding of 'structuration' as an essential aspect of 'narrativity'. However, it is a very specific kind of structuration that is foregrounded.

This is apparent in Bennett and Royle's definition, which describes narrative in Aristotelian terms as 'a series of events in a specific order – with a beginning, middle and an end' (2004: 53), or more specifically as 'the establishing of some (causal/temporal) relation between them' (2004: 324), and therefore as being 'characterised by its foregrounding of a series of events or actions which are connected in time' (2004: 53). The same is also emphasized by Martin Gray, who sees narrative as 'a story, tale or recital of facts', where 'a selection of incidents is made so as to suggest some relationship between them', highlighting the fact that 'to create a narrative or narrate a story' is to 'recount and establish some connection between a series of events' (2007: 188–9).[12] Similarly, Julian Wolfreys states that 'Most fundamentally, to *narrate* is to tell a story, to give a sequence of events a particular form so as to produce a significance produced as, or greater than, the sum of the parts' (2004: 163), a definition that includes both aspects of its etymological heritage, highlights the crucial role of form, but also (and most importantly) determines that the significance of a narrative resides in the effect of its totality – in the signified 'ideal' which the organized text refers to.

Although the mere existence of both concepts points to the irreducibility of one to the other, it is only since the twentieth century that there has been a sustained effort by narratologists to 'provide a rigorous definition of "narrative" while reserving the term "story" for a quite separate concept' (McQuillan 2000: 3). Gray, for instance, reminds us that although 'any sequence of events told so as to entertain is a "story"', in narrative theory the word has a wholly distinct meaning, signifying 'the list of events that represent the bare, chronological

---

[11] M. H. Abrams and Geoffrey Harpman, for instance, define the term bluntly as 'a story, whether told in prose or verse, involving events, characters and what the characters say and do' (2014: 233), and Bennett and Royle open their discussion of narrative in their *Introduction to Literature, Criticism and Theory* (2004) by talking extensively about stories and using both terms in a manner that suggests their interchangeability.

[12] To this, Gray adds that 'History is a narrative, though the word is more commonly associated with fiction' (2007: 89), showing both the postmodern tendency to reject the etymological heritage of narrative as knowledge and the inflation of the term as a result of the narratological endeavour to demarcate its confines, which paradoxically resulted in their widening.

framework, out of which the narrator builds the plot' (1992: 274). The reason behind this endeavour to differentiate between the two concepts was that, for the first time, there was a specific focus on narrative form, not just as a linear model consisting of three parts and working in the service of content but as an infinite number of possibilities for organizing a text, highlighting once again the double dimension of narrative as both a certain content (be it knowledge or fictive events, etc.) and its structure or form.

If the differentiation between narrative and knowledge (resulting from the discrimination of *mythos* and *logos*) resulted in a foregrounding of form as one of its crucial aspects (a criterion determining narrativity),[13] the (post)modernist problematization of this dichotomy directed the focus explicitly onto the question of structure and opened up narrative to a new horizon of formal possibilities. Starting with the Russian Formalist distinction between '*fabula*' and '*sjuzhet*' ('*histoire*' and '*récit*' in the Francophone tradition or 'story' and 'discourse' in the Anglophone one), narratologists have striven to discriminate between the two concepts and demarcate the constituent components of narrative, with the aim of providing an in-depth delineation of the term. By drawing a distinction between its syntagmatic and semantic dimensions, narratologists defined all stories as narratives, albeit not all narratives as stories. If a story is the sequence of events in their natural, chronological order, a narrative is not just said story but its plot, that is, 'that organised (but not necessarily chronological) arrangement that is the actual narrative' (Gray 2007: 274). Consequently, it is through the *fabula/sjuzhet* distinction that narrative becomes understood as 'a process of grammatical structuration within language' consisting of both 'the events of a story' and 'the way those events are told in a narrative' (McQuillan 2000: 4).

In very general terms, therefore, narrative existed as a 'form of knowledge' prior to Plato, it then became equated with 'story' as a result of the Aristotelian theorization of plot and the transcendentalization of knowledge consolidating mimesis as its *telos* and linearity as its inherent model, and remained largely as such until the notion of teleology (and of disinterested knowledge) was problematized in the late nineteenth century – most famously by Nietzsche. His work had crucial implications for the understanding of narrative form because his critiques of language, teleology and absolute truth entailed a renewed

[13] Yet, while this differentiation entailed a foregrounding of form, since it was the specific way in which events were structured that made the recounting of these events a narrative, it also brought about the consolidation of conventional narrative structures, rather than a process of formal experimentation.

understanding of narrative (given its inherent relationship with said ideas), inspiring the transition from the (Platonic) perception of literature (as a series of events or elements organized with a didactic purpose) to the understanding of narrative as an intricately organized aesthetic object, consisting of both a story and a discourse, whose sense and value exist beyond its teleological significance. Moreover, the transition from the ostensibly clearly defined notion consisting of a *fabula* and a *sjuzhet* to the poststructuralist view that considers all speech acts as narrative is also to some extent the result of Nietzsche's critique of Platonism, which, while perhaps inadvertently, prompted a revaluation of the concept in the twentieth century.

Prior to this revaluation, however, there seems to have been little reflection upon the different formal possibilities of narrative. While the discrimination between *mythos* and *logos* emphasized form as a crucial requisite of narrativity, this did not lead to a process of formal experimentation but to the hegemony of the linear narrative structure. Characterized by a broadly chronological arrangement of the central elements of its plot, which develop as a result of a causal logic and in a linear or consecutive fashion, the linear form encompasses the type of narratives described by the Aristotelian model of plot, with its clear beginning, middle and end. A linear text may indeed abide by the three-part Aristotelian model or have a conventional structure of development in which the action passes through the phases of *exposition, complication, climax* and *denouement or resolution*. Yet, it may also be incomplete, or deviate from the traditional Aristotelian paradigm or other linear models (such as the seventeenth-century doctrine of the 'three unities'), seemingly breaking with linearity through techniques such as beginnings *in medias res, prolepses, analepsis, metalepsis* or *ellipsis*, without hindering the underlying structure of the story, which remains linear. Even in those cases where a narrative's discourse is consciously constructed so as to blur the linear development of its story through certain devices or omissions, its underlying structure habitually reveals an underlying linear story all the same.

Since the significance of linear narratives resides in the opposition of beginning and end through the discernible contrast of both status quos, their overall meaning and value are inevitably teleological, given that it is the end which exposes the causal and cohesive structure underlying its different elements. So the pervasiveness of linear narrative forms is not a consequence of the fact that writing is inherently linear (that words succeed one another on the page). Linearity must be consciously constructed and preserved through the causal connection of the central elements of the plot, as well as through the revealing of a *denouement* in which a change has taken place in the initial state of affairs, providing the text with an overarching significance: the implications of such change.

The ensuing analysis will show how the linear form became gradually conceptualized and established as the paradigmatic narrative structure as a result of two specific phenomena: the imitation of the structural formulas advanced by some of the major narratives of Western literary history and the consolidation of these formulas through the leading analyses and theorizations on these works. Certainly, if we accept the 'genealogical assumption' that concepts or 'basic categories' (such as 'narrative form') are in fact 'produced' and reshaped by those 'discursive practices' (Culler 2011: 8) that engage with them in what deceptively appears to be a purely retrospective process, it is evident that the linear form not only surfaces as a paradigmatic narrative structure due to its currency; it is determined as such by the different historical conceptualizations of literature. Thus, we shall now examine a range of texts, both literary and critical, that show how the concept developed over time (from narrative as knowledge to narrative as story, etc.), how this affected the way in which narrative form was understood and how, as a result, linearity became the prototypical structure of narrative.

The genealogy of linearity (I): The linear form as myth

Seeing as the first-known narratives were in fact myths, it is necessary to start by making some general observations about the structure of mythology. As Campbell famously argued in his landmark study *The Hero of a Thousand *Faces* (1949), regardless of their nature or origin most myths have the same underlying narrative structure, that is, they conform to 'The standard path of the mythological adventure of the hero', which is, in essence, 'a magnification of the formula represented in the rites of passage' consisting of three broad phases: 'separation – initiation – return' (2008: 27). The narrative structure that Campbell refers to is the monomyth, a model that has been reappraised as one of the paradigmatic motifs in narrative throughout history. Although often described as circular (a description popularized by the conventional diagram used to elucidate the structure) – given that the hero sets out into the world and arrives back home – this narrative form is in fact linear (or at best cyclical) since it entails a sense of progress through the gradual development that comes to light during the course of the story.

Given the monomyth's ubiquity, when discussing the central features and significance of the structure of mythology it is perhaps sufficient to cite Claude Lévi-Strauss' remark that the substance of a given myth 'does not lie in its style, its original music, or its syntax, but in the story which it tells' (1955: 430). Lévi-Strauss contends that 'Myth is the part of language where the formula *tradduttore tradittore* reaches its lowest truth value' because meaning is autonomously present not in its 'gross constituent units' but in the manner in which these are combined (1955: 430). Having a moral or didactic (rather than an aesthetic) purpose, myth demands linearity, because it requires a teleological structure through which to express its teachings effectively. Meaning is not present independently in the description of characters, events or their 'isolated relations'; the actual 'constituent units' of a myth are 'bundles of such relations', since 'it is only as bundles that these relations can be put to use and combined so as to produce a meaning' (Lévi-Strauss 1955: 431). A myth's value resides in the totality that emerges as the result of the singular way in which its 'gross constituent units' are combined, rather than in the way in which it elaborates or presents these or even in the unveiling of the story,[14] since the myth's central purpose is that of expressing a specific idea or teaching.[15] The structuring of the 'gross constituent units' is hence not arbitrary or governed by an aesthetic urge but subordinated to the expression of meaning.

To be sure, early narratives such as *The Epic of Gilgamesh* (arguably the oldest surviving work of literature) are clearly representative of this predilection. Although the tale is structured (physically) through its division into a series of tablets, each of which corresponds to an independent 'thematic unit',[16] these units only acquire their full significance through their combination. So, as Lévi-Strauss argues, meaning is constructed from the bundles of relations of the constituent units. Furthermore, according to its internal structure, *Gilgamesh*

---

[14] In most cases, a myth's audience would be familiar with the story being described. The value of the myth thus resided in the didactic significance of its story (rather than in the story itself): the assimilation of knowledge through the experience of narrative.

[15] This also accounts for the fact that, in many cases, there exist several versions or slight variations of the same myths, as is the case with 'the earlier (Homeric) versions of the Oedipus myth' where 'some basic elements are lacking' (Lévi-Strauss 1955: 430). It is for this reason that 'the quest for the true version' of a myth is senseless, since, regardless of slight discrepancies or variances, the overall meaning of the myth remains constant and one may therefore 'define the myth as consisting of all its versions' (Lévi-Strauss 1955: 435).

[16] In the standard Akkadian version, for instance, the first tablet introduces an initial 'problem' by describing Gilgamesh's unjust ruling of Uruk, Enkidu's birth and education; the second portrays the resolution of this problem through Gilgamesh and Enkidu's battle and reconciliation; and so on.

is also divided into several episodes, each bearing a presentation, development, climax and resolution, and at the same time fulfilling these exact functions within the overall story. This system of underlying relations constitutes the overarching structure of the epic – and therefore also determines which elements are crucial or superfluous within the narrative. The structure is clearly linear, not only because the events succeed one another chronologically but because they develop in a strictly causal fashion (every event is the direct result of a former one), each one leading coherently to the next with a common purpose. The narrative thus works towards a single aim. Beginning with a presentation, in which we are introduced to Gilgamesh and Enkidu, and continuing with a rising action, in which both characters travel to the Cedar Forest to fight Humbaba, a climax, in which Enkidu dies, and a resolution, where the hero finally accepts his mortality, all of the events have the combined function of transmitting several existential teachings, such as the importance of friendship, of coming to terms with the loss of loved ones and with one's own mortality. *Gilgamesh* is in fact a paradigmatic linear narrative, culminating, as it does, with the hero's death: a unified and structured sequence of casually connected events whose *telos* is to teach acceptance of mortality, as well as values such as love, compassion, friendship, bravery and so on.[17]

Although with some divergences, the same is true of the first major narratives of classical Greek literature, Homer's *Iliad* and *Odyssey*. These texts share so many structural features with *Gilgamesh* that critics such as M. L. West argue that the latter 'accounts for major elements of the *Iliad*'s plot, structure, and ethos' (2003: 347), and the same could be said about the *Odyssey*. In both cases the story is made up of several episodes that can be recomposed into an overarching linear structure giving the text its overall meaning. Like *Gilgamesh*, the *Iliad*

---

[17] Even if the story originates from five independent poems (each of which may be viewed as an autonomous whole), it only becomes *The Epic of Gilgamesh* (and acquires its full significance) when tablets I–XI (of the Akkadian version) are read successively to produce a unified account of Gilgamesh's journey towards the acceptance of mortality. Thus, the Sumerian poem entitled 'The Great Wild Bull Is Lying Down' and tablet XII of the Akkadian version (which paraphrases the Sumerian poem 'In Those Says, in Those Far-off Days') exist only as a kind of disjointed sequel and prequel to the epic. Indeed, this idea is reinforced by the fact that the old Babylonian versions broadly cover the same content and follow the same structure as the standard Akkadian version – either coinciding fully or adding certain details which do not affect its basic significance. So, although the epic appears fractured (given its division into tablets and the different variations of some episodes) it is not truly so, since all tablets broadly relate the same events and therefore express essentially the same teachings. The disjointed constituent units (the five previous poems and tablet XII) can therefore be considered as surplus (regardless of the fact that the five poems are older than the final Akkadian version), since they do not affect the significance of its underlying story, stressing that the core of the work resides in the 'bundle of relations' of the narrative's central elements, rather than within these elements themselves.

and *the Odyssey* depict their hero's emotional (and physical in the case of the *Odyssey*) journey: a 'suite of emotions and mood changes' that endows each narrative with 'its artistic unity, determining its beginning, its end, and its basic structural framework' (West 2003: 334). As happens in most ancient epic poetry, these texts present the subject matter around which the whole text orbits at the beginning of the text. In the case of the *Iliad*, it is the rage (*menin*) of Achilles that constitutes the narrative's basic structuring principle – since all of the text's central elements work towards the exploration of this theme. In the *Odyssey*, it is the figure of Odysseus that structures the narrative, since it is the total sum of his actions and experiences that allows him to become the man that he is at the resolution, and this development corresponds to the overall development of the narrative.

Unlike *Gilgamesh*, however, the discourse of Homer's texts does not follow a strict chronology, beginning in medias res and having numerous analepses and prolepsis through which the whole story emerges. Nevertheless, the underlying story is itself chronological, and all the events can be easily mapped onto an overall linear sequence. These epics' linear form is constructed progressively through the combination of several storylines that exist in various temporalities, all of which revolve around the same central theme, constituting the structure's nucleus. Consequently, despite deviations from the natural sequence of time, a single underlying linear storyline emerges gradually throughout the text. The epics' linear character is stressed further by the fact that, as Georg Danek argues, despite the various digressions, time is always 'represented as a continuum, as the primary narrator never looks back in time when he switches to a different storyline' (cited in Grethlein and Rengakos 2009: 277). Even if flashbacks or simultaneous events abound – as is the case with many epic poems – an underlying linear structure conforming to the overarching sequence of the events is discernible in the midst of these. A narrative's 'story' can hence be fragmented, owing to ramifications or voids in its plot, and still become unified and linear through the unveiling (sometimes implicitly) of an underlying causal relation that progresses towards a final resolution, endowing the different events or elements that make up the story with an overall significance.

As Katherine King observes, Homer's narratives 'became the touchstone for all Classical literature created in Athens, Alexandria, and Rome', shaping, as they did, the 'Greek and Roman concepts of narrative structure' (2012: 6). Texts such as Hesiod's *Theogony* (8 BCE), Aesop's *Fables* (6 BCE), the tragedies of Aeschylus, Sophocles and Euripides or the comedies of Aristophanes all base their forms on

Homer's epics. Besides, even when poets did not imitate Homer they imitated each other, perpetuating the same formal conventions. This is evident if we consider that most Greek tragedies followed the same five-part structure,[18] consisting of a prologue, a parode (which is itself divided into the strophe, antistrophe and epode), episode, stasimon and exode; while most comedies adhered to the parallel structure of prologue, parode, agon, parabasis (divided into ode, epirrhema, antode and antepirrhema), episode and exode. Thus, even before narrative form had been explicitly conceptualized (notably by Aristotle), the imitation of existing narratives (mostly Homer's, but also of subsequent authors as these became increasingly popular) served to consolidate linearity as the paradigmatic framework of narrative.[19]

Furthermore, long before the appearance of the *Poetics*, several discussions of rhetoric by the Greek sophists (the origin of literary theory) had already provided a theoretical basis for the linear form by outlining certain formal features of 'good literature' – at least in relation to prose. Among these, Corax's rhetoric – described by Barthes as a kind of 'proto-rhetoric', since it was a 'rhetoric of the syntagm, of discourse, and not of the feature, of the figure' (1988: 17) – is significant for being one of the earliest surviving theorizations on literary form. Corax outlines a structural model consisting of five basic units: '1. exordium; 2. narration or action (the relating of facts); 3. argument or proof; 4. digression; 5. epilogue' (Barthes 1988: 17). This is the earliest formulation of a proto-literary (linear) structure in prose – one which, as Barthes notes, 'has kept its main organisation' even in the academic writing of the present day as 'an introduction, a demonstrative body, a conclusion' (1988: 17). This model also bears clear resemblances to the linear structure of early drama and epic poetry as theorized in Aristotle's *Poetics*. The Coratian outline mirrors the linear narrative form, having the same teleological nature and working towards its purpose in the same basic manner: through a five-part division which develops the text's subject matter gradually, with each segment roughly equating to the basic components of the previously mentioned model and likewise culminating in the unveiling of the text's overall meaning in its resolution. Corax hence achieves

---

[18] Even in those cases where authors deviate from this structure by changing the order of the parts or excluding some of them, the narrative's linear character is preserved.

[19] The formal and stylistic features of the literary text carried little importance at this time, ostensibly present as an inherited precondition, yet assuming no true significance or value within the literary work: that is, verse was a mere conventional standard. The general framework of myth (form in the service of meaning) thus underlies all Classical narratives, rhetorical or poetic figures apparently existing only as a practical tool (aiding memory) or as an imitation of the music of the lyre which accompanied the recitation of poems.

the first theoretical sketch of the formal arrangement of a literary text, even if it refers to a kind of speech aimed at persuasion, rather than to the fictional speech of poetry.

Yet, it would not be until Gorgias of Leontium (484–376 BCE) that rhetorical models were applied to prose, allowing it to become a specialized discourse and aesthetic object, ancestor of literature.[20] This was a significant stage in the development of literary form because the aesthetic properties of verse (rhyme, rhythm, etc.) were substituted by a number of formal aspects 'immanent to prose' yet bearing equal aesthetic properties to the lost features of verse – techniques such as the usage of 'words of similar consonance, symmetrical sentences, antitheses reinforced by assonance, alliteration, [and] metaphor' (Barthes 1988: 18). The analysis of these pseudo-poetic figures opened prose to the realm of stylistics, accomplishing its first characterization as a proto-literary genre. Gorgias' endeavours must thus be highlighted as a general foregrounding or revalorization of form and aestheticism within literature, a stance that would be contrary to the ensuing Platonic poetics.

The genealogy of linearity (II): Plato, Aristotle and the poetics of linearity

Plato challenged Gorgias' views by reproving literature (poetry *and* rhetoric) on moral and didactic grounds and commending 'truthfulness' instead, causing the concept of form to experience a major redetermination. Plato's Socrates denounces literature on account of it being an irrational (since it emerges from inspiration rather than knowledge) imitation, unable to depict truth: a degraded 'copy of a copy', countering the views not only of Gorgias but of other sophists such as Thrasymachus who valued literature for its capacity to represent, but also to produce reality through its power of persuasion.

What is most important about Plato's challenging of pre-Socratic rhetoric, however, is that it was achieved through dichotomizing the concept into a 'good' rhetoric, that of law, whose aim is to depict the truth, and a 'bad' rhetoric (of fact), which simply aims for verisimilitude and therefore applies to any other kind of writing. This division placed all forms of literary art under the totalizing

---

[20] This turn came as a result of a shift in the composition of 'funeral panegyrics (threnodies)' from verse to prose, leading to the birth of a new genre, the '*epideictic*', constituting the 'advent of a decorative prose, a prose-as-spectacle' (Barthes 1988: 17–18).

negative category of the rhetoric of fact, devaluing literature and establishing *psychagogy* as the sole type of artistic speech.[21] In this way, literature becomes defined teleologically, given that truth is identified as the end and measure of real art.[22] Furthermore, by claiming that literature can only lead us further way from truth (given that it is a representation of what is already a copy: the accidents of the world of ideas), its formal features (which ornament content) were deemed a hindrance for it to achieve the status of art. Plato subordinates *mythos* to *logos*, art to science, pleasure to truth, the poet's knowledge to that of the philosopher, instigating a devaluation of form in relation to content. He inaugurates a tradition which is to re-emerge repeatedly throughout the history of literary scholarship by identifying didacticism as the *telos* of the imitative arts and rejecting aesthetics through the prioritizing of content as the potential expression of truth. Nevertheless, these determinations were overturned by Aristotle, who achieved a reversal of the Platonic devaluations of poetry and rhetoric, by claiming that literature can reveal truth through its power of imitation.

Be that as it may, Aristotle's distinction between the two types of literature is again teleological (to convey an idea or to convey an image), implying that the form of these discourses is determined by such an aim. This happens in relation both to rhetoric (by emphasizing reasoning rather than elocution) and to poetry, which he defines as a structured whole where every part is related and works towards a single objective. Thus, despite holding an antagonistic view to Plato, and hence revaluating literature's function and value, Aristotle preserves the hierarchy established by the original view of narrative as the transmission of knowledge (or Plato's didacticism) where form works in the service of content.[23]

Aristotle reconceptualized the phenomena of discourse in *Technè rhétorikè* and *Technè poiétikè*. The first outlines a model for the structure of speeches

---

[21] Since the aim of psychagogic art was '"synoptic" knowledge' and its object 'the correspondence or the interaction which unites types of souls to types of discourse', the dialogic form or *adhominatio* was implicitly established as the quintessential structure of 'good rhetoric' and thus of 'true art' – so that Plato is deeming his own works art, while dismissing other kinds of literature, even if, as Barthes notes, he 'sets writing aside and seeks out personal interlocution' (1988: 19).

[22] These views were developed gradually throughout Plato's dialogues: particularly in *Gorgias*, where Socrates critiques the sophist's rhetoric, disqualifying it as art; in *Ion*, where he discusses the nature of knowledge and poetry, establishing the latter as a kind of 'divine madness' rather than as an artistic expression; and in Book 10 of *The Republic* (possibly his best-known criticism of art), where Socrates condemns poetic imitation, claiming that it is ruinous to the understanding and concluding that the creators of 'imitative arts' should be expelled from the ideal state and not be permitted to return unless they can prove that their art is both pleasant and useful to humanity.

[23] Aristotle's analysis was not groundbreaking since he was merely formulating the practices of famous writers of his time (such as Homer), which were already seen as the standard practice.

consisting, in essence, of two parts: a 'statement of the case' and its 'proof', and which may not consist of more than four parts: 'Introduction', 'Statement, Argument, and Epilogue' (Aristotle 2004: 13). Again (as with Corax's rhetorical paradigm), this structure is very similar to the linear model he proposes for the formal arrangement of poetry – which revolves around unity, gradual progression and the aim to convey a concrete message through the presentation of an initial state of affairs that is either reinforced or overturned in the resolution. Therefore, venturing to define what he claims has 'hitherto been without a name', that is, literature: the 'art which imitates by means of language alone, and either in prose or in verse' (2018: 9), Aristotle opens the *Poetics* by identifying 'the structure of the plot' as a 'requisite to a good poem' (2018: 7), foregrounding form as a fundamental element of the literary text. However, this foregrounding only serves to emphasize the teleological function of literature: imitation, since he claims that all forms of narrative poetry are modes of *mimesis*, which he deems to be an 'instinct of our nature' (Aristotle 2018: 15).

Having identified *mimesis* as narrative's *telos*, Aristotle pursues the logic of his reasoning by claiming that since 'Tragedy is the imitation of an action', the 'arrangement of the incidents' (the plot), being also 'the imitation of the action', is its most essential part (2018: 25). So, although his description of literature is primarily formal, it establishes form as a mere means towards *mimesis*, rather than as an aim in itself. He even downplays the importance of formal features such as verse as a requisite for a text to be poetry, claiming that Empedocles should not be deemed a poet simply because he writes in verse. It is imitation which acts as the compulsory condition for a text to be poetic and therefore its content or significance (rather than its form) what gives it its value and defines it as literature. Accordingly, while he claims that what is 'most important of all is the structure of the incidents', since 'the incidents and the plot are the end of a tragedy; and the end is the chief thing of all' (Aristotle 2018: 25, 27), he is in fact referring to a very specific kind of structure, a mimetic one (the linear form). Aristotle goes on to outline this 'proper structure', claiming that it must be 'complete, and whole, and of a certain magnitude', that is, comprised of a 'beginning, middle and an end' and neither 'exceedingly small' nor too 'vast', so that 'the unity and sense of the whole' is preserved (2018: 27, 29, 31). 'Unity of plot', then, is stressed as a crucial feature of a narrative's form, taking the Homeric epics as a reference:[24]

---

[24] See Aristotle (2018: 33).

the plot, being an imitation of an action, must imitate one action and that a whole, the structural union of the parts being such that, if any one of them is displaced or removed, the whole will be disjointed and disturbed. For a thing whose presence or absence makes no visible difference, is not an organic part of the whole. (Aristotle 2018: 35)

All is in favour of unity, even size. Aristotle admits that although 'the greater the length, the more beautiful will the piece be by reason of its size', this is only true insofar as 'the whole be perspicuous' (2018: 33). Consequently, plot is not defined as any organization of the events of a narrative but as one of a specific kind: a cohesive whole composed of three main sections and structured coherently on the basis of 'logical necessity'.[25] Aristotle criticizes episodic narratives as the worst form, hierarchizing plot structures according to their complexity and contending that a 'well-constructed plot' should be 'single in its issue, rather than double as some maintain', unfold according to the 'necessary or the probable' and contain a resolution that displays both a reversal of the initial situation and a recognition on the part of the protagonist of his or her fate (2018: 39, 41, 47). The *Poetics* thus sketches out, explicitly and for the first time, a theoretical basis for linear narrative form, identifying it as a unified, harmoniously developing whole, led by logic and causality, that unveils its overarching significance through a reversal or a recognition in its resolution.

Overall, ancient Greek literature from Homer to Apollonius, Aeschylus to Aristophanes, displays the same basic underlying formal character, coinciding with Aristotle's theorization of tragedy. *Mimesis* is the key concept underlying the preponderant views of literature at the time, with ideas such as truth, morality or didacticism being closely associated to it. The linear form therefore emerges as the sole conceivable structural arrangement for narrative, providing the cohesion and logical coherence that a unified work aiming to depict a single and specific notion must have.

By and large, these same views and norms were replicated by the Romans, who adopted Greek standards, consolidating them as literary conventions. To be sure, the narratives of ancient Rome share with those of ancient Greece the same underlying formal character. We can appreciate clear similarities between the tragedies of Aeschylus, Sophocles and Euripides and those of Livius Andronicus, Nevio, Ennio, Pacuvio and Accio; between the comedies of Aristophanes and

---

[25] Aristotle places so much importance on plot that he argues that 'The poet or "maker" should be the maker of plots rather than of verses', since 'he is a poet because he imitates, and what he imitates are actions' (2018: 37).

those of Plautus and Terence; and between the epic and the didactic poetry of Virgil, including *The Aeneid* (1 BCE), and that of Homer. Even new genres such as the satire (which although originated in Greece was only developed as a specific genre in the early days of the Roman Empire) or other groundbreaking forms, such as Ovid's anti-epic *Metamorphoses* (8 CE), innovate with regard to the subject matter, themes and characters depicted in the plays but not in their structures. The foremost writers of ancient Rome are thus responsible for solidifying the Greek's compositional practices as maxims for literary creation, giving way to the establishment or reinforcement of certain literary canons.

Horace, for instance, reinstates many of his predecessor's ideas, claiming that young poets should also follow their steps, a tendency which is evident in both literature and criticism. His discussion of the in medias res technique in *Ars Poetica*[26] is a clear development of Aristotle's analysis of drama, exhibiting how Homer was still a reference at this time. Moreover, Horace reconciled his Greek predecessors: like Plato he stresses morality and like Aristotle he aligns literature with imitation, adding to these notions that of 'decorum', by declaring that poetry's *telos* is to combine usefulness and pleasure in order to both instruct and delight. Thus, for Horace, it is still unity, cohesion and appropriateness which constitute the central features of poetry and therefore dictate the structural organization and need (or lack thereof) for rhetorical features in a literary work. The principle of decorum determined that the part should fit the whole, the subject the genre and the language the character. Form was hence again subordinated to content. Although narratives should strive to delight through imagery and other aesthetic means, these were not intrinsically valuable but purely instrumental. Horace's concept of the 'purple patch' (unnecessarily ornamental passages) exemplifies this well, since it reveals his belief that all aesthetic considerations are secondary to the transmission of meaning. Alternative structures to the linear model were therefore not even considered; if the purpose of narrative was a mimetic didacticism, linearity fulfilled this aim perfectly. Unity of form thus becomes crucial to Horace (as it was to Aristotle) because it is through this unity that a text can instruct most adequately. Indeed, Horace seems to be paraphrasing the Greek philosopher when he states: 'let it be what you will, but let it be simple and unified' (2001: 124).

---

[26] The poem's maxims were adopted by numerous ensuing poets (Geoffrey of Vinsauf, Pierre de Ronsard, Nicolas Boileau, Alexander Pope, Lord Byron, Wallace Stevens, etc.).

Among the many Roman poets who took on Aristotle's discussion of drama in relation to the structure of narrative, it is important to mention Theon's *Progymnasmata*, which furthered the conceptualization of the linear form by identifying five possible alternative configurations for narrative (middle-beginning-end,[27] middle-end-beginning, etc.). None of these constitute alternatives to the linear model, but rather different possibilities for its elaboration. It is also worth mentioning the anonymous treatise *On the Sublime* (attributed to Longinus), since it replaced *mimesis* with *ekstasis* (an ecstasy triggered by the expression of inner feelings and thoughts which aims to have an uplifting effect)[28] as the *telos* of literature, praising ornamental form, yet again subordinating it to narrative's underlying function (*ekstasis*), so that while form is identified as a 'source of sublimity' it remains subjected to other aspects. Quintilian[29] also developed certain Aristotelian notions by substituting Horace's *in medias res* for *a mediis vel ultimis*, echoing Theon's five structural possibilities and producing an analysis of literary tropes that helped contemporary authors intensify the vibrancy and interest of their writings (to aestheticize literature). Yet, Quintilian continues to subordinate form to content by establishing referentiality as the foremost function of words – with other (figurative) uses being subordinated to it – implicitly safeguarding the hierarchy established by Plato's *logos/mythos* dichotomy. He thus replicates Horace's maxim 'delight and instruct', emphasizing the importance of the first term but only in the service of the second. Finally, Plotinus' revision of Plato must also be highlighted as another attempt to reconcile the arts with the latter's idealism. In 'On Intellectual Beauty', Plotinus contests Plato's view of literature as a degraded copy of a copy, establishing beauty as a means to access the 'world of Forms' (or first *arché*) through the power of the intellect, as a way to become unified with 'the One'. However, although Plotinus reconciles Platonism with art, he reaffirms literature's teleological status as a referential object that aims to signal certain aspects of the 'world of Ideas', safeguarding once again the content/form hierarchy deriving from such a view.[30] This understanding of literature as a mimetic-didactic phenomenon would remain almost unchallenged until the Romantic period.

---

[27] As in Homer's *Odyssey*.
[28] Longinus is one of the earliest critics to argue in favour of literature as expression and is thus an ancestor of the Romantic movement.
[29] Although a rhetorician, his ideas became extremely influential by the Middle Ages for poetic theory as well as rhetoric because he used Homer, Virgil and Horace's poetry to illustrate his arguments.
[30] As a strict dualist, Plotinus still contends that the material world is subjected to the world of ideas and thus that the underlying idea or content of a literary work is more important or valuable than its specific shape.

The genealogy of linearity (III): The medieval linear form

Like the Romans, the European writers of the Middle Ages also adopted and developed the conventions and narratological analyses of their predecessors, largely producing continuations of their work. Certainly, thinkers such as Plato, Horace or Plotinus were still extremely influential among medieval and Renaissance writers. Plotinus' ideas, for instance, were reappraised by Christian scholars such as Augustine, who claimed that since human language reflects the *logos* it must guarantee this unity by striving for absolute transparency, rejecting rhetorical or figurative uses that may blur its connection to truth[31] – views that were shared by authors such as Macrobius and Boethius. Similarly, Hugh of St Victor and Geoffrey of Vinsauf, among others, engage with Plato's ideas: the first by arguing that the reading of literature parallels the 'reading' of the world and therefore that one may be beneficial to the other; and the second by reviewing Horace's principle of decorum, claiming that the poet should seek new ways of portraying traditional themes rather than new subject matter. However, while both highlight the importance of aestheticism, it is still subordinated to an underlying didactic *telos*.

The impact of the Classical legacy clearly extends beyond the realm of scholarship. As John Reynell Morell observes, 'much resemblance may be traced between Hector, Achilles, Roland, and Richard of the Lion-heart' (1984: 10), not only in the content of these works but in their forms too.[32] Overall, the principal Classical storylines, themes, genres and stylistic conventions were safeguarded in the Middle Ages, the literature being still mostly poetic (romances and heroic poems) and influenced by paganism in the un-Romanized territories and by Christianity in the regions influenced by Roman culture. Like in ancient Greece and Rome, the lyric and epic were still the customary branches of poetry, though, unlike in Classical literature, drama was almost non-existent until the emergence of the Mysteries (religious plays). The main genre of the Classical period, the

---

[31] Dante famously applied Augustine's distrust of figurative writing to his own *Divine Comedy* (1320), in his 'Letter to Can Grande'.

[32] Although I refer to the literature of the Middle Ages as a coherent whole due to the strong similarities found across countries, there existed a divide between the narratives of Italy, France and Spain, which were strongly influenced by Roman culture and those of the Gothic-Teutonic and Slavic peoples (see Morell 1984: 4). One of the main differences between these two groups was that the territories that were not subdued by the Romans retained their vernacular languages while the subdued kingdoms produced 'a current written literature, consisting of what critics have called Low Latin', which developed into the Romance languages (Morell 1984: 4). This divide seems non-existent in relation to literary form.

epic poem, was still one of the most important literary forms in the early Middle Ages, as we see from the prominence of works such as the Old English *Beowulf*. Yet, this form soon decayed, especially in France and Spain, being replaced by the courtly romance and the *chanson de geste*. Many of the *trouvères* would have been familiar with writers such as Virgil and Ovid, especially with the latter's *Ars amatoria*, which they reappraised in their own treatises, sometimes without acknowledging the author; while most romancers were familiar with the classics, from which they appropriated material for their own narratives.

The Germano-Christian influence also gave way to the birth of the sagas and the songs of the troubadours, which shared some affinities with the epic, although mostly written in prose. In fact, while prose is initially rare it gains increasing terrain on poetry, especially in Spain and Iceland but later also in France, soon becoming the primary medium for the composition of sagas and romances (See Morell 1984: 10). These were distinct from the epic on account of their magnitude and thematic content, but very similar in relation to the significance, structural arrangement and overall function of their form. The romance utilizes essentially the same structure as the epic but for more concrete purposes: focusing the action on a specific goal and aiming to depict a specific tangible theme rather than a broad abstract ideal. Both share a linear plot structure, although whereas in epic poetry it is centred on 'national or cosmic problems', in romances it is 'oriented towards a specific climax' (Klarer 2013: 10). Established as an independent genre, many ancient romances initially employ verse forms, as is the case in the anonymous fourteenth-century Middle English Arthurian Romance *Sir Gawain and the Green Knight*. However, they increasingly turn to prose and tend towards 'a focused plot and unified point of view' that condenses the action and orients the plot 'toward a particular goal' (Klarer 2013: 10).

The reason for this gradual focalization (and hence distancing from classical Aristotelian form) is that while still didactic, medieval authors tended to give more importance to entertainment, increasingly composing romances as interlaced narratives that stand as sequels or prequels to existing texts, rather than as autonomous or self-contained stories – privileging multiplicity and surprise instead of the Classical notions of unity, wholeness and so on. These divergences gradually led to the emergence of new genres such as the story cycles (the Arthurian cycle or the *Roman de Renart*), which, in turn, gave way to collections of novellas such as Boccaccio's *Decameron* or Chaucer's *The Canterbury Tales*. The increasing presence of these vast, disjointed, plural or interlaced narratives, which lie between unity and multiplicity, makes the origins and story of their development a fundamental 'chapter in the history of medieval narrative form', becoming, as Eugene Vinaver notes, 'one of the fundamental esthetic issues of thirteenth-century literature' (cited in Ryding 1971: 17). This progressive distancing from Classical forms can be attributed to the fact that although most early medieval texts mirror Classical ones in terms of imagery, subject matter, thematic content and structure, this was more a result of the direct imitation of Greek and Roman narratives than of adherence to specific theories such as Aristotle's, which were mostly ignored at this point.

In fact, the *Poetics* was almost completely disregarded until the sixteenth century, to the extent that some critics have explicitly labelled early medieval literature as 'anti-Aristotelian' (see Ryding 1971: 9). Notable divergences between Aristotle's model and the literature of the early medieval period include the writing of continuations of existing narratives (the epic cycles) rather than separate, self-contained stories, thereby rejecting Aristotle's principle of unity, and composing texts with multiple storylines and characterized by surprise rather than by the Classical principle of inevitability. This situation would culminate in what came to be known as 'the Italian controversy', a series of polemics lasting from 1548 to the end of the sixteenth century regarding the structure of narrative. The controversy unfolded between the 'ancients' and the 'moderns', the former calling for a return to the Aristotelian narrative model and the latter for a critical acceptance of the new forms that had emerged during the early medieval period. This 'quarrel' was less the result of an unawareness about the *Poetics* (since it had been translated into Arabic by Averroes and into Latin by several authors) than of a general neglect of the treatise. Trissino began the controversy[33] by condemning those texts that did not follow the Classical convention of narrative unity or a single action, which had become so popular at the time. The debate continued with Giraldi's response,[34] which dismissed Trissino's condemnation by distinguishing three equally valid genres of heroic poetry: the Classical epic, describing a single action of a single protagonist; the biographical romance, recounting various actions of a single protagonist; and the Romantic epic in the manner of Ariosto, recounting various actions of several protagonists. It was Torquato Tasso who put an end to the debate with his *Discorsi dell' arte poetica* (1564), mostly known in its latter revision, entitled *Discorsi del poema eroico* (1594).

---

[33] In *Italia liberate dai Goti* (1548).
[34] In *Discorsi intorno al comporre dei romanzi* (1549).

Tasso reappraised Aristotle's theory, directing his criticism specifically against Ariosto's *Orlando furioso* (1532), a text deviating from the Aristotelian model by breaking with the conventions of wholeness, length and unity and representing the culmination of a long tradition that had begun to develop in France in the twelfth century by combining the epic and the romance, the two major genres of the Middle Ages.[35] Tasso divides his discussion of narrative structure into three parts, according to the notions of length, unity and the question of beginning, middle and end. In each part, he begins by paraphrasing Aristotle, after which he adds his own remarks, refining the philosopher's ideas in various ways. In relation to the question of beginning, middle and end, Tasso notes that for a story to be complete it must contain everything needed for it to be understood: 'the causes and the origin of that enterprise which one aims to deal with are expressed, and through the appropriate means one is led to an end that leaves nothing not well concluded or not well resolved' (1875: 569; my translation). Every element related to the story must be included (causes, origins, etc.), its development must be gradual and coherent, and the ending must resolve everything. About length he remarks that 'in little poems one praises their grace and acumen rather than their beauty or perfection' (Tasso 1875: 572). Hence, magnitude is required if beauty or perfection is to be achieved, although the narrative's size must not challenge the reader's memory. Tasso also stresses that the poet's art achieves perfection only when it is able to make the events of his narrative follow one another according either to necessity or to probability. This is important because it explicitly highlights logical sequencing and coherence as a fundamental feature of the linear form. Tasso resolves Trisino's and Giraldi's debate on unity by taking Aristotle's side, albeit cautiously, since he attempts to reconcile unity with variety by establishing a parallelism between epic poetry and the universe: 'which, for all its variety, remains one in form and essence' (Ryding 1971: 14).

By claiming that writers should construct narratives that have a unity like that of the cosmos and describing form as a 'complex piece of machinery in which every gear and lever performs a necessary function with respect to the whole' (Ryding 1971: 15) – a logical sequencing determined by necessity or probability – Tasso reformulates the linear form, reinstating Aristotle's ideas,

---

[35] Although defining *Orlando furioso* as an antagonist to Aristotelian form may seem rather harsh since, despite clear differences, both forms are essentially linear, with figures such as Robortelli or Tasso, Aristotle's analysis is adopted in 'a more systematic and absolute form' than in Aristotle himself, given the 'fires of controversy' in which it was reappraised (Ryding 1971: 10).

albeit more systematically. In emphasizing logical progression as the key feature determining both adequacy of length and unity, Tasso denoted the overall structure of narrative as a unified linear continuum: self-sufficient, all-inclusive, developing as a result of logical coherence and aiming to convey a specific narrative universe that expresses a concrete moral code. By equating the ideal narrative to the cosmos (due to its complex and plural unity) he also accounts for disruptions in this continuum (beginning in medias res, prolepses, analepses or even the fragmented structures of episodic and interlaced narratives), seemingly encumbering linearity but not precluding it. Furthermore, his metaphor reveals exactly what the linear form represents: a way of seeing the world as an ordered, coherent and intelligible machine working according to an internal logic (which is precisely what Nietzsche rejects).

Tasso's impact was such that following the debate, his analysis became crucial in ensuing discussions of narrative form. If, before him, deviation from the Classical models had not been subject to criticism, with figures such as Joachim du Bellay, Jacques Peletier or Rebeleis overtly praising certain aspects of those texts or even adhering to this trend, from the late sixteenth century most authors committed themselves to the Tassian-Aristotelian narrative model, encouraging writers such as Montaigne to deride the medieval forms and define himself as a knowledgeable Classicist. Numerous critics also furthered Tasso's efforts. Julius Caesar Scalinger, for instance, writes in 1561 that drama must aspire to be verisimilar, emphasizing that plays should not have many settings or actions. And similar determinations can be seen on the part of Lodovico Castelvetro in his *La poetica di Aristotele vulgarizzata* (1570), which elaborated a 'neo-Aristotelian theory of unity' that differentiated between narrative and dramatic methods in relation to their treatment of time and space, yet emphasizing unity, albeit of different kinds, in both cases. Thus, by 1580 the controversy had been settled once and for all. Aristotle's ideas were gradually disseminated throughout Europe, and the linear, teleological model became a norm in the composition of narratives.

Echoing the effort of the Italian neo-classicists, Philip Sidney's *An Apology for Poetry* (1595)[36] continued this tendency by amalgamating Classical and continental views to achieve a synthesis of 'two voices', a first 'in the manner of Boccaccio, Politian, and Tasso' and a second 'in the manner of Scaliger, Castelvetro, and Ben Jonson' (Hardison 1997: 77). Sidney argues in favour of

---

[36] It is important to note that the term 'poesy' included prose narrative, since Sydney himself composed romances in prose.

the value of poetry by identifying it as 'the first light-giver to ignorance, and first Nurse' (1860: 63), echoing a Horatian maxim which had also been paraphrased by Boccaccio in his *Genealogia deorum gentilium* (1360) and by Angelo Poliziano in his Neo-Platonist *Nutricia* (1491). Sidney highlighted the importance of inspiration and redefined the Aristotelian concept of mimesis by claiming that *poesy* does not imitate, but creates a new world. This does not mean, however, that he rejected Aristotle's or other Classical views. On the contrary, he adapted them to his particular understanding of literature, claiming that although the poet 'goes hand in hand with nature' he is 'not enclosed within the warrant of her gifts' but ranges 'only within the zodiac of his own wit' (Sidney 1860: 68). He also restated the Horatian motto that poetry has the capacity to both teach *and* delight, merging Classical views in a way that, as O. B. Hardison notes, makes it seem as though 'Plato, Aristotle, and Horace were all in complete agreement concerning the function of poetry' (1997: 69).

Sidney hence paved the way for writers such as Shakespeare, whose plays both adhere to and deviate from the Classical dramatic norms (especially in relation to the unity of time and setting). Yet, while straying from the neo-classical conventions, writers such as Shakespeare continue to devise their narratives as linear teleological constructs. Even Cervantes, whose chief work, *Don Quixote de la Mancha* (1605), is in many ways contrary to the Aristotelian standard, explicitly criticized the early medieval form, echoing Tasso, Sidney and others. Not only that, he explicitly disqualified all those medieval texts where the middle does not correspond to the beginning or end as 'a chimera or a monster' (cited in Ryding 1971: 18), and the Aristotelian ideas expressed by one of his characters, his Canon of Toledo, even became a sort of model for later seventeenth- and eighteenth-century criticism. The 'defenders of the ancients'[37] thus achieved a synthesis of the major literary conventions of the Classical and Medieval periods, extrapolating certain new notions from them (doctrines such as that of the three unities – of action, place and time), which would become dogmas in the production and interpretation of literature for centuries to come.

In France, a similar debate took place in the second half of the seventeenth century revolving around the 'Quarrel over *Le Cid*' and the 'Quarrel of *La Princesse de Clèves*'.[38] In the former (during the mid-1630s), Corneille's tragicomedy is targeted for deviating from the traditional conventions. This controversy was also resolved with a consensus on the importance and value of the pseudo-

---

[37] Barthes also mentions Gerardus Vossius (see 1988).
[38] See Altman (2008: 3)

Aristotelian notion of unity of action, a resolution that becomes manifest within the decade, with most French playwrights abandoning those anti-Aristotelian features of pastoral and epic poetry and striving for unity instead. Almost fifty years later, a second 'quarrel' (revolving around Madame de Lafayette's text) takes place in the form of various anonymous monographic critiques touching on several key formal questions, among which the notion of unity is again crucial. What is most important about this second quarrel, however, is that unity of action is for the first time applied directly to narrative prose, having such an impact that from that moment on the multiple plots prototypical of the epic and romance would be considered unacceptable in French narrative.

The neo-classical endeavour continued to be fostered throughout Europe by writers such as William Congreve, John Dryden[39] and Samuel Johnson, who championed the Classical conventions while at the same time arguing in favour of granting authors the liberty to innovate (anticipating the inclinations of the Romantic writers in the second half of the eighteenth century). This call for invention was therefore paradoxically still coincident with a continued demand to adhere to the basic Classical framework. Johnson thus highlights the importance of tradition while defending playwrights such as Shakespeare against those who criticized him for combining elements from tragedy and comedy, and transgressing Classical norms such as that of the unity of time and setting, helping to popularize his work further. Indeed, the currency of this view was such that when Alexander Pope asserts in his *Essay on Criticism* (1709) that writers should 'Learn hence for Ancient Rules a just Esteem; / To copy *Nature* is to copy *Them*' (1841: 18) he is describing the literary Zeitgeist, rather than providing a personal opinion. So, while Aristotle's ideas (and those of his ensuing counterparts) were reappraised, synthesized and refashioned into a 'set of rules' for the creation of narratives, essentially they only determined that the action 'should follow a linear plot' (Klarer 2013: 151).

The genealogy of linearity (IV): The linear form and the rise of the novel

Consolidated as standard for the composition of narrative through Europe after the seventeenth century, the influence of the linear model soon extended

---

[39] Notably in his 'An Essay of Dramatic Poesy' (1668).

to novel writing too. In fact, it is arguably the case that the double process of Classical influence and narrative focalization brought about by the romance actually led to the emergence of the novel. Altman for one stresses that as the novel's popularity rapidly increased, 'the very notion of what constitutes a narrative' became 'retooled to match neo-Classical prescriptions of proper narrative construction':

> The new definition of narrative adopted during this period was carefully matched to novelistic production. Fallen from grace, many prior narrative traditions were no longer considered worthy of attention and thus were no longer taken into account in defining narrative itself. (Altman 2008: 4)

Narrative became explicitly conceptualized according to neo-classical standards, so that aside from the stir caused by medieval literature (resolved in the 'Italian controversy'), the homogeneous picture regarding form prevails – through a continued adherence to linearity. This homogeneity was owing in great measure to a continuous belief in the referential function of literary texts, in their status as signifiers: as a single and coherent structure that aims to represent the world in order to signify a certain extra-textual reality.[40]

Although disparaged at first, the novel was soon advocated by well-known writers such as Samuel Johnson, yet only so long as it continued to resemble past literature in its drive to represent human nature and specially to be morally didactic. Consequently, the popularization of the novel triggered a paradoxical double movement, with writers at the same time allowing and even encouraging innovation, but also affirming that literature ought to mimic the classics. Novelty in the eyes of writers such as Johnson consisted in being both unpredictable yet still easily recognizable, which mostly meant that even if the content of a novel was innovative, its form should follow the traditional framework. Thus, while a number of theories of the novel emerged as a result of its increasing popularity (Huet, Blackenburg, et al.), they focused on the discussion of thematics and didactics rather than structure.[41] The formal features of narrative were mostly ignored in critical discussions about the novel until the late nineteenth century, perhaps owing to the fact that as this new genre became increasingly popular novels tended to strive towards verisimilitude (even in the early works of

---

[40] It is important to keep in mind that while many medieval narratives went against the Aristotelian notions of form, they did not break with linearity. The teleological linear syntagmatic form is preserved even in the so-called anti-Aristotelian narratives of the early Middle Ages.
[41] See Hühn et al. (2014: 333).

novelists such as Defoe or Richardson) to the point where scholars such as Ian Watt have argued that the break between the prose romance and the novel essentially became the degree to which a text was verisimilar or aspired to be realistic.[42] Although this argument has been criticized due to its emphasis on formal realism as an inherent feature of the novel – a tendency which did not become ubiquitous until after the decay of Romanticism – it serves nonetheless to show how Realism was gradually established as the central literary movement of the nineteenth century.

The development of the novel, first towards Romanticism and later towards Realism, can be traced through the gothic, sentimental and historical novels: starting with texts such as Horace Walpole's *The Castle of Otranto* (1764) through to Goethe's 1774 *The Sorrows of Young Werther* (perhaps the paradigmatic Romantic novel) and culminating with works in the style of Walter Scott's *Waverley* (1814). Yet, prior to the consolidation of Realism, it was the Romantic-era novel that set the bar in prose writing, prompting a search for new, personal (though also purportedly objective) means of expression. However, for all of Romanticism's emphasis on the importance of originality, subjectivity and individual sensibility by notable pre-Romantics such as Edward Young or even David Hume, formal experimentation is still largely absent in the narratives of this period. Romantic novels display much innovation in terms of content or subject matter but still adopt conventional linear forms when treating these new topics:

> Most eighteenth-century novels, like *Pamela*, follow a narrative of progress: from rags to riches; from captivity to freedom; from illegitimacy to legitimacy; from wandering to homecoming. And even those that end unhappily, like *Clarissa*, do not question the value of the story being told, or their own capacity to transmit it. To generalize, for the eighteenth-century novel, stories of individual lives have a pedagogical value for their readers, and the novel, as a genre, has the capacity to transmit that value. [. . .] In the Romantic-era novel, however, the confident didacticism of the eighteenth-century novel tends to dissipate under the pressure of a thorough ongoing critique of both the form and value of individual life stories, as well as an interrogation of the novel's own generic capacity to transmit them. [. . .] Romantic fiction is persistently drawn to lives that end not in redemption or transcendence, but in ruin or failure. Foregrounding the end over the beginning, Romantic novels tend to start not with their protagonists'

---

[42] See Watt (2001: 10).

birth, but with an announcement of a devastation wrought by his or her life's disaster. (Heydt-Stevenson and Sussman 2010: 24)

Hence, although they challenge the value and structure of forms such as the 'marriage plot' and the *Bildungsroman*, they do so without troubling the idea of a linear development or presenting alternatives to it. Even if there is a reversal in the content and aim of narrative, displayed through an overturning of certain aspects (such as the foregrounding of the end rather than the beginning or of failure rather than triumph), the same paradigm governs the structure of these texts, albeit reversed. If, prior to the eighteenth century, novels were overtly optimistic or idealistic in their aspiration towards didacticism, with Romanticism they become representative of a terrible pessimism, which is nonetheless formally constructed in the same essential manner.[43]

Be that as it may, the concept of literary form does experience a major theoretical development in the late eighteenth century owing to the influence of Kant, who, in his *Critique of Judgement* (1790), associated it with subjective perception and the increasing importance of philosophical aesthetics. Indeed, it is Kant who for the first time identifies form as the most important aspect of art, stating that in painting, sculpture and in all the 'formative arts' it is the 'design' that is most 'essential', and claiming that 'what pleases by its form' rather than 'what gratifies in sensation' is 'the fundamental prerequisite for taste' (2007: 56). As Leighton remarks, Kant's emphasis on form is such that he often uses the term in order 'to express the art form itself', and while he does not consider it as such, he does employ it 'as the maidservant of more conceptual abstractions: truth, taste, or judgement, for instance' (2007: 4). Kant separates beauty from charm, the 'intrinsic' from mere 'ornamentation' (2007: 68), equating form with the former terms and thus establishing 'finality of form' as the criterion determining 'a pure judgement of taste which is uninfluenced by charm or emotion' (2007: 65). He not only deems form to be a vital feature of art but claims that beauty 'ought properly to be a question merely of the form' (Kant 2007: 65), identifying it, for the first time, as a crucial aspect of literature.[44] So, although Theodore

---

[43] The Romantics continued to have a functionalist perception of literature, since they still identified *mimesis* (albeit as an emotional or psychological mimesis rather than as the mere representation of nature) as its function. Romantic narratives therefore still have an overarching *telos*: to convey the artist's genius or to depict his inner world.

[44] Despite Kant's insistence on the importance of form, it should be noted that his definition of literature is still teleological, so although form is emphasized, it is in itself insufficient to establish a certain speech act as literary – its function is in fact its essential characteristic and quality. Consequently, he still perceives literature in a way which disallows the possibility of true formal innovation.

Uehling is right to point out that Kant's concern 'is not with any property of an object but fundamentally with the disposition of the cognitive faculties of producer and perceiver' (cited in Leighton 2007: 4), he nevertheless implicitly highlights the importance of literature's form by continuously invoking the arts, and indeed poetry in particular, which he claims is in 'the first rank among the arts' (Kant 2007: 101).

The *Critique of Judgement* is also crucial to the history of narrative for developing and underscoring the concept of disinterest, which would become 'the forerunner of Walter Pater's fin-de-siècle doctrine of *l'art pour l'art*' (Hutchinson 2011: 2). Kant's claim that 'The liking that determines a judgment of taste is devoid of all interest', which serves as the title to the second section of Book I, was to be understood by later writers as a call both to judge art exclusively according to its own standards and to strive for aesthetic excellence through disinterestedness.[45] Though, as Leighton notes, if it is Kant who provides the nineteenth century with 'a language for aesthetic disinterestedness', it is Schiller who gives it 'a powerful and influential account of form' specifically as 'art form' (2007: 5–6). In a much-cited section of his *On the Aesthetic Education of Man* (1794), Schiller states that 'In a truly successful work of art the content should effect nothing, the form everything' and therefore that 'the real secret of the master in any art' resides in making 'his form consume his material' (cited in Leighton 2007: 4). Yet, for all the currency that these German philosophers gave to the discussion of form, most Romantics seem to have ignored the question of narrative structure altogether.

The continued adherence to the linear model, even in the face of explicit calls for formal experimentation, was perhaps also owing to the fact that although the novel experienced a boom during the Romantic era, it was still not considered as a serious branch of literature and was therefore rarely the specific focus of literary criticism. Thus, claims such as Schiller's were taken up by both Romantic and Realist narrative writers, albeit with radically antagonistic results – perhaps because they were considered exclusively in relation to rhetorical rather than syntagmatic questions of narrative form. If, for a Romantic-era novelist, emphasis on form meant highly symbolic imagery, meticulous description and ornamental prose, for a Realist it meant absolute transparency, rigour and precision; but in neither case did this focus apply specifically to the question of structure. Furthermore, with the rise of the Realist movement the linear form is

---

[45] Taken up first by the Romantics and later by the Decadents.

explicitly consolidated. Emerging from the Cartesian and empiricist belief that truth can be discovered through reason and the subject's senses, it is no wonder that Realist writers did not seek to find alternatives to the linear model.

Consequently, in both Romanticism and Realism form is still essentially a function of content, still principally functional. It would not be until the modernist rejection of Realist aesthetic principles that the value and function of form were reconsidered. Flaubert anticipates this shift when he claims to want to write 'a book about nothing, a book dependent on nothing external, which would be held together by the internal strength of its style' (1980: 154). However, such a book would not be possible through a pure reliance on stylistic innovation: the structure of narrative would also need to be rethought in order to rid the text of its ideological implications. This is precisely what Nietzsche's critiques emphasize: that art (and thus form) is in fact never disinterested, since being a physiological process, the expression of interpretative will to power,[46] it is inevitably biased (or interested): the imposition of a subjective order on the chaos of reality, directed towards or resulting from a specific *Weltanschauung*. So, despite the interest in disinterest, the new attempts at re-introducing the formal paradigm and the movement from 'pure form' to 'purely form',[47] it was above all Nietzsche who encouraged modernist writers to turn their attention to the question of structure. It is Nietzsche who, as Marilyn Farwell rightly puts it, made it clear that 'the linear plotting and its concomitant realism [...] encodes bourgeois values of universal subjectivity and a normative closure', and thus who identified linearity, or 'the master plot', as 'an ideological monster' (1996: 47).

* * *

As the preceding analysis has shown, the various ways in which literature was understood historically were crucial in the conceptualization of the linear form. That linear model remained largely unchallenged up until the twentieth century, when the structure of narrative becomes the subject of detailed consideration for reasons that are at once political and philosophical. As Mihály Szegedy-Maszák claims in 'Nonteleological Narration', while 'before the twentieth century the structure of most works of narrative fiction was based on some kind of teleology', from the early decades of the twentieth century a 'post-Nietzschean doubt began to undermine belief in linear succession' (1997: 273).

---

[46] See Rampley (1993).
[47] See Hutchinson (2011: 2).

This is not to say, however, that Nietzsche's impact should be understood as a direct influence, but rather, as acting upon certain 'existential views', which in turn affected or shaped the prevailing understanding of related concepts such as narrative and form. Although perhaps inadvertently, his thought paved the way for modernists to consider some of the same issues he was discussing in relation to the literary practices and movements of their time (as well as in those of their predecessors). Nietzsche's gradual unmasking of the various theological vestiges inherited from Christianity culminated in his analysis of the question of nihilism, an inquiry that would epitomize his critique of the linear form since it implicitly established linearity as a nihilistic structure. Nevertheless, as mentioned at the outset of this introduction, the decision of modernist writers to abandon the linear teleological structure is conceivably not so much a direct consequence of their having read Nietzsche, as the result of their having to address the question of nihilism themselves and creating narratives that responded to it.

In any case, if prior to Nietzsche narrative form was subordinated to content and mostly considered as a rather insubstantial aspect of the literary text, from the turn of the century this situation changes completely: a collective interest in structural experimentation becomes clearly apparent. As we shall see, Nietzsche's philosophy revealed linearity as an artificial model, representative of a specific world view, and fuelled by this same realization many modern writers decided to devise alternatives to the linear structure by employing 'original temporal arrangements that broke radically with the Victorian convention of a largely chronological narrative' (Richardson 2002: 603). Driven by an ambition to challenge the assumed structure of experience, many authors sought ways to stop, reverse time or break with its linear sequence by disorganizing their texts and rearranging events so as to blur their connections or even providing several alternatives for a narrative's resolution. Yet, possibly the most striking of these innovations is the appearance of a variety of circular structures. The central aim of this book is to identify the major exponents of this tendency in narrative construction, with a view to discussing the significance and the effects of these deviations from the linear model.

First, however, we must turn to the elucidation of Nietzsche's ideas, since aside from their potential impact in encouraging certain writers to use circular forms, they provide us with an analytical toolbox and framework with which to think about the significance of these narratives. We will thus begin Chapter 2 by examining Nietzsche's early critiques, his discussion of the concept of nihilism and his idea of eternal recurrence, in order to show how these concepts follow a logical progression that underlies his thinking on the 'death of God'. This analysis will also clarify the full import of this idea by outlining both its pre-Nietzschean history and its specific significance in the work of the German philosopher. Having considered these aspects of Nietzsche's philosophy, the book will then focus on the scrutiny of some of the most prominent examples of anti-teleological narratives in which a circular structure is adopted. Our analysis will seek to account for the different ways in which circularity can be configured, as well as to elucidate the aesthetic and philosophical implications of the works under scrutiny.

The close readings have been grouped chronologically into four chapters, each composed of various sections. Every section begins by exploring the relationship between the authors and Nietzsche's ideas, and then continues with an analysis of the nature and effects of the texts' circular form. It is important to underscore at this point that while the way in which the close readings have been grouped may unintentionally suggest a perfectly progressive linear development, this was clearly not the case, since the texts studied emerged independently and in many cases their authors were unaware of each other's work.

Chapter 3 offers close readings of August Strindberg's *The Dance of Death* (1900), Gertrude Stein's 'Melanctha' (1909) and Azorín's *Doña Inés* (1925). Chapter 4 analyses Raymond Queneau's *The Bark Tree* (1933), Vladimir Nabokov's 'The Circle' (1934), Daniil Kharms' *Elizabeth Bam* (1928) and two of his short stories, 'A Tale' (1935) and 'How an Old Woman Tried to Buy Ink' (1935). Chapter 5 focuses on James Joyce's *Finnegans Wake* (1939), Jorge Luis Borges' 'The Circular Ruins' (1940) and various plays belonging to the Theatre of the Absurd (by Eugène Ionesco, Samuel Beckett and Arthur Adamov). Finally, Chapter 6 examines novels by Alain Robbe-Grillet, several of Julio Cortázar's short stories – although focusing particularly on 'The Continuity of Parks' (1964) – Italo Calvino's *If on a Winter's Night a Traveller* (1979) and Maurice Blanchot's *The Madness of the Day* (1949/1973). We will thus turn now to the analysis of Nietzsche's ideas, in order to illustrate why their consideration may have encouraged writers to abandon the linear form in search of structural alternatives.

2

Nietzsche's bequest

Buddha's shadow and the 'greatest burden'

Long before proclaiming God's death, Nietzsche had already developed a number of critiques that were to become decisive in his identification of form as an ideological construct and his critique of linearity. This line of thought begins with a radical theory of language (elaborated during his years as a professor of philology) that professed a distrust in its capacity to render reality, which in turn gave way to a full-blown sceptical epistemological critique (specifically in relation to the notions of disinterested knowledge, absolute truth, teleology and metaphysics) and which eventually led to the extended discussion of the question of nihilism and, finally, to the idea of eternal recurrence. Thus, by the late 1860s Nietzsche had written several texts which, although unpublished during his lifetime, became decisive in the gradual assembly of his 'philosophical system'. These consist essentially of a series of critiques: of Schopenhauer's work, of the concept of teleology, of language and of the problems of human perception. More specifically, these analyses further Kant's and Schopenhauer's endeavours to examine teleology and metaphysics from a materialistic or scientific viewpoint.[1]

Inspired by the reading of Friedrich Albert Lange's *History of Materialism* (1866), Nietzsche begins to question the reality of metaphysics and to dwell upon its relationship to language and art. He also reflects upon the question of teleology and, using Kant's *Critique of Judgement* as a basis, produces an extensive critique of this notion. By 1868 he had already devised voluminous notes conforming to the outline of a work that he claimed was 'half philosophical, half natural science' (Nietzsche in Crawford 1988: 105) and which was otherwise[2] identified as 'Concerning Teleology since Kant'[3] (Förster-Nietzsche 1895: 269). Nietzsche

---

[1] See Crawford (1988: 66).
[2] Namely by Elisabeth Förster-Nietzsche in her biography of Nietzsche.
[3] Nietzsche's sister claims he wrote them 'during his convalescence in March and April (1866)' (Förster-Nietzsche 1895: 269).

began to formulate his own thoughts on the notion of teleology by critiquing Kant's concept of the organic, Schopenhauer's two essays 'Critique of the Kantian Philosophy' and 'On Teleology' (both in *The World as Will and Representation* (1819)), and the ideas on teleology found in Kuno Ficher's *Immanuel Kant und Seine Lehre* (1824). As Claudia Crawford argues, the notes show that Nietzsche's sceptical epistemology derives specifically from his equally sceptical theory of language, since his 'continuing critique of metaphysics [. . .] uses as its primary tool his understanding of the limits of language and conceptuality' (1988: 106). The result is a critique that equates metaphysics with teleology with the aim of overthrowing or undermining both notions under the awareness of their inherent theological nature, their lack of an actual ontological status and therefore of absolute value.

Nietzsche's bequest (I): The early critiques

In his famous posthumously published essay 'On Truth and Lies in a Nonmoral Sense' (written in 1873), Nietzsche combines and develops some of the key ideas found in the early notes on 'On Teleology' and the two early unpublished essays 'On the Origins of Language' and 'Notes on Ancient Rhetoric' to produce a deconstruction of language's capacity to represent reality, the value of human experience and the notion of absolute truth. As Ben Hutchinson notes, such texts would become extremely influential in 'founding a scepticism as to the epistemological status of language that would underlie much twentieth century thought and literature' (2011: 30). In the following passage Nietzsche highlights the clear connection between the aforementioned ideas, arguing that an awareness of perspectivism leads to the understanding that the alleged 'absolute' laws of nature are in fact subjective conventions that we cannot know 'as such' but purely through their 'relations to other natural laws', which 'always refer back only to one another and are absolutely incomprehensible to us in their essence' since we know of them only 'what we add to them – time, space, hence relations of succession and number', and therefore that the metaphysical enterprise is senseless, theological and driven by faith:

> Everything marvelous that we admire in the laws of nature and that promotes our explanation and could mislead us into distrusting idealism, consists exclusively of the mathematical stringency and inviolability of time- and space-

perceptions. But we produce these perceptions within ourselves and out of ourselves with the same necessity as a spider spins its web. If we are compelled to grasp all things only under these forms, then it is not surprising that in all things we really grasp only these forms: for they all must carry the laws of number in themselves, and number is the very thing that is most astonishing about things. All the regularity which so impresses us about the course of the stars and in the chemical process coincides fundamentally with the properties which we ourselves project into things, so that we impress ourself with it. (Nietzsche 1989a: 253–4)

By claiming that even the inherent human understanding of the concepts of time and space are but subjective perceptions, fictional constructs, Nietzsche unveils the bias and fragility of the ostensibly solid bases upon which any understanding of the world rests. This ferocious critique dismisses all forms of disinterested knowledge, encouraging his readers to rethink these bases, to reconsider the significance and look for alternatives to the models that had been deceptively accepted as being intrinsic to nature.

Nietzsche continued to develop these ideas with his critique of teleology in the first of his *Untimely Meditations* (1876), 'David Strauss, the Confessor and the Writer', arguing that while natural scientists refrain from 'asserting anything as to the ethical or intellectual value' of the laws of nature, historicists (such as Strauss) fall into a deceptive 'religiosity' and 'pursue a consciously dishonest kind of natural science' when they assume that 'all events possess the highest intellectual value and are thus absolutely rational and purposeful' (2007: 31–2). The idea is elaborated further in his second essay, 'On the Uses and Disadvantages of History for Life', culminating in the total rejection of what Hollingdale calls 'the progressive or whiggish consequences' that derive from the historicist assumption that 'every aspect of human life is unavoidably conditioned by history' – in other words, the 'rather unexamined teleology that usually accompanies' historicism (cited in Nietzsche 2007: xv). Moreover, in this essay Nietzsche also antagonizes those 'pure thinkers [. . .] whom knowledge alone will satisfy and to whom the accumulation of knowledge is itself the goal' to the historicists, who, under the spell of teleology, observe and value life purely for its 'ends [. . .] and thus also under the domination and supreme direction of these ends' (2007: 77). 'Pure' intellectual thinking is thus opposed and prefixed to teleological thinking – making the necessity to overcome the latter unequivocal.

More importantly, however, Nietzsche relates his critique of teleology explicitly to the question of narrative in this second essay:

To think of history objectively [...] is the silent work of the dramatist; that is to say, to think of all things in relation to all others and to weave the isolated event into the whole: always with the presupposition that if a unity of plan does not already reside in things it must be implanted into them. Thus man spins his web over the past and subdues it, thus he gives expression to his artistic drive but not to his drive towards truth or justice. (Nietzsche 2007: 91)

To support his case, he goes on to cite the Austrian dramatist Franz Grillparzer's description of history as the way in which man 'imposes his concept of purpose from without upon a whole which, if it possesses a purpose, does so only inherently' as well as his claim that since every human being has a different 'individual necessity' it is 'impossible to establish any all-embracing necessity prevailing throughout all events' of life (cited in Nietzsche 2007: 91). So, Nietzsche argues that perspectivism discloses the falsehood of teleology. Furthermore, history is here revealed as the 'narrativization' of life and by extension the subliminal theological reliance that (linear) narratives have on teleology is also exposed.

Despite the fact that this second meditation is centred on the discussion of history (rather than literature), Nietzsche also identifies the major weakness of narrative linearity very clearly in this text when he states that 'If the value of a drama lay solely in its conclusion, the drama itself would be merely the most wearisome and indirect way possible of reaching this goal' (2007: 92). Although not intended as a comment on narrative per se, the passage inadvertently exposes the in-built problem of linearity – namely, as Beckett would later put it in his novel *Murphy* (1938), in linear narratives 'the end' irremediably 'degrades the way into a means'. Besides, Nietzsche develops this critique by characterizing the teleological thinking of historical culture as a 'senile occupation, that of looking back, of reckoning up, of closing accounts, of seeking consolation through remembering what has been', making a connection between teleology and theology by describing the former as 'A religion which of all the hours of a man's life holds the last to be the most important' (2007: 101). This connection and its subsequent line of reasoning are expounded throughout the remainder of the essay, stressing the underlying assumption that after God's death teleological thinking should be dead too.[4] Overall, then, by uncovering the bias of teleology in the study of history, Nietzsche unveils its contingency in narrative, implying that if history should overcome teleology, then so should literature.

---

[4] The extended (and fragmented) critique of teleology in *Untimely Meditations* comes to a close in the third essay, 'Schopenhauer as Educator', in relation to 'the cultivation of exemplars' (see 2007: 161–4) and to 'nature' (see 2007: 177–9).

A similar, albeit more explicit, effort is apparent in some sections of *Human, All Too Human* (1878). While Nietzsche deals with the discussion of teleology tacitly in his *Untimely Meditations* (without ever using the term to delineate his argument), in this text the concept is discussed univocally on two occasions. It first appears in the sixth section of the preface, where he claims that in order to become a 'free spirit' one must 'grasp the sense of perspective in every value judgement – the displacement, distortion and merely apparent teleology of horizons' (Nietzsche 2005: 9). This phrase synthesizes his prior *Untimely* critique by characterizing teleology as a deceptive appearance, and drawing the connection again between the awareness of perspectivism and the awareness of the teleological illusion.[5] The second reference appears shortly after the first, in the second section of the book's opening essay: 'On First and Last Things'. The fragment bears the title 'Family Failing of Philosophers' and in it Nietzsche criticizes philosophy's 'lack of historical sense', by which he means that philosophers take 'the most recent manifestation of man' (which is historically contingent) as being its 'fixed form from which one has to start out' (2005: 13). What is most important about this fragment, however, is that he identifies teleology as a result of this misconception: 'the whole of teleology is constructed by speaking of the man of the last four millennia as of an eternal man towards whom all things in the world have had a natural relationship from the time he began' (Nietzsche 2005: 13). Furthermore, the topic is reappraised in aphorism[6] 247 (though there the term 'teleology' is absent), 'Circular Orbit of Humanity', where the idea of an ultimate progressivist triumphant end of history is mockingly substituted by a circular return to a human 'apelikeness' (Nietzsche 2005: 117). Finally, in section 135 ('Means and End') of the addition *The Wanderer and His Shadow* (1879), the critique is reiterated again in a passage where the idea of theodicy is discussed in relation to art (bearing some resemblance to the previously mentioned quotation from Beckett's *Murphy*): 'In art the end does not justify the means, but holy means can justify the end' (Nietzsche 2005: 244).

The same is true of the pre-Zarathustrian texts *Daybreak* (1881) and *The Gay Science* (1881). In the first, Nietzsche deems teleology a 'sentimentality' (in aphorism 49, 'The Fundamental Feeling: Our Final Corruptibility'), blaming

---

[5] There are also a number of further reiterations of his epistemological scepticism, for instance in section 14, where, while commenting on the apparent unity of thought and feeling, he claims that '[t]Here too, as so often, the unity of the word is no guarantee of the unity of the thing' (2005: 19).
[6] Critics such as Karl Jaspers have expressed their reluctance to define Nietzsche's style as aphoristic, even if Nietzsche himself described the format of his passages as aphorisms in *Mixed Opinions and Maxims* (§129). (See Westerdale 2013: 14–15.)

Christianity for giving it a widespread currency. He also discusses the concept in the year of *Daybreak*'s publication in his letters to Overbeck, drawing a parallelism between himself and Spinoza given their shared denial of 'the freedom of the will, teleology, the moral word order, the unegoistic, and evil' (Nietzsche 1976: 92). *The Gay Science* also contains numerous restatements of the critique, beginning with a passage that shall be discussed later in this chapter due to it being one of the earliest announcements of the idea of eternal recurrence: the aphorism 'Let us beware'. In it, Nietzsche pushes his ideas one step further by characterizing teleology as an 'aesthetic anthropomorphism' (1974: 109), a characterization which is all the more telling considering its context, since it is drawn in the midst of an oblique antagonism between a rational, ordered and teleological cosmos, and a chaotic and eternally recurring one. Even more explicitly, however, Nietzsche fosters his sceptical epistemological critique in relation to causality, by arguing (in aphorism 112, 'Cause and Effect') that notions such as 'lines, surfaces, bodies, atoms, divisible times, divisible spaces' do not correspond to reality and hence that all explanations using these concepts are merely human delusions produced as a result of a theological urge (1974: 110). He also restates this idea in aphorism 121, 'Life Not an Argument', making again the connection between the illusion upon which cosmological or scientific explanations of life are reliant and narrative:

> We have arranged for ourselves a world in which we are able to live – by positing bodies, lines, planes, causes and effects, motion and rest, form and content; without these articles of faith no one could endure living! But that does not prove them. Life is not an argument; the conditions of life might include error. (Nietzsche 1974: 117)

Thus, by the time Nietzsche wrote *Thus Spoke Zarathustra*, his critique of linearity had already been tacitly yet almost fully accomplished. Having elucidated the implications of perspectivism, questioned the power of the senses to perceive reality, the capacity of language to render it and produced an extensive critique of our 'aesthetic anthropomorphisms' (such as the notions of a divisible time and space, causality and specially teleology), all of which would gradually lead to his extensive discussion of the question of nihilism, he had already set the ground for writers to consider these same issues in relation to narrative, to replace linearity with Zarathustra's circularity – to take time back to its circular roots. First, however, Nietzsche was to take up the notorious discussion of the question of nihilism: a necessary prerequisite for the full-blown development of his idea of eternal recurrence.

Nietzsche's bequest (II): Buddha's shadow[7]

The term 'nihilism' does not appear in Nietzsche's writings until 1880, by which time he had already published *The Birth of Tragedy* (1872), *Philosophy in the Tragic Age of the Greeks* (1873), *Untimely Meditations* (1873–6), *Human, All Too Human* (1878) and *Mixed Opinion and Maxims* (1879). Although initially the word only surfaces sporadically in his notes, and in these early appearances is not given significant attention, it gradually becomes one of his central concerns, starting, as Shane Weller points out, with the famous sentence found in a notebook dated autumn 1885–autumn 1886: 'Nihilism stands at the door: whence comes to us this uncanniest of all guests?' (Nietzsche 1968: 7).

The first published book where Nietzsche discusses nihilism explicitly is *Beyond Good and Evil* (1886); however, at this point he also reworks some of his earlier texts to incorporate the term, including the preface for the revised edition of *The Birth of Tragedy*, the appendix of songs the fifth book of *The Gay Science* (1882). In the revised preface of *The Birth of Tragedy* he makes nihilism the central force behind the necessity of advocating an aesthetic interpretation and valuation of life, and therefore of considering the Apollonian-Dionysian opposition. In *The Gay Science*, he incorporates a passage (§345 'Our question mark'), which not only gives an overview of the history of nihilism (Christianity, Buddhism, pessimism) but elucidates the concept with the purpose of averting the inevitable dilemma that it entails: '"Either abolish your venerations or – yourselves!" The latter would be nihilism; but would not the former also be – nihilism?' (Nietzsche 1974: 204). So, in the works written after the 1885-6 notebook that Nietzsche either saw published during his lifetime or intended for publication, the term appears frequently, with the most extensive analyses of the concept being found in the third section of *On the Genealogy of Morals* (1887), where he focuses mostly on the relationship between nihilism, art and science – and where he also declares his intention to write a 'History of European Nihilism' (see §27). The concept is also discussed, although to a lesser extent, in

---

[7] Parts of this section were modified and expanded into an essay entitled 'Nietzsche's Shadow: On the Origin and Development of the Term Nihilism', published in *Philosophy and Criticism* in December 2020 (https://doi.org/10.1177/0191453720975454).

The Anti-Christ (1895), principally in relation to Christianity and Buddhism (see sections 6, 7, 9, 11, 20).

Nevertheless, the ideas which constitute the basis for his thought on nihilism are already present in his texts written prior to 1885. In his 'On Truth and Lies in a Nonmoral Sense', for instance, Nietzsche's epistemological distrust (which might at first sight seem to be a form of epistemological nihilism) unveils the problematics of science and positivism as nihilistic devaluations of life. In his *Untimely Meditations* too, the preoccupation with nihilism is evident in his repudiation of David Strauss' progressivist 'new faith' and in the revaluation of life (as opposed to knowledge) in the second 'Meditation' (1874). Even in his adoption of the 'aphoristic' style, initially in a work that may be perceived as being ostensibly hedonistic, *Human, All Too Human* (1878), the influence of the concept is palpable since this choice of form constitutes in itself a statement against systematization and hence a denunciation of logic, reason and structure – nihilistic values for Nietzsche, given their inherent positing of a superior metaphysical dimension in regard to physical existence. So while the most extensive discussions of nihilism are found in the works written after 1885 and, above all, in the *Nachlass*, the key ideas underlining this discussion were also developed progressively within his early published works.[8]

In any case, all these instances may be regarded as evidence of the development of a preoccupation which was later synthesized under the proclamation of the 'death of God', in section 108, 'New Battles', of Book 1 in the first published version of *The Gay Science* (1882):

> After Buddha was dead, they still showed his shadow in a cave for centuries – a tremendous, gruesome shadow. God is dead; but given the way people are, there may still for millennia be caves in which they show his shadow. – And we – we must still defeat his shadow as well! (Nietzsche 1974: 109)

This proclamation marks Nietzsche's first announcement of the perpetual threat that nihilism entails, the analysis of which would constitute his primary concern throughout his subsequent work.

---

[8] He begins in *The Birth of Tragedy*, where Nietzsche takes the first step towards this end as a critique of the moral interpretation of life; continues in *The Gay Science*, where all his fundamental concepts related to the question of nihilism are already present (perspectivism, the death of God, eternal recurrence, etc.); and culminates in *Thus Spoke Zarathustra*, one of his most iconic works (a sort of recapitulation of his philosophy) containing his most extensive discussion of the notion of eternal recurrence.

Hence, even if the first published use of the term 'nihilism' is not found until *Beyond Good and Evil*, its advent had already been proclaimed in *The Gay Science* (even prior to its 1887 revision) and its repercussions (the birth of the Overman and especially the necessity of eternal recurrence) discussed extensively in *Thus Spoke Zarathustra* (1883).[9] Yet, while the importance of the problem of nihilism is already evident from Nietzsche's first published text, the in-depth analysis of the concept does not occur until his announcement of the 'death of God', which triggers a gradual and ever more extensive consideration of its implications in his ensuing works. In these, his thought on nihilism follows a threefold development. Nietzsche begins by establishing Socratism and Platonism as forms of nihilism. He then equates these philosophies with Christianity (as well as with Buddhism). He defines Christianity as 'nihilistic in the most profound sense', since 'it negates all aesthetic values – the only values recognized in *The Birth of Tragedy*'; stresses that nihilism is 'rooted' in 'one particular interpretation, the Christian-moral one' through its positing of a superior reality that undermines life; and argues that Christianity is itself 'the cause of nihilism', given that it inevitably entails the eventual devaluation of those same values that it posits (Nietzsche 1968: 271, 7, 13–14). Finally, Nietzsche declares that nihilism is intrinsic to Western thought, at the same time a condition of the past, present and future: beginning with Platonism, developing into Christianity and reaching out into the pessimism of the nineteenth century but also announcing its advent everywhere 'in a hundred signs' (1968: 3), an advent that will mark the era of 'the next two centuries' (1968: 3).

It is not only nihilism's temporality that is paradoxical. The task of its announcement and overcoming also calls for the same contradictory necessity of 'look[ing] back when relating what will come; as the first perfect nihilist of Europe who, however, has even now lived through the whole of nihilism, to the end, leaving it behind, outside himself' (Nietzsche 1968: 3). In other words, as Weller puts it:

> nihilism is that which belongs to the past in the sense not just that it commenced with Plato, or that it follows upon 'pessimism' in the period 1830-50 [. . .] but

---

[9] Although Nietzsche's earliest proclamation of the 'death of God' appears in *The Gay Science*, it is in *Thus Spoke Zarathustra* that the question of nihilism is first considered fully and perhaps described most effectively. In *Zarathustra*, Nietzsche does not expound his thoughts dogmatically or systematically (an approach that he himself repudiated) but through parables that require interpretation, making his style an essential part of its meaning. Moreover, the work's poetic nature also highlights the importance that literature (and art in general) had for Nietzsche.

also that it has already been surpassed in the one who announces its coming and who takes it as his task to write its history before its arrival. (2008: 15)

So, in the same way that the development of the concept of nihilism can be separated into three distinct phases within Nietzsche's thinking, his definition is also comprised of three basic elements. As Gilles Deleuze points out, for Nietzsche nihilism is at one and the same time 'the value of nil taken on by life', 'the fiction of higher values which give it this value' and 'the will to nothingness which is expressed in these higher values' (1983: 147).

If Nietzsche begins by tracing the origins of nihilism back to certain fundamental aspects within Socrates' philosophy it is because it establishes reason as an 'instrument' or mechanism with which life can be judged from an external point of view, creating a problematic dichotomy – 'the problem "of the real and the apparent world"' (1989a: 16) – that is discussed in his first published mention of the term 'nihilism'.[10] For Nietzsche, then, Socrates' philosophy is a 'symptom of decadence'; he represents 'a moment of the profoundest perversity in the history of values', a decadence emphasized through his final 'rejection of life' (discussed in section 340 of *The Gay Science*) (1989b: 430). On the other hand, Platonism is also condemned on account of its elaborating Socrates' philosophy by arguing that given its (alleged) inherent objectivity, reason logically posits an overarching, metaphysical, transcendent 'true' world, with regard to which the real, physical world is no more than a 'perverted copy' (Diken 2009: 17).

In other words, Nietzsche describes Platonism as the belief that 'the more subtilized, attenuated, transient a thing or a man is, the more valuable he becomes; the less real, the more valuable' (1968: 308). This, Nietzsche claims, is Platonism's inexorable effect:

> Plato measured the degree of reality by the degree of value and said: The more 'Idea', the more being. He reversed the concept 'reality' and said: 'What you take for real is an error, and the nearer we approach the "Idea", the nearer we approach "truth"'. (1968: 308)

Thus, by subjugating the existing world to 'a supra-sensory realm beyond earthly life', Plato not only demeans life, earthly experience, its values and truth but also makes it impossible, as Bülent Diken points out, 'to create new values that are in accordance with this world' (2009: 17). Consequently, Nietzsche argues that by positing these views, Socrates and (especially) Plato give rise to nihilism

---

[10] See section 10, part 1, of *Beyond Good and Evil*.

since they annihilate life in order to emphasize a superior world, the superior realm of the world of ideas or eternal and perfect forms, an annihilating process which would subsequently be 'popularized and turned into a mass movement by monotheistic religions' (Diken 2009: 17).

This Socratic and Platonic (and Christian) 'devaluation of life' is at the same time an affirmation of three central values: 'the concept of "aim" [*Zweck*], the concept of "unity" [*Einheit*], and the concept of "truth" [*Wahrheit*]' (Nietzsche 1968: 13). It is also a moral interpretation of life as opposed to an aesthetic one – in absolute contrast with Nietzsche's view as expressed in *The Birth of Tragedy*, where he states that 'only as an aesthetic phenomenon can existence and the world justified eternally' (1967: 24). However, the Socratic/Platonic/Christian affirmation is one that 'turns back upon itself, and judges itself as a falsification', devaluating those central values that it posits, owing to both internal reasons – 'the internal logic of moral interpretation' (Weller 2008: 16) – and external or historical ones, such as the decline of faith in religion and the rise of pessimism, a process which is tersely articulated in the notorious claim 'God is dead'. The consequence of this realization is what Nietzsche describes in a passage dated spring–fall 1887 as 'The most extreme form of nihilism', the awareness that 'every belief, every considering-something-true, is necessarily false because there simply is no true world' (1968: 14).

Nietzsche identifies two possible responses to nihilism: active and passive (see 1968: 17). He deems active nihilism to be the only true answer, since passive nihilism remains in essence a moral valuation and therefore inherently nihilistic, given that 'morality is a way of turning one's back on the will to existence' (Nietzsche 1968: 7). Passive nihilism considers 'existence as punishment', which is precisely what Nietzsche condemns in Socrates' philosophy (1968: 11). Thus, Arthur Danto is right to argue that although Nietzsche's conception of nihilism can be traced back to the pessimism or 'Nihilism of Emptiness' of the 'Buddhist or Hindu teaching', through this Oriental pessimism he is able to construct an affirmative attitude towards life, a 'new way to say "Yes"' (1965: 28–9). The overcoming of nihilism by the active nihilist is paradoxical not only in that it is a negation which is in itself the greatest form of affirmation: that of life as such, but also in that to overcome nihilism, one has to counter it constantly, in a continuous effort to overcome the values, norms and structures imposed by culture and tradition – to re-evaluate existence relentlessly in order to avoid the grasp of nihilism. For this to be achieved, one must stand at the same time before, within and beyond, but also inside, on-the-limit and outside of nihilism.

This highly paradoxical time and place, Nietzsche claims, is that of art: 'It is in art that the question of the limit – and, above all, the limit between negation and affirmation – becomes critical' (Weller 2008: 21).

Accordingly, Nietzsche's way of overcoming nihilism is not in itself an ideology but a re-evaluative or deconstructive call to arms. It is the proclamation that since all aspects of life, as well as all the ideological systems that attempt to explain them (science, philosophy, art, religion), are merely the products of 'the will to power' – 'an impulse and a drive to impose upon an essentially chaotic reality a form and structure', to transform it into 'a world congenial to human understanding while habitable by human intelligence' (Danto 1965: 12) – one must revaluate existence continuously in order to destabilize those values that have been assumed as true and therefore engage in a constant process of creation and becoming. Given Nietzsche's assertion that 'the measure of the desire for knowledge depends upon the measure to which the will to power grows in a species', meaning that 'a species grasps a certain amount of reality in order to become master of it, in order to press it into service' (1968: 267), the values that all ideological systems posit will necessarily devaluate themselves. The only possible response to nihilism is hence 'a Dionysian yes [*Ja-sagen*] to the world as it is, without exceptions, exemptions or deductions' (Nietzsche in Danto 1965: 15). For this reason, nihilism can only achieve its culmination in the notion of the 'eternal recurrence of the same' (*ewige Wiederkehr des Gleichen*), since the existence of a universe which repeats itself ad infinitum is, in Nietzsche's view, the only real alternative to a teleological understanding of the world and the idea of progress, or in Nietzsche's own words: '"the eternal recurrence." That is the most extreme form of nihilism: (the "meaningless") eternally!' (1968: 36).

One can therefore summarize Nietzsche's thought on nihilism as a twofold process: nihilism as the negation of life through its subordination to a 'higher realm' and nihilism as the consequence of the 'death of God' – in other words, as the realization of the fictitiousness of this higher realm. Moreover, the question of nihilism leads Nietzsche to the idea of the eternal recurrence of the same. The relationship between these two concepts is established as a logical and intrinsic necessity, a fundamental characteristic of both. The sole proposed response to nihilism (active nihilism) cannot take place without the idea of eternal recurrence, since without a perpetual affirmation in the face of the eternal recurrence of the same escape from existence remains a (devaluative) option, its absence precluding the true fulfilment of nihilism. The eternal recurrence is necessary if nihilism is to achieve its most extreme form – and if it is to be overcome. It is therefore necessary to proceed with the analysis of Nietzsche's key concept in the understanding of nihilism (for some even in the totality of his thought), in order to clarify its precise nature as Nietzsche understood it, its antecedents or precursors, and the reasons for considering it necessary for the realization of active nihilism. This will help us understand how this ultimate expression of nihilism relates to the process of formal experimentation taking place in twentieth-century European literature and leading to the emergence of a circular narrative trend.

Nietzsche's bequest (III): Ouroboros

In a frequently cited anecdote found in the section on *Thus Spoke Zarathustra* in the posthumously published autobiography *Ecce Homo* (1908), Nietzsche writes that the idea of eternal recurrence came to him as a revelation while he was 'walking through the woods along the lake of Silvaplana; at a powerful pyramidal rock not far from Surlei' (2010: 295). The intriguing passage (which bears striking similarities to the description of a divine epiphany) recounts how, having experienced this abysmal insight, Nietzsche decided to render his 'thought of thoughts' hastily on a piece of paper through the beautifully poetic yet obscure inscription: '60,000 feet beyond man and time' (2010: 295). However, regardless of his claim, and as several critics point out, the idea of eternal recurrence is not so much the innovative product of an uncanny revelation as a revision or appropriation of a notion of circular time present in a number of ancient theologies.

Circular conceptions of time appear in the religions of ancient Egypt and Babylonia, in Norse mythology, in several Asian spiritual traditions such as Vedism, Jainism, Hinduism, Buddhism and Taoism, in the Mayan and Aztec Mesoamerican civilizations, in Mazdaism and Ismailism, and in the beliefs of the Native American Hopi tribe, among others. Certainly, prior to the rise of the monotheistic traditions, most societies seem to share a circular conception of time. Yet, far from appearing repeatedly in an immutable fashion, these notions are of a very distinct nature. In some instances, the concept of circularity merely refers to patterns of natural events (such as the cycle of night and day or the seasons) that either recur within an underlying dimension of eternal linear time or are taken as paradigmatic of its overall nature (which is accordingly deemed circular). In others, it refers to the cycle of creation and destruction of the earth or even of the whole cosmos; in these cases, too, circularity may or may not coexist with a supra-dimensional notion of linearity. And still in other traditions eternal recurrence is a phenomenon that affects human and animal life, so that it is not only the planet or the universe that recurs in cycles but the beings that exist within it that are repetitively reincarnated into different bodies.

Moreover, in other spiritual traditions (such as Buddhism) the notion of time as a true substance is discarded altogether as an illusion. Nevertheless, even in these cases the concept of recurrence habitually prevails as the ostensible pattern encouraging individuals to be deceived into perceiving time as a real or ontological substance. What is more, although in some of these creeds circularity is subjugated to, or coexistent with, an overarching notion of linear time (which is only perceptible, however, to the deities that stand outside of the cyclic recurrences), in other instances the gods (and hence, time itself) are also subject to the endless circular pattern of creation and destruction. Needless to say, these divergent notions are not mutually exclusive and appear in all sorts of miscellaneous combinations.

Thus, in ancient Egypt, one of the earliest recorded instances where the nature of the cosmos was 'based upon the principle of the eternal return' (Antelme & Rossini 1998: 2), the notion of circularity was combined with a belief in a hidden demiurge (the great Atum, creator of the universe, from whom the world originated and to whom all will eventually return), an afterlife (which was simply considered as a transition where individuals were to await the beginning of a new cycle) and a conception of linear time (as evidenced by the existence of the terms '*neheh*', meaning circular time, and '*djet*', linear time). The ancient Egyptian conception of eternal recurrence not only explained the cyclical processes of the world, such as the flooding of the Nile or the daily journey of Ra (the sun god), but also described the general pattern of the cosmos, which was thought to recur in its entirety. A similar belief was present in the Mayan and Aztec civilizations, which also combined a circular understanding of the creation and destruction of the planet (the Mayans, for instance, believed that the earth had been destroyed four times and created five times) with a polytheistic pantheon and a notion of afterlife. This belief is also found in the religion of the Babylonians, who held that all events in the cosmos, including the periodic creation and destruction of the earth, recurred in what was called a 'Great Year', which some 'commentators set [. . .] at 36,000 years' (Morris 1986: 18).

In the ancient Vedic texts, time is also considered as both the 'manifestation of Brahma (God in his aspect as creator of the universe)' and therefore linear (emanating from God), but also essentially circular: since 'the act of creation recurs along with everything else' in cycles, with each cycle being divided into four stages or Yugas, vast periods of time having a 'character of its own that dominates the age' (Benedict 2011: 21).[11] However, in two of the spiritual traditions that emanated from Vedism – Hinduism and Buddhism – circularity acquired an added significance. Although in Hinduism time is also often posited as a manifestation of God and its flowing described as circular (the cycle of time is called Kalachakra, and, as in Vedism, it is divided into Yugas), eternal recurrence also conforms to the pattern of the process that individuals undergo after death, returning to life through a transmigration of the soul. Yet, since Hinduism is not so much a religion per se as a 'collection of religions', where 'one person's sacred scripture is by no means necessarily someone else's', even the concept of reincarnation 'is *not* a universally accepted part of Hindu teaching and faith' (Lipner 1994: 2). This type of recurrence, in which life is presented as an evaluative trial that individuals undergo with the ultimate aim of escaping earthly existence, is also present in Buddhism, albeit in this creed it is merely considered as 'a function of mind' that 'has no reality of itself' (Benedict 2010: 21).[12] Finally, another extreme form of theological circularity is present in Norse mythology, where all that exists (including the deities that created and govern the earth) was thought to be subjected to a circular process of total destruction and renewal.

Circularity was therefore generally presented either as a quality of earthly existence or as the overarching condition of the cosmos, in many cases coinciding with the existence of eternal beings and (accordingly) with a notion of linear time. However, some ancient civilizations also display a far more extreme form of eternal return (one that has considerable affinities with Nietzsche's idea), where linearity is rejected altogether and replaced with an entirely circular conception of time. This type of recurrence was discussed in Greece, among others, by Eudemus of Rhodes,[13] who commented on an idea original to the Pythagoreans (but also adopted by the Epicureans and later by the Stoics). Eudemus noted that if all things do in fact recur infinitely in exactly the same way, then everything actually happens only once. Driven by this insight, he distinguished between

---

[11] In Taoism, the universe and time are the same thing, an infinite number of cycles.
[12] Thus, the Buddhist Wheel of Life (Samsara) does not represent an ontological truth but a model of the human perception of earthly existence.
[13] Although the idea was not originally Eudemus', he was the first commentator to relate the Pythagorean notion of recurrence to the concept of 'sameness', bearing evident similarities with Nietzsche's description of the eternal return.

two types of recurrence. The first is present in the 'natural order of things': the 'movements of the heavenly bodies and the phenomena produced by them, such as solstices and equinoxes', which although deemed 'the same' are in fact numerically different and therefore 'exist a number of times' (Ouspensky 1997: 468). The other kind is one in which 'numerically the same things recur', a form of absolute recurrence where 'there exists no difference in time, because if [. . .] things are the same, what occurred before and what will occur afterwards are also the same', so that 'Everything is the same and therefore time is the same' (cited in Simplicius 2014: 142). Eudemus also describes the repercussions of such a notion at a personal level in a fragment that bears significant resemblances to some of Nietzsche's latter formulations, arguing that if such a cosmological model were true, 'then I also will romance, holding my staff, while you sit there, and everything else will be the same' (cited in Simplicius 2014: 142).

The two types of circularity distinguished by Eudemus, as well as the numerous varieties of eternal recurrence found in the different ancient religions (some of which do not fit into his paradigm), can be synthesized and subdivided into two fundamental or overarching categories of circular time. In the first, circularity is subdued to the figure of a deity and coexists with a notion of linear time, acquiring a specific significance: be it evaluative (as a means to assess the mortal beings which experience it), dualistic (as a reflection of the ambivalent nature of the gods and existence) or hierarchical (as a manner in which to emphasize the subordinated nature of the entities subjected to the processes of decay and recurrence in relation to the omniscient status of the eternal deities that are exempt from these cycles). On the other hand, we find an antagonistic type of circularity which is not subordinated to linearity or serves a specific purpose but represents the epitome of meaninglessness. Nietzsche's eternal recurrence is an example of this second category. In instances of the first type – where circular time coincides with an overarching sense of linearity or 'eternity' – the former generally functions as a representation of the concept of 'becoming' while the latter represents the category of 'being'. In the second sort the notion of 'being' is eradicated and replaced by a perpetual 'becoming'.[14]

The previous survey of ancient conceptions of time shows that the idea of circularity was very common prior to the rise of Abrahamic theology. In fact, its replacement by linearity was a direct legacy of the Judaeo-Christian tradition[15]

---

[14] Being exists only as the being of becoming.
[15] See Cahill (2010).

and previous monotheistic religions such as Zoroastrianism. A brief overview of the history of the perception of time reveals that the notion of linearity and the understanding of time as an absolute substance were repeatedly challenged prior to the rise and expansion of the Abrahamic faiths (especially in ancient Greece), but scarcely thereafter up until the twentieth century.[16] This is arguably a result of both Christianity's hegemony after the fourth century and the adoption of the linear model in Newtonian physics.

Nietzsche's efforts to assert the idea of eternal recurrence against the Abrahamic notion of linearity may therefore be better understood as the logical result of his full-blown attack on these 'nihilistic' doctrines – an attack on the notions of teleology, eschatology and theodicy, which the linear model entails – rather than as a direct appropriation of previous theological notions of mythical time. Furthermore, many of these ancient conceptions of circular time are fundamentally distinct from Nietzsche's idea of eternal recurrence. While in most ancient theologies time was established as a bi-dimensional concept, in which circularity was subordinated to linearity, Nietzsche argued the opposite: linearity as a mirage hiding the ultimate reality of circularity.

Nietzsche's bequest (IV): 'Second as farce'

Even if we disregard the preponderance of circularity in ancient religion as the source of Nietzsche's idea, other extreme forms of eternal return, bearing striking similarities to Nietzsche's concept, are present in the work of a number of previous and contemporary thinkers. They can be found, for instance, in several texts which were either owned or known to have been read by Nietzsche, and even in the work of some predecessors and contemporaries possibly unknown to him, such as Giambattista Vico's *The New Science* (1725),[17] Louis-Auguste Blanqui's *Eternity by the Stars* (1872) or Gustave Le Bon's *Man and Society* (1881). Among Nietzsche's contemporaries, Eugen Dühring discussed eternal recurrence (although to dismiss it) in his *Kursus der Philosophie* (1875), a copy of which Nietzsche owned and commented. Furthermore, a text that he was reading during the summer of his supposed revelation, Johann Gustav Vogt's *Die Kraft* (1878), also contains references to a similar notion. Besides,

---

[16] Giambattista Vico's circular theory of history (which is discussed in detail in Chapter 5) is one of few examples.
[17] Donald Verene claims that Nietzsche never read Vico (see Verene 1994).

Heinrich Heine, whom Nietzsche considered (along with himself) 'by far one of the foremost artists in the German language' (2010: 242), also describes the idea in almost exactly the same terms as Nietzsche later discusses it in a letter to his lifelong friend Carl Freiherr von Gersdorff – as well as in aphorism §1062 of the posthumously published *The Will to Power*:

> For time is infinite, but the things in time, the concrete bodies are finite [. . .] Now, however long a time may pass, according to the eternal laws governing the combinations of this eternal play of repetition, all configurations that have previously existed on this earth must yet meet, attract, repulse, kiss, and corrupt each other again. . . . And thus it will happen one day that a man will be born again, just like me [. . .]. (Heine in Kaufmann 1956: 318)

Based on this evidence, many scholars insist that Nietzsche's notion of eternal recurrence is no more than an appropriation of previous conceptions of circular time. Pierre Brunel, for instance, emphasizes that there is 'apparently nothing original' in Nietzsche's thought of thoughts, since he was merely 'returning to the idea of the infinite recurrence of the same events formulated by Chrysippus, and to the active fatalism of Epictetus' (1996: 420). Nietzsche himself acknowledged his awareness that the idea featured in ancient Greek philosophy (both in the Pythagoreans and in the Stoics), referencing them, for example, in the second of his *Untimely Meditations*, or remarking in *Ecce Homo* that the idea '*could* possibly [. . .] also have been taught by Heraclitus', or in any case by the Stoics, 'who derived all their fundamental ideas from Heraclitus, [and] possessed traces of it' (2010: 274). However, Nietzsche does not avow a direct adoption of the idea, since he includes and italicizes the word 'could' when stating that Heraclitus (and, subsequently, the Stoics) had 'possibly' also taught the eternal recurrence, highlighting the distinction between his notion and that of other thinkers. Indeed, even if echoes of the ancient idea of recurrence are plentiful, his own conception differs significantly to that of his predecessors because it contains several fundamental implications in relation to his critique of modernity, such as that of allowing for the fulfilment of active nihilism: the ultimate affirmation of life.

Moreover, regardless of whether Nietzsche experienced a revelation in his walk through the Swiss woods or appropriated the idea from a contemporary or earlier thinker, the fact is that the situation in Europe during the first half of the nineteenth century was an evident source of inspiration for the elaboration of such a notion. Beginning with the Napoleonic Wars (1803–15) and the failure of the Congress of Vienna (1814-15) to put an effective end to the tensions they awoke, the social, political and economic landscape of the continent experienced an unprecedented transformation that would forever change its sociopolitical structure.

The destruction caused by the resistance to Napoleon gave rise to various agrarian and industrial problems, which, in turn, caused a generalized economic crisis, not only in Europe but throughout the world. The population in Europe also increased to the point of doubling that of the preceding century and with this growth came noteworthy effects, such as the expansion of cities, which transformed the labour market, the occupational and social structure and the organization of nation states. This led to harsher living conditions but also facilitated social cohesion, organization and mobilization inspired by the circulation of new ideas calling for economic and political improvements (such as the establishment of representative governments). Thus, by 1830 the situation in Europe was ideal for revolutionary upheaval, and it was not long before the dissatisfaction of the masses materialized in the form of a series of revolutions which, in the space of thirty years, spread across the continent (France, Italy, Prussia, Austria, the Italian states and the West German states). This situation proved that the spirit of 1789 remained alive and that ideas such as popular sovereignty, equality and labour rights had permeated throughout Europe, resulting in the flourishing of political and social struggle. However, by 1850 the optimistic vision awoken by such revolutionary activity had been shattered, perpetuating an economic, political and social precariousness, and encouraging many to doubt whether true social and political progress was possible.

The failure of the revolutionary upheavals of 1830-48, added to the failure of the French Revolution, the subsequent fiasco of the Napoleonic empire and the ineffectiveness of the Congress of Vienna, made the enlightened faith in the ideal of progress or the Hegelian concept of development as the result of the materialization of dialectical struggle seem to many no more than a fantasy, among both the more conservative and the more liberal members of society. Marx, who (with Engels) had published his *Manifesto of the Communist Party* in 1848 and observed the succession of revolutionary uprisings with a sort of expectant optimism, soon saw his expectations crushed by the worker's democratic election of Louis Napoleon III in France. Such events demonstrated not only that nationalism could work against communism but that class struggle could result in a return to a former unjust (classist) sociopolitical structure, rather than in progressive change. This led Marx to declare that 'history repeats itself, first as tragedy, second as farce'. So, it is not surprising that by as early as 1873 Nietzsche was criticizing Hegelian idealism on the basis of its assumption that there is a 'final aim' and *'reason'* in world history (1976: 39), proposing instead an alternative model that rejected Hegel's belief in a goal, purpose or meaning to life and emphasizing, instead, that any affirmation of an alleged intrinsic sense to existence or world history is but the mere imposition of a subjective interpretation.[18]

The exhausted optimism of the revolutionary movements and the ongoing political instability crystalized after 1848 in the form of nationalism, leading to the unifications of Italy in 1870 and Germany in 1871. As a result of these unifications, and the re-establishment of the republic in France, the balance that had been upheld in Europe since the end of the Napoleonic Wars was broken, positioning Germany as the central continental power. Nietzsche, who at twenty-seven was already a professor at Basel when Germany became a unified nation state, had initially been hopeful about the possibilities of the unification,[19] but by as early as 1871 considered the whole process a calamity. His participation as a medical orderly in the Franco-Prussian War (which led to the unification) opened his eyes to the banality of the endeavour, since he felt that rather than demonstrating intellectual or cultural superiority it confirmed that Germany had given up genuine cultural development in exchange for a vulgar hunger for political domination and material gain. Indeed, as Walter Kaufmann points out, if there is a single enemy to which Nietzsche directs the fierce criticism of his earlier works, it is the State, 'which is pictured as the very Devil' (1956: 103). Nietzsche positioned himself in diametrical opposition to the Hegelian conception of the nation as that which could make possible the 'supra-social enterprises' of the 'realm of Absolute Spirit' (Kaufmann 1956: 104). The reason for this was that while both of them 'considered customary morality essentially social and hence bracketed it with the State' (Kaufmann 1956: 104), Hegel defended this notion whereas Nietzsche rejected it, considering the modern political nation to be responsible for the deterioration of culture through a mediocre education that levels society through demagogic and populist educational policies.

The events of 1848, added to the subsequent rise of nationalism and the processes of national unification, also brought about a sudden and radical scepticism towards organized religion. The church increasingly lost its power and credibility, resulting in a general feeling of disaffection that encouraged a

---

[18] See 'Notes' (1873), in Kaufmann (1956: 39).
[19] See Young (2010: 71).

significant part of society to abandon their faith. This collapse of religious belief was replaced by a more 'modern faith' in politics and science, a senseless shift in Nietzsche's eyes, since he considered both of these disciplines as correlatives of religion: intrinsically tied to faith and morality, and thus providing human beings with nihilistic (in the sense of life-negating) values and references with which to interpret, understand or lead life. If Nietzsche describes politics and the State as 'the coldest of all cold monsters' and 'the new idol', respectively (1976: 160), science is likewise criticized for its underlying belief that 'truth is more important than everything else' and hence for resting on the same 'metaphysical faith' as religion (1974: 281). It is the emergence of these 'modern faiths' that would lead Nietzsche to condemn the nihilistic process by which ideologies posit values that ultimately and inevitably lose their apparent importance, once their lack of worth is made palpable by history.

The socio-economic and political changes discussed earlier, added to the shift from theology to politics and science, may well have led Nietzsche to see life as characterized by perpetual change, with no purpose, meaning or end. However, these same conditions led to the rise of 'realism' in the latter part of the nineteenth century. In the literary world, this phenomenon took shape in the form of the rise of the Realist novel and the escalating importance of the periodical and journal as literary media. In science, it came largely as a result of Darwin's *On the Origin of Species* (1859), which challenged the traditional notion of what a human being is by emphasizing that natural selection was a random process and not the result of a logical or idealized progress. In politics, it came in the form of Bismarckian *Realpolitik* (ideology shaped by the belief that 'the end justifies the means'). Thus, overall, the study of society came to be characterized by a 'cold-eyed view', resulting from the realization that mankind was not inherently different from the rest of the animal kingdom and that there was no underlying force, be it spiritual, intellectual or dialectical, behind human history. In other words, reason had led to the destabilization of the human being within the universe. For Nietzsche, the major logical inference to be drawn from this climate was the disavowal of the Hegelian notion of history as a developmental progressive process shaped by dialectical conflict or even of the subsequent Marxist notion of dialectical materialism.

Nietzsche's work marked, then, the opening of a new era, where God, along with any alternative metaphysical values, was deemed dead. In so doing he was rejecting a philosophical tradition which had dominated Western thought from Plato to the Enlightenment. By questioning the value systems of modernity and rejecting the validity of all traditional values, Nietzsche rejected 'the ideal of progress as posited by enlightened rationalism, according to which (especially in Hegel) progress is defined as the evolutionary materialization of reason in history' (Golomb 2004: 219). If Hegel saw historical progress as following the pattern of an ascending spiral, which developed as a result of the dialectical struggle between opposing forces, Nietzsche contradicted this view by positing the idea that the process of change which unfolds as an outcome of this conflict does not lead to progress but to a circular pattern of infinite recurrence. This notion was soon to be reinforced by the succession of conflicts (the Russian Revolution, the Spanish Civil War, the two world wars) which shattered Europe both physically and spiritually, exposing the extent of humanity's destructive power and the questionable nature of the values that had led to such horrors.

As a result, for an increasing number of intellectuals (of which Nietzsche is the clear precursor) these political and social crises revealed that conflict did not lead to progress at all. On the contrary, they appeared to point to the fact that history repeats itself (even Marx admitted as much) and that struggles undertaken in the name of improvement actually resulted in the opposite: relapse and regression. Hence, to many it became clear that the French Revolution's attempt to eradicate absolutism had failed, begetting the exact same sociopolitical conditions that it sought to eliminate, by leading to the establishment of an autocracy (the Napoleonic empire); that the Congress of Vienna's attempt to avoid revolutionary upheavals through a return to absolutism also failed, leading to an unstable climate out of which revolution was able to re-emerge in 1848; that these revolutions, aimed at freeing the numerous absolutist European nations from their monarchical yoke, paradoxically gave way to the re-establishment of such monarchies, as well as to the emergence of new nation states that explicitly undermined the nationalistic values which had led to their formation; and so on. In short, the linear (or helical) progressivist models of world history (such as Hegel's) seemed to be manifestly contradicted by the history of the nineteenth century viewed from the 1870s and beyond. This questioning of the idea of history as a form of progress would only be exacerbated with the outbreak of the First World War, which, for many Europeans, only confirmed Nietzsche's diagnosis.

So, as the preceding analysis suggests, although the concept of eternal recurrence is by no means original to the German philosopher, his idea stands apart from other circular conceptions of time, having a direct relevance to the historical period and specific implications for the philosophical thinking of his era. Given the disparity of the theological, ontological and ideological implications of Nietzsche's conception of eternal return, and the crucial significance of the sociopolitical context in inspiring (consciously or unconsciously) the creation (or revelation) of such a notion, it is important to set his idea alongside other (prior and contemporary) notions of circularity. More than a metaphysical framework, Nietzsche's idea worked as a direct critique of linearity (as the inherent structural paradigm of modernity) imposed in Western thought through Judaeo-Christian (or Zoroastrian) theology. Consequently, it is now necessary to consider those texts in which he introduces and elaborates upon his notion of eternal recurrence, in order to grasp the (plural) significance of his 'thought of thoughts'.

Nietzsche's bequest (V): The 'greatest burden'

Although *The Gay Science* is generally credited as the first work mentioning the idea, an early allusion to the eternal return can be found in the second of the four *Untimely Meditations* ('On the Uses and Advantages of History for Life'), originally published in 1874. There, Nietzsche refers to the Pythagorean belief that 'when the constellation of the heavenly bodies is repeated the same things, down to the smallest event, must also be repeated on earth' (2003:70). Yet, at this point the notion is presented not only as an uncanny hypothetical but as one voiced by the ancient Greek philosophers rather than by Nietzsche himself. Besides, it is discussed in a manner that suggests its utter implausibility, since Nietzsche mentions it in a section where he is arguing against the need for a monumental consideration of history, and the Pythagorean idea of recurrence is brought up as one of the single instances where this kind of 'historiological way of considering history' would be adequate or necessary (Löwith 1995: 133). Consequently, in Nietzsche's first textual reference to the idea of eternal recurrence, the notion is implicitly repudiated.

As a Nietzschean concept, however, eternal recurrence is presented in a wholly contrasting light. It is referenced for the first time in §109 of *The Gay Science* ('Let Us Beware'), a section that constitutes a plea for the 'de-deification' of nature. Here, Nietzsche describes the universe as a 'musical mechanism' which 'repeats eternally its tune' (1974:109), alluding to the Pythagorean characterization of the cosmos. The passage is preceded by the aphorism 'New Battle' (where the 'death of God' is first announced), thus revealing the inherent connection between the two concepts. In fact, §109 is clearly an elaboration of the ideas expressed in 'New Battle', since Nietzsche is warning the reader precisely against that which constitutes the key idea of the previous section: to perceive the universe as something more than an eternal chaos, 'a lack of order, organization, form, beauty, wisdom, and whatever else our anthropomorphisms are called' – in other words, of keeping alive 'the shadows of God' (1974: 109).

It is also important to note that the eternal recurrence is only referred to in passing at this point, making the section an enigmatic 'preview' to its full-blown development later in the book, possibly devised to awaken the reader's curiosity. Such a direct and ephemeral presentation of what is undoubtedly an eccentric idea, added to the fact that in this first instance Nietzsche does not refer to it explicitly as the eternal return, has led scholars to dismiss its literal meaning, since, as Maudemarie Clark remarks, it may be 'easily interpreted as a metaphor, and by itself, certainly provides no basis for a cosmological construal of eternal recurrence' (1990: 254). However, Nietzsche's use of metaphors and symbolic imagery is not a reason to disregard the meaning of his texts, since most of his writing is poetic in nature and, as Heidegger observes, it would be senseless to make a distinction between poetic and theoretical writing in his work, especially in relation to the idea of eternal recurrence, given that 'In Nietzsche's thinking of his fundamental thought the "poetical" is every bit as much "theoretical," and the "theoretical" is inherently "poetical"' (1984: 73). Moreover, scholars such as Clark appear to ignore the importance of music in the cosmological interpretations of the Pythagoreans.

Be that as it may, the first and only time Nietzsche denotes the concept by means of his notorious phrase in *The Gay Science* is in §285, 'Excelsior'. As in the case of §109, the reference here is also extremely brief, although this time it is qualified by an allusion to a specific sort of recurrence, that of 'war and peace' (Nietzsche 1974: 162). Yet, taking into consideration both the poetic nature of Nietzsche's writing and his understanding of struggle, both as a necessary requisite for the fulfilment of the individual and as a quintessential condition for the production of art, the concepts of war and peace should perchance be understood metaphorically (as in most of Nietzsche's deployments of these concepts) rather than literally. They must be read as referring to a broader notion of existence encompassing the fundamental dichotomy underlying the struggle of life. In fact, Heraclitus describes all being as a 'war' or 'strife' between opposites, in his famous claim: 'We must know that war is common to all and strife (*eris*) is justice, and that all things come into being through strife necessarily' (cited in Preus 2015: 153), making Nietzsche's words a clear allusion to this pre-Socratic's philosophy. Life is described as '*essentially appropriation, injury, overpowering of what is alien and weaker; suppression, hardness, imposition of one's own forms, incorporation, and at least, at its mildest, exploitation*' (Nietzsche 1989a: 203). A process recurring incessantly – eternally.

Nietzsche discusses the idea of eternal recurrence in detail for the first time in §341, 'The Heaviest Weight'. However, before analysing the passage in question, it is important to consider its title: '*Das größte Schwergewicht*'. The word '*Schwergewicht*', the literal translation of which is 'heavyweight' (translated by Kaufmann and Nauckhoff as 'weight' and by Levy and Krell as 'burden'), bears connotations that are of critical importance, since it alludes to the related term '*Schwerpunkt*', which means 'center of gravity' (Krell in Heidegger 1984: 20). So, as David Krell points out, with the use of the word '*Schwergewicht*' Nietzsche wishes to convey the notion of recurrence as something that may 'stablize us or wear us down, but which will most certainly deflect us from our former trajectory' (cited in Heidegger 1984: 20). *Schwergewicht* should not be understood simply as weight, load, burden or problem but as a centrifugal force that draws all to itself, as an abyss that must lie at the heart of every individual's consciousness and around which all other thoughts must orbit.

The second preliminary aspect that needs to be considered in §341 is that Nietzsche introduces the concept as a direct question to the reader through the words 'What if [. . .]?' (1974: 273). Although this initial formulation has led scholars to disregard the notion as a cosmological interpretation and consider it simply a thought experiment, such a construction can also be read in other ways. To begin with, this formulation may have been motivated by the desire to confront his readers directly with the idea, since it univocally demands our engagement. Additionally, Nietzsche may have decided to introduce the notion as a hypothetical and to adorn it through the use of poetic language and fantastical imagery because he understood that a view of such uncanniness could not be expressed effectively through direct communication. If his readers were to consider the question seriously and in all its magnitude, a conventional and coherent elucidation of the idea would not be appropriate in the first instance. The challenge was to present the thought in a way that would shock, captivate and compel his readers to consider its implications at a moment in history when Christianity (and later science) had long established linearity as the sole coherent model for the understanding of time.

Accordingly, in this initial formulation the idea is not only constructed as a question but posited through lyrical language and highly symbolic imagery, immediately acquiring a dramatic pathos. Even before it has been articulated, the question already achieves this pathos in its presentation, since rather than being voiced by the writer, it is pronounced by a demon. Besides, this demon does not merely appear before the reader at any given moment: he 'steal[s] after [him] into [his] loneliest loneliness' (Nietzsche 1974: 273). The reader is hence made immediately vulnerable, so that even before any question has been uttered, the dramatic tension has already achieved its height. The effectiveness of the construction also lies in the fact that the question conceals a number of subsequent queries, all of which reinforce the overarching notion and make its dreadfulness overpowering and unbearable, so that the initial 'what if' implicitly repeats itself. What if 'a demon was to steal into your loneliest loneliness'? What if 'this life as you live it and have lived it you will have to live once again and innumerable times again'? What if 'there will be nothing new in it'? What if 'every pain and every joy and every thought and sigh and everything unspeakably small or great in your life must return to you, all in the same succession and sequence'? (Nietzsche 1974: 273).

The fantastical imagery in this passage also allows Nietzsche to play with the ambiguity of the concept. Thus, the demon is said to appear in 'some day or night', symbolically anticipating the twofold nature of the knowledge of recurrence (Nietzsche 1974: 273). The character of the demon, which initially serves the purpose of allegorically presenting the idea as the epitome of dreadfulness, is also successively overturned and deemed a god to express the notion's ambivalent nature, which can represent either the most terrible of thoughts or the greatest divine prospect. The thought's ambiguous dualism and the demon-god's oxymoronic identity echo Nietzsche's attack on the notions of good and evil, emphasizing that both concepts are the result of divergent perceptions of events or entities, which are inherently neither one nor the other. Consequently, the section concludes with the postulation that eternal recurrence is neither dreadful nor blissful per se but wholly dependent on the disposition (or attitude towards life) of the individual who faces the challenge of such knowledge.

Finally, the decision to introduce the idea by means of a question can also be explained by the specific situation in which the extract appears. Although most scholars tend to ignore §341's context (given that Nietzsche's text is purposely disjointed and each section given an independent title), the fact is that the passages which surround it are extremely significant for any consideration of its overall significance. 'The Heaviest Weight' follows a section where Nietzsche criticizes Socrates for what he takes to be the philosopher's gravest fault: stating at his deathbed 'O Crito, I owe Asclepius a rooster', which Nietzsche interprets as 'O Crito, *life is a disease*' (1974: 272). According to this interpretation, Socrates is not only taking the extremely pessimistic (or decadent) stance of negating the intrinsic value of life but establishing death as the sole escape from the suffering caused by this 'disease'. As a result, §341 may be read as a direct response to such a view of existence, symbolically addressed to Socrates and constituting a refutation of both the validity of this view and the conclusions drawn from it.

In other words, to Socrates' claim that life is a disease and death its only possible cure, Nietzsche responds with the question: What if that which you claim to be a cure is actually the opposite (an infinite return to that life that you consider a disease)? What would that make of this diagnosis and its proposed solution? Nietzsche's question undermines Socrates' stance and identifies the diagnosis itself as the disease. This reading would establish Nietzsche's question as a warning against viewing life through Socrates' decadent prism, rather than a mere thought experiment. So, understanding the passage exclusively as a call to consider the idea's hypothetical implications is possibly an oversimplification. In any case, the section stands as a preamble for its discussion in Nietzsche's next and 'most important' text *Thus Spoke Zarathustra*. Having introduced the idea as the enigmatic yet overwhelming conclusion of *The Gay Science*, Nietzsche conceivably expected his readers to dwell upon the demon's questions and seek further elucidation of the concept in his next book.

In the preface to *Ecce Homo*, Nietzsche declares *Zarathustra* to be his most important work, one which 'stands by itself' among his other works: 'not only the highest book that there is' but the 'greatest gift [mankind] has ever been given' (2010: 219). He identifies the principal role of the eponymous protagonist to be the teaching of eternal recurrence. Both the importance that Nietzsche attributes to the book and the position which the idea of eternal recurrence has within it clearly emphasize the significance of the idea, not only for this text but in his philosophy more generally.[20] Besides, Nietzsche's incapacity to expose the thought himself, his need for a tragic hero such as Zarathustra to think and express it poetically, evidences its magnitude. The idea is too heavy a burden to be carried by a normal human being: 'its teaching requires a unique teacher'

---

[20] Given Nietzsche's assertions, the scholarly attempt to undermine the importance of both the idea of eternal recurrence and *Thus Spoke Zarathustra* is wholly unjustifiable and can only be understood as biases against fundamental aspects of Nietzsche's philosophy.

and its formulation a specific discourse, a poetic register that allows Nietzsche to portray the 'sense' and 'truth' of the doctrine 'in the realm of the sensuous' (Heidegger 1984: 32, 35).

Yet, before Zarathustra can summon the courage to confront the thought internally and discuss it openly with others, it is foreshadowed several times in the text. There are a number of vague allusions to an enigmatic idea, as well as to obscure omens about its impending revelation in some of the final chapters of Part Two ('The Dancing Song', 'On the Great Events' and 'The Soothsayer'). It is also the central teaching in the section 'On Redemption', and it is implied in the question posed by that which speaks 'without voice' in 'The Stillest Hour', forcing Zarathustra to retire to his solitude until he gathers the strength to proclaim the thought. Finally, it is also implicit in the protagonist's realization that 'Peak and abyss [. . .] are now joined together' in 'The Wanderer' (Nietzsche 1965: 267). However, eternal recurrence is not mentioned explicitly until Zarathustra has prepared himself to undertake this task, and this does not take place until Part Three of the book – in the chapters 'On the Vision and the Riddle' and 'The Convalescent' – and in 'The Drunken Song' of Part Four.

'On the Vision and the Riddle' constitutes the first explicit elucidation of the thought of recurrence. In it, Zarathustra, who is crossing the sea from the blessed islands, talks of it to the sailors he is travelling with after spending two days in complete silence. Even before the notion is discussed, the place, time and audience chosen by Nietzsche to introduce the idea characterize its nature and significance. Zarathustra has chosen 'the bold searchers, researchers and whoever embark with cunning sails on terrible seas' as those worthy of hearing the riddle-vision for the first time and the open sea as the appropriate place to do so (Nietzsche 1965: 267–8). So, prior to its announcement, Nietzsche has already prepared the terrain methodically for the proclamation. It is only after two days of silence, in which Zarathustra contemplates whether the place, time and audience are right, that he decides to speak. His 'heaviest of burdens' is a notion that is intended to be considered only by the most courageous of men, and far from the tranquillity and familiarity of the blessed islands.

After two days of silence, then, Zarathustra finally proclaims the idea of eternal recurrence through an allegory. He describes how upon mounting a path 'that ascended defiantly through stones, malicious, lonely' (setting the allegorical tone which is to characterize the passage), he is confronted by the 'spirit of gravity', a dwarf that he carries on his shoulder 'dripping lead into [his] ear' and dragging him down as he struggles to climb the arduous mountain path (Nietzsche 1965: 268). Zarathustra understands that he needs courage to confront this dwarf, a courage that is defined as 'the best slayer', capable of slaying 'death itself', so great that it would allow one to say 'Was *that* life? Well then! Once more!' (Nietzsche 1965: 269). Accordingly, in this first part Nietzsche is again preparing the ground for the unveiling of the idea. If in the preface to the tale he identified the necessary setting, time and audience for the revelation to take place, he now identifies 'courage' as the fundamental weapon to confront his 'thought of thoughts'.

Having determined these preliminary aspects, Zarathustra finally ventures to describe the notion openly for the first time. In this first exposition the idea is articulated in an attempt to rid himself of the dwarf once and for all – underscoring its unbearable nature. Hence, he tells the spirit of gravity his 'abysmal thought', certain that the dwarf will be unable to bear it. The spirit then jumps from his shoulder and Zarathustra shows him a gateway, which he identifies as the 'Moment', indicating that there are two infinite roads leading to and from it, past and present. He then asks the spirit if he believes that the paths 'contradict each other eternally?', to which the dwarf replies: 'All that is straight lies [. . .]. All truth is crooked; time itself is a circle' (Nietzsche 1965: 270). Infuriated by his dismissal, Zarathustra proceeds to describe the thought more fully:

> Behold [. . .] this moment! From this gateway, Moment, a long, eternal lane leads *backward*: behind us lies an eternity. Must not whatever *can* walk have walked on this lane before? Must not whatever *can* happen have happened, have been done, have passed by before? And if everything has been there before [. . .] Must not this gateway too have been there before? And are not all things knotted together so firmly that this moment draws after it *all* that is to come? Therefore – itself too? (Nietzsche 1965: 270)

Zarathustra uses the description of the gateway 'Moment' to counter the dwarf's dismissive response to the revelation. With it, he seeks to cast off the spirit of gravity by signalling the terrible reality that past and future do not converge in a distant infinity but in the eternally recurring present 'Moment'. Consequently, one cannot merely observe the gateway as a bystander (as the dwarf intends to) but must experience it ceaselessly. For we live within that eternal 'Moment', which constitutes the point where past and future converge, and where whoever experiences it 'lets what runs counter to itself come to collision, though not to a standstill, by cultivating and sustaining the strife between what is assigned him as task and what has been given him as endowment' (Heidegger 1984: 57).

This passage is also Nietzsche's first attempt at presenting the idea as the result of a logical deduction. He endows the notion with a dialectical proof and verisimilar bases by stating that given an infinite amount of time and a finite number of items and combinations, the same combination would necessarily recur infinitely. However, far from aiming to identify eternal recurrence merely as the result of a rational deduction, Nietzsche incorporates this dialectically sound argument in the midst of a fantastic scene full of symbolic imagery. He returns to some of the imagery present in §341 (such as the spider or the moonlight), not only emphasizing the magnitude of eternal recurrence (which encompasses everything, from the vastest objects and most significant events to the smallest and most trivial) but relating it to the 'realm of the sensuous'. Furthermore, the passage is drawn to a close through the description of its most extreme and uncanny aspect, that which makes eternal recurrence most difficult to believe and hardest to bear, echoing both Eudemus' and Heine's formulations: 'and I and you in the gateway [. . .] must not all of us have been there before? [. . .] – must we not eternally return?' (1965: 270).

Once Zarathustra has described the notion in detail for the first time, the dwarf and the gateway disappear, and, as if woken from a dream, Zarathustra encounters a shepherd bearing 'a heavy black snake' in his mouth (Nietzsche 1965: 271). The image of the shepherd asphyxiated by the snake (which evidently symbolizes Zarathustra's attempt to cope with the thought of eternal recurrence) has the added significance of foreshadowing the internal struggle which he later experiences in 'The Convalescent'. This foreshadowing, as well the description of the howling dog which sparks in Zarathustra a remembrance of his early childhood, has been identified by Paul S. Loeb[21] as Nietzsche's attempt to insert the notion of eternal recurrence into the actual plot of the text, so that (like Plato in *Phaedo*) he makes the text commit to the doctrine at a 'metanarrative level'. The visions suggest that Zarathustra is able to foresee events as prospective memories that he has already experienced in a previous iteration, making the story (albeit not its structure) implicitly circular.

The first Zarathustrian exposition of eternal recurrence may therefore be divided into three distinct parts: a first in which he introduces the 'spirit of gravity' and identifies courage as the necessary virtue to confront the thought,

[21] In 'Eternal Recurrence' (2013).

a second depicting this confrontation and providing a rational explanation of the idea, and a third where, having apparently cast away the spirit, Zarathustra presents the shepherd's allegory. Apart from the evident symbolism of Zarathustra's internal struggle and subsequent acceptance of the eternal return, this allegory also acquires the added significance of signalling, through the shepherd's transformation into a man, Zarathustra's realization that the thought is not a lesson to be learned by all. The idea of eternal recurrence cannot be taught to the herd: it requires a very specific audience. He who undertakes the role of its teacher cannot be a shepherd seeking to guide a flock, but rather an individual who must share his knowledge only with others like him – such as the courageous adventurers of the sea, those who in *Human, All Too Human* are identified as 'free spirits'. Besides, his decision to articulate this final thought in the form of an allegory, which Zarathustra urges the sailors to interpret, compels the reader once again (as in §341 of *The Gay Science*) to engage with the thought directly, precluding the possibility of regarding it passively or dismissively.

Consequently, 'On the Vision and the Riddle' amplifies the ideas introduced in §341 of *The Gay Science* in several ways. First, Nietzsche draws the reader's attention to the fact that not everyone is able to bear the thought of eternal return, so that the question presented in §341 (which has no specific addressee) is now directed only to those who are well disposed and courageous enough to confront it (implying that it was a lack of courage which drove Socrates to negate life by asserting that death would be its cure). This connects the idea of recurrence to that of the *Übermensch*. Moreover, Nietzsche stresses that the question requires an active engagement on the part of the individual who aims to confront it. It is an eternal question demanding an eternally recurring answer (of affirmation). Subsequently, he provides some logical proof for his thought by describing it as the result of deductive reasoning. Finally, he suggests that it entails the possibility of a prospective memory, hence implicitly awarding his narrative a circular tone.

Although references to the eternal recurrence reappear in ensuing chapters (it is the central theme, for instance, of 'On Involuntary Bliss', where Zarathustra is still struggling to accept the thought, and is also mentioned in 'On the Old and New Tablets'), it is not elucidated further until 'The Convalescent', towards the end of Part Three. In this episode, Nietzsche describes how Zarathustra rises one morning shouting 'like a madman', suddenly overcome by the need to awaken his 'abysmal thought' (1965: 271). As the thought rises in him, however, Zarathustra becomes nauseous and falls unconscious. Upon awakening, he lies motionless for seven days while his animals remain by his side and gather food for him. On the seventh day, and as Zarathustra rises, his animals speak to him, and it is in this speech that we find the fullest elaboration of the notion. It is worth noting that, once again, Nietzsche has relayed the exposition of the idea to the voice of a highly symbolic entity. If in §341 the thought was pronounced by a phantasmagorical demon-god and in the previous major elucidation it appears in the form of a riddle-vision as an internal conversation with 'the spirit of gravity', here too, the speakers Nietzsche has chosen to voice the thought are significant. It is Zarathustra's animals who speak, and Nietzsche has consciously left unspecified which animal is in fact speaking. Rather, the voice is collectivized under the pluralized noun, implying that it is nature that speaks to him, and consequently life itself, in place of a specific entity. This symbolic collectivized speaker also suggests that the protagonist has reached a stage of development in which he is now able to understand nature, the world, life itself, allowing him to hear the words of his animals.

Zarathustra's creatures encourage him to leave his cave, insisting that a new knowledge has come to him and that he should therefore experience the world through the light of this new knowledge. To this he replies dismissively that although their words delight and refresh him, they are nothing but 'chatter': 'illusive bridges between things which are eternally apart' (Nietzsche 1965: 328). This means that they are unable to reveal the reality to which they are referring and thus deceive the listener by failing to disclose what is dreadful in that reality. So, in the same way that the spirit of gravity's reply to Zarathustra's first mention of eternal recurrence reduced it to an overly simplistic assumption that neglected its profundity, Zarathustra sees his animals' chatter as a 'deception of sounds' (Nietzsche 1965: 329). However, instead of falling silent and disappearing as the dwarf did, the animals reply:

> to those who think as we do, all things themselves are dancing: they come and offer their hands and laugh and flee – and come back. Everything goes, everything comes back; eternally rolls the wheel of being. Everything dies, everything blossoms again; eternally runs the year of being. [. . .] eternally the ring of being remains faithful to itself. In every Now, being begins; round every Here rolls the sphere There. The center is everywhere. Bent is the path of eternity. (Nietzsche 1965: 329–30)

This paragraph elaborates previous elucidations of the idea by presenting it no longer as a hypothetical question, riddle or thought experiment but as the reality of existence. It establishes the world as a world of becoming. Everything becomes: only the eternal process of creation and decay, which recurs infinitely, can rightfully adopt the category of being (the being of becoming). However, to this novel exposition of the thought Zarathustra again replies dismissively, for he feels that the animals talk lightly and joyfully of a notion that has first to be suffered if one is to understand and *know* it. He also blames the animals for turning the abysmal truth into a 'hurdy-gurdy song' and regarding him impassively as he was being suffocated by the notion, watching his 'great pain as men do', with the 'lasciviousness' they call 'pity' (Nietzsche 1965: 330). In order to be able to speak of the 'thought of thoughts', one must necessarily undergo the monster's suffocation, bite off its head and lie 'weary of this biting and spewing' in convalescence (Nietzsche 1965: 330). Thus, the focal point of the chapter becomes not only what eternal recurrence *is* but *how* it must be understood.

By drawing a parallelism between the animals' conduct during his convalescence (which he claims was motivated by pity) and human behaviour, Zarathustra produces a critical analysis of man as 'the cruellest animal against himself' (Nietzsche 1965: 331). He also explains why he was choked with nausea at the awakening of the 'abysmal thought', asserting that the monster that choked him was in fact the 'great disgust with man' and especially the awareness that 'the small man' too must recur eternally (Nietzsche 1965: 331). Zarathustra also remarks that the soothsayer he met earlier in the book was right in claiming that 'All is the same, nothing is worthwhile, knowledge chokes'; and that both the greatest man and the smallest are 'all-too-similar to each other [. . .] all-too-human. All-too-small the greatest' (Nietzsche 1965: 331). Hence, it is the idea of the eternal recurrence of the smallest that causes Zarathustra's suffering and nausea, a sensation which cannot be overlooked and must be experienced and overcome, since its testimony is perpetually inscribed in the eternal 'Moment' where past and future converge.

Having partly uncovered the abysmal nature of his thought to the animals, they at once plead with Zarathustra to stop talking, urging him to go out into the world so that he can learn how to sing from 'the songbirds', since they claim he must learn how to sing before he can talk again: 'For singing is for the convalescent; the healthy can speak' (Nietzsche 1965: 331–2). To this, again, Zarathustra replies contemptuously that although he agrees with them (as in the previous cases) and understands that he must sing as a medium of comfort during his period of convalescence, they must not turn the idea into a 'hurdy-gurdy song', since this singing is not the result of a superficial understanding of eternal recurrence but the consequence of overcoming it. Zarathustra can now sing because he has understood that the recurrence of suffering and the smallest man is also necessary; he has overcome the abysmal, bitten off and spat out the dark monster's head. He is finally ready to sing, but his new songs will be completely different. Consequently, the animals urge him to fashion himself 'a new lyre' with which he can chant these new songs, cure himself and fulfil his destiny by becoming 'the teacher of the eternal recurrence' (Nietzsche 1965: 332).

Following this, the animals reiterate their exposition of what will constitute Zarathustra's central teaching:

> that all things recur eternally, and we ourselves too [. . .] that there is a great year of becoming, a monster of a great year, which must, like an hourglass, turn over again and again so that it may run down and run out again; and all these years are alike in what is greatest as in what is smallest. (Nietzsche 1965: 332)

This reiteration emphasizes that Zarathustra has now understood and overcome the thought: not only that it is necessary that the smallest also recur but that the smallest and most abysmal is itself part of the greatest and highest. It is also interesting to note here that the cycle of recurrence is described as 'a great year', recalling the Babylonian use of the term and indicating Nietzsche's will to illustrate the ancestral heritage of the concept, which Zarathustra, however, as its teacher, is the first to fully understand.

The chapter concludes with a further restatement of the thought where the notion of the *Übermensch* and the concept of nihilism are explicitly linked as constituting the essence of Zarathustra's teaching: 'to teach again the eternal recurrence of all things, to speak again the word of the great noon of earth and man, to proclaim the overman again to men' (Nietzsche 1965: 333). The animals' discourse draws to a close by determining that Zarathustra's 'going under' is finally over. He also displays this realization himself by remaining silent and in conversation with his soul at the end of the chapter. Rather than responding to the animals' final words (as throughout the rest of the chapter), he has come to accept that if *all* is to 'cohere and recur', then 'even the greatest teaching, the ring of rings, itself must become a ditty for barrel organs' (Heidegger 1984: 60).

Although the idea of eternal recurrence is referred to repeatedly throughout the book's ensuing episodes (it is alluded to in all the chapters of Part Three following 'The Convalescent'), it is not discussed again in an extensive manner. Nevertheless, 'The Drunken Song' in Part Four also features the idea as its central theme, although in this case it is portrayed in a different light.

Zarathustra's roundelay, first introduced after his conversation with Life in 'The Other Drunken Song', is expounded in this chapter, illustrating its connection to the eternal return. The ideas emphasized in this elucidation, however, differ greatly from the unbearable and abysmal implications that were highlighted earlier. Here, the description of eternal recurrence acquires the jubilant tone of the animal's 'hurdy-gurdy song', yet without falling into the trap of dismissing its true depth by producing a condescending tune. Zarathustra's new song proclaims that 'the world is deep' and 'Deep is its woe', but at the same time it is filled with a joy 'deeper yet than agony' which exists eternally (Nietzsche 1965: 436). Joy thus becomes the key emotion in this final elucidation. It is joy which 'wants deep eternity' (Nietzsche 1965: 436), because it is fuelled by a love for life and fate, a joy which is deep because it encompasses all woe, agony and pain.

Aside from the importance of joy, this lyrical closure to the book emphasizes another crucial aspect of the idea: its atemporality. The temporal perspective, which is implicitly underlined in the animals' exposition by way of their reference to 'a great year', an 'hourglass' or by stating that they will all 'come again', is completely omitted in this chapter. In fact, the notion of 'recurrence' itself is almost obliterated from the text and 'eternity' becomes the focus of this final exposition. The dreadfulness of the 'coming back' of all that is great and small vanishes, and instead an eternal joy takes its place. This emphasis on the notion of eternity over that of recurrence also stresses the idea present in 'On the Vision and the Riddle' that the return will not happen in an infinitely distant moment which allows it to be disregarded or overlooked but that it is *in* the moment, that the moment is *eternal*. The word 'recurrence' (*Wiederkehr*) is consciously replaced in this chapter by 'eternal ring', destroying the temporal implications of the former and thereby asserting a 'timeless modality of eternal existence' (Seung 2005: 326).

The reason for striving towards such a destruction is twofold. First, because, as Thomas K. Seung argues, the 'temporal connection' causes 'disgust and nausea', given that 'its casual powers crushes autonomous will', while the 'eternal connection' generates 'love and joy' in its assurance of 'the harmonious union of the individual with the cosmic self' (2005: 326). It is this second dimension that Zarathustra now seeks to emphasize. Second, through its annullation of the eternal return's temporality, 'The Drunken Song' constitutes what Kaufmann calls 'the ultimate apotheosis of the supra-historical outlook, the supreme exaltation of the moment', an acclamation of the present which impedes a nihilistic escape through 'any faith which pins its hopes on infinite progress' (1956: 277). By establishing eternal recurrence as an eternal present rather than as an infinite cycle of recurrence, Nietzsche impedes all conceivable escape from the 'Moment', abolishes any possibility of its devaluation and proclaims an infinite love for the deep joy of life. Hence, although the concept is not explicitly expounded in 'The Drunken Song', the chapter epitomizes the characterization of eternal recurrence by stressing a different facet to that of previous chapters: as an infinite atemporal flux, an eternal and endlessly changing present moment.

The eternal return does not feature frequently or extensively in Nietzsche's later works. The only other book published during his lifetime which includes a significant reference to the idea is *Beyond Good and Evil*, and even in this case its discussion is extremely limited.[22] The reference appears in §56, in the third part of the book ('What Is Religious'), where Nietzsche presents the concept once again as 'the ideal of the most high-spirited, alive, and world-affirming human being' (1989b: 68). This section adds to previous elucidations of the notion in several decisive ways. First, the concept is presented here not as a hypothetical thought experiment or lyrical doctrine of his godless demigod Zarathustra but as a direct insight signed and uttered by Nietzsche himself, asserting that the highest ideal of the most vital individual is necessarily the eternal affirmation of life as suffering and its recurrence. Second, and most importantly, the notion is deified or at least its potential deification is put forward as a possibility: 'And wouldn't this be – *circulus vitiosus deus*?' (1989b: 68). With this rhetorical question Nietzsche defines eternal recurrence as the god of the most vital human being, who wants all that 'was and is' eternally (1989b: 68). He withdraws God in order to establish existence as god, an eternal existence perpetually inscribed in the 'Moment'.

The fact that the eternal return is mentioned only sporadically and vaguely in the writings published after *Zarathustra* has led some scholars to see this as proof of Nietzsche's hesitation concerning the idea or even as a rejection of it. However, the evidence in the writings that were not intended for publication actually points in the opposite direction. As Nietzsche himself states on several occasions, his avoidance of any consideration of eternal recurrence stems instead from his belief that a stronger man, 'younger, "heavier with future"', should and can be the only one apt to communicate this thought appropriately (1989b: 96). Indeed, in the notes published after his death, the idea of eternal return appears

---

[22] It is also mentioned fleetingly in *The Twilight of the Idols* (1889) but not elaborated upon.

repeatedly and in a manner which shows that far from losing interest in the notion or thinking about rejecting it, he was working towards consolidating and reaffirming it by all possible means (even seeking scientific confirmation of his arguments).[23]

The unpublished notes collected in the polemical *The Will to Power*[24] show ample evidence of this attempt to prove the doctrine, as well as of Nietzsche's infatuation with it precisely in the period where it is absent from the published texts (1887–9). Thus, writings such as the selection of notes dated 10 June 1887 (1968: §55) or some of the passages belonging to the 1883–8 notebook (1968: §417) reiterate many of the ideas present in his published works. The idea of eternal recurrence is established as the epitome of meaningless, as a pantheistic anti-theological cosmology, and as an unbearable notion for the decadent. It is a countering force to 'disintegration and incompleteness', and a 'new *center*' or burden (Nietzsche 1968: 224). The *Will to Power* also includes further evidence of Nietzsche's exploration, reformulation and attempt at a consolidation of the concept in the years following the publication of *Beyond Good and Evil*, such as a plan for a book entitled *The Eternal Recurrence: A Prophecy*. Furthermore, the passages compiled in *The Will to Power* and the philosopher's other *Nachlass* not only continue with the characterization of the thought set forth in his published texts; they also reveal that Nietzsche tried to reconcile those ideologies opposed to his philosophy (such as Platonism) with his own thought by means of the idea of eternal recurrence (see Nietzsche 1968: §1061).

Given the professed importance of this uncanny notion, its changing characterization and continual development throughout the published and unpublished texts, the scholarly attempt to come to terms with the idea has led to a wide range of contrasting interpretations.[25] The heterogeneity of these

---

[23] See, for instance, §1063 of *The Will to Power*.

[24] According to Kaufmann, *The Will to Power* was (erroneously) considered as Nietzsche's magnum opus and the 'most systematic work' during the first half of the twentieth century owing to the Nazi ideologue Alfred Baeumler's edition and study *Nietzsche: Der Philosoph und Politiker* (1931). However, after the Second World War most scholars adopted the antagonistic stance of disregarding the text entirely, influenced by Schlechta's *Werke in drei Bänden* (1954–6). Nevertheless, Kaufmann argues that both positions are actually untenable, since *The Will to Power* 'contains a good deal that has no close parallel in the works Nietzsche finished [...] on nihilism [...] and the attempts at proofs of the doctrine of the eternal recurrence of the same events' (1959: xiv). Although Kaufmann's edition of *The Will to Power* follows the initial systematic order of the passages, he insists that the work is in no way 'a carefully wrought systematic text' but a 'selection from Nietzsche's notebooks of the years 1883 through 1888' (1959: xiv). The text should be read as a collection of 'disjointed jottings', many of which did not 'satisfy him' and therefore 'do not represent his final views', rather than a consciously unified assortment of passages (Kaufmann 1956: xix).

[25] According to Lawrence Hatab, for Karl Jaspers eternal recurrence is essentially a 'response to the death of God, a worldly replacement for traditional constructs and an antidote to nihilism' in the

interpretations reveals that Nietzsche's 'abysmal thought' can be read in many ways. Most of these, however, are not mutually exclusive. In fact, considering them in conjunction enriches the understanding of eternal recurrence, as a true 'thought of thoughts', irreducible to 'barrel organ songs', an idea with considerable potential for the pragmatic application of its theoretical framework. Nietzsche's discussion of eternal recurrence establishes it as a plural notion that develops gradually throughout his work, displaying its myriad implications. This development commences with the ephemeral presentation of the idea (in §109 and §285 of *The Gay Science*) aimed at awakening the curiosity of the reader and establishing recurrence as an unquestionable cosmological trait. It continues with the hypothetical formulation (in §341 of *The Gay Science*) which defines the notion as a challenge to decadence, the utmost thought experiment and ultimate means for the affirmation of life. This is followed by Zarathustra's elucidations, which present it as the abysmal understanding that past and future converge in the 'Moment', and that the thought needs to be embraced and suffered before it can finally be sung as a nuptial hymn to the eternal marriage of the (over)man to life. Finally, it culminates by defining it as an anti-theological, anti-nihilistic pantheism: no meaning, no coming from somewhere, no going anywhere, only an eternal present, recurring eternally.

Thus, the manner in which the notion is articulated varies significantly and gradually in Nietzsche's work, both published and unpublished. However, within all these formulations, the same inherent implication remains. In opposition to the philosophical theodicies of Leibniz and Hegel, in which the negative aspects of life are but a minor side of its overall 'positive picture', and to Schopenhauer's (and Socrates') life-denying pessimism which posits that non-existence is preferable to existence, Nietzsche presents an absolute affirmation and love for life, both in its most 'positive' and in its most 'negative' aspects, undermining the moral valuation of existence as a nonsensical 'sickness'. Consequently, the idea of eternal recurrence is not only the most extreme logical consequence

absence of theology (2005: 124). Karl Löwith reads it as the reversal of the nihilistic 'will to nothing' that emerges out of a godless world by the 'radical nihilist', who 'attempts "to want to have nothing different" from what it is, already was, and also will be again' (1997: 57). For Klossowski, it is a criterion to identify strength and weakness (or vitality and decadence), in the way that Nietzsche implicitly confronts Socrates with the question in §341 of *The Gay Science*. For Heidegger, it is Nietzsche's 'fundamental metaphysical position', a doctrine containing 'an assertion on being as a whole', the 'roots' of his thought (1984: 5). For Deleuze, it is an 'ontologizing of becoming' where 'becoming' is 'a philosophical primum that must inform all thinking' (Hatab 2005: 124), or in Deleuze's own words: 'Returning is the being of that which becomes' (1983: 48).

of the rejection of Platonic-Christian nihilism and other equivalent modern ideologies, nor as the sole way to devise a milieu in which the most extreme form of 'active nihilism' can be accomplished, but as the ultimate assertion that it is life itself that is valuable, not its results, structure or understanding. *It is, in short, a rejection of life as plot*. A positing of reality as that which points towards nothing but itself: an eternal, irreducible life which exists (and must be affirmed) perpetually in the present moment. The idea of eternal recurrence is the absolute affirmation of *this* life, one which removes the possibility of its devaluation through the positing of 'purpose', 'meaning', 'afterlife' or even death. As we shall see, the narratives studied in the ensuing chapters aim to underline many of these same ideas through the use of circular structures.

* * *

So, the eagerness to find alternatives to the linear model cannot be attributed simply to a gratuitous urge for innovation. What prompted this trend was the awareness that linear narratives, being teleological, express or are representative of a specific world view, one that is essentially theological. Nietzsche's ideas made it apparent that, in the same way that the linear structuring of time was a vestige of Christianity, the linear form was not the necessary and implied logical structure of narrative but a theological and didactic eventuality. His critiques exposed the assumed natural structure of narrative (linearity) as a complete contingency, an arbitrary imposition, uncovering the frailty of its underlying assumptions: that the world can be explained (disinterestedly) and that said explanation can be communicated. Beyond that, his work compelled the question: How can narratives aim to transmit values if the value system collapses? The task at hand hence became to devise narratives that would surpass the limitations of teleology and the grasp of theology. Indeed, the break with the Victorian convention of a chronological sequencing was, in great measure, a result of the fact that said model had been unveiled as a religious residue in the age of the rise and increasing hegemonization of scientific atheism. Consequently, the reason for the new-born interest in formal experimentation in the European literature of the twentieth century was an awareness about linearity's ideological backdrop.[26] It is the combined force of the collapse of the

---

[26] The same logic exposing teleology's reliance upon theological premises (and its implicit assertion of a theological world view) also revealed linearity's dependence upon, and assertion of, empiricism and positivism. Since the plot of linear narratives develops as a result of the changes that certain (kernel) events trigger in the state of affairs, revealing a causal relationship among the elements causing

assumption that linearity constituted the essential or natural character of life (and thus of narrative) and the realization that in linear texts 'only the end can finally determine meaning' (Brooks 1984: 22) that prompts the urge to abandon the linear model.

this development, they also suggest that the world can be explained by dividing it into causes and effects. Linear narratives entail an empiricist or positivist understanding of existence because they construct progression by mirroring the general framework of human cognition. In other words, linearity implicitly postulates the belief that causality (and thus logic) and sensory perception are apt modes for the interpretation of reality. Therefore, they express an inherent reliance on truth as causality, logic, empiricism (in general) and logical positivism (in particular). Even those texts that contradict these naturalistic notions of truth thematically (through the description of events, characters, actions or settings that challenge such an understanding of the world) simply do so as part of a 'fantastic pact': an inferred agreement between writer and reader implicit within the understanding that literature is fiction. Hence, these fantastical elements become assimilated into the logical positivist framework of the narration, reinforcing said world view, even as they seem to undermine it.

3

The birth of circularity
Strindberg, Stein and Azorín

Although linear structures were paradigmatic for most nineteenth-century realist and naturalist narratives, the first circular texts did not emerge as a direct reaction against these representational literary trends. In fact, many of the experimental forms appearing in the European literature of the early twentieth century grew out of the same conventions which they inevitably overcame. The same interests and preoccupations that had motivated the development of these trends (realism and naturalism) also led to their surpassing. In many cases, it was because writers aimed for an ever more rigorous realism that they began to see the linear form as unnatural or unrealistic and thus felt the need to look for alternatives.

Consequently, the myriad formal innovations taking place at the turn of the century were not so much the result of a self-contained desire for novelty or a conscious reactionary struggle to do away with the practices then in vogue. Rather, they emerge as a consequence of a growing alertness regarding the fictiveness of the linear model. The first narratives to break with linearity continued to remain trapped in the threads of past conventions in many respects, and those writers who were able to overcome them only succeeded in severing these threads very gradually. In most cases, such a break was at first neither conscious on the part of the author nor recognized in its reception by the work's critics. Nevertheless, while retaining strong ties to realism and naturalism, the texts analysed in this chapter are the first evidence of a transvaluation of narrative in the European literary field, through a striving to reconfigure what had for many centuries been considered as its inherent or ideal structure. Moved by an urge to overcome the artificialities and limitations of teleology and the linear model, authors such as August Strindberg, Gertrude Stein or José Augusto Trinidad Martínez Ruiz paved the way towards a new kind of literature through the use of a range of circular forms.

August Strindberg's *The Dance of Death* (1900)

An innovator in both his writing and artwork, August Strindberg anticipated many of the developments that were to take place in modern art and literature in the first half of the twentieth century. Although best known for his drama, Strindberg's 1879 novel *The Red Room* is generally acknowledged as the first modern Swedish literary work, making him one of the first precursors of the modernist movement, both in his native country and in Europe more widely. Strindberg's literary career commenced at the age of twenty when he published his first work, *A Namesday Gift* (1869). He began by writing historical plays but gradually turned to more contemporary subjects, depicted in a realistic style. However, having written a number of works during the 1880s, which may be characterized as psychological naturalism, he decided to leave playwriting aside for several years, only to return to the theatre in 1898 with the publication of the first part of *To Damascus*. This innovative text represented a radical break with his earlier work, inaugurating a new and decisive stage in his writing life, marked by a choice of dramatic structures that deviated from the Aristotelian linear model.

Considered as a dangerous writer, living in self-imposed exile partly due to the hostility that his collection of satires *The New Kingdom* (1882) had earned him and having been tried for blasphemy for his collection of stories *Getting Married* (1884), Strindberg found it extremely hard to publish in his native country during this time. Nevertheless, at the turn of the century he was able to return to Sweden, finding a new acceptance in his homeland.

During his exile, Strindberg had come into contact with some of the leading figures in the emerging modern artistic movement, such as Paul Gauguin, Edvard Munch and Frederick Delius, inspiring him to transform naturalism into what Robinson calls an 'associational' art that 'was eventually to facilitate the emergence of his later modernist theatre' (cited in Strindberg 2008: xx). The post-1898 plays display a shift in focus from 'ephemeral political and social so-called questions' to what he described as an 'artistic-psychological writing' (Strindberg 2008: ix). The structure of his plays also changed drastically after his 1890 rupture. If his 1887 play, *The Father*, has in many respects a clearly traditional Aristotelian structure, where even the formatting corresponds to the classical dramatic conventions (it has a different scene for every entry and exit – see Robinson in Strindberg 2008: x), his post-1898 works move away from these norms, developing a new kind of naturalist writing which is largely the result of an increasing preoccupation with and questioning of the distinction between fiction and reality. These works display a repeated insistence on the problematic nature of this dichotomy and a breaking down of the opposition between truth and fantasy, dream and reality, life and literature, that is clearly reminiscent of Nietzsche's ideas.

In his move towards this new kind of naturalism, Strindberg also began to perceive and portray identity as a heterogeneous construct in perpetual flux, shifting incessantly as a result of the different stimuli (physical, social and psychological) that configure and reconfigure it throughout one's life. His new dramaturgy thus aimed to do away with the meticulous character representations typical of realism or naturalism in order to show the '"characterless character", or *multiplicité du moi*', that constitutes an identity (Robinson in Strindberg 2008: xi). Strindberg defined his protagonists as 'conglomerates of past and present stages of culture, bits out of books and newspapers, scraps of humanity, torn shreds of once fine clothing now turned to rags', drawing a connection between the way in which he created his characters and the process by which our identity is 'patched together' (2008: 60). Similar to his distrust of the fact/fiction opposition, this view of identity (which is one of the notions that initiated his gradual deviation from, or reconfiguration of, naturalism) has a clear Nietzschean ring and may actually be linked to his relationship with the German philosopher.

Strindberg described Nietzsche's impact upon him vividly (and even grotesquely) as 'a tremendous ejaculation of sperm' into the 'uterus' of his 'mental world', which had left him 'like a bitch with a full belly' (2008: xv). The catalyst of this relationship had been Georg Brandes, who initially lent Strindberg a copy of *Beyond Good and Evil* (1886), while also making Nietzsche aware of the playwright's work, prompting an epistolary relationship between the two. Strindberg rapidly familiarized himself with many of Nietzsche's works, some of which – such as *The Genealogy of Morals* (1887) and *Twilight of the Idols* (1888) – were sent to him by Nietzsche himself. The two writers shared a critical stance towards Christianity, a sceptical outlook on the idea of truth, an interest in the relationship between the conscious or the intellect and the instincts or the unconscious, and in the tension between mediocrity and exceptionality, an idea that Strindberg had already discussed in his *Vivisections* (1887) (see Robinson in Strindberg 2008: xv). This affinity was strengthened by their shared interest in psychology, with both writers developing intricate analyses of the human mind. It was only with Nietzsche's mental breakdown (patent in his last letter to Strindberg, which he signed as 'The Crucified') that their correspondence came to an end. Thus, if the playwright's desire to renovate drama was not inspired (at least to a certain extent) by Nietzsche's call to transvaluate all values, it unquestionably derives from a common *Weltanschauung* or set of philosophical preoccupations.

In the last decade of the nineteenth century, Strindberg moved beyond naturalism into a new epoch of literary composition. While this shift begins with the publication of *To Damascus*,[1] *The Dance of Death* (1900) is perhaps the best example to illustrate the way in which his choice of an unorthodox structural configuration led to the development a new kind of theatre. Although *The Dance of Death* may initially strike one as a conventional realist or naturalist play, perhaps a more desolate version of his earlier play *The Father*, or, as Szalczer argues, 'a somewhat anachronistic post-*Inferno* naturalist play' or 'bourgeois marriage tragedy' (2009: 100), there are striking differences between this and his previous work. The most significant of these differences is that it does not have a linear plot, making it, as Joe Martin suggests, paradigmatic of a desire to find a new dramatic language, which was 'neither naturalism nor expressionism' (cited in Strindberg 1997: 21). Yet, regardless of the specific literary trend with which we may wish to associate the play, what is clear is that with this text Strindberg takes the first steps towards the transvaluation of drama, and this is done through the use of circularity.

The work moves beyond the trends in vogue at the time by recuperating many of the features of medieval drama. For one, allegory rather than mimesis seems to motivate the composition and to constitute the underlying essence of the narrative. Overall, the play takes the form of an allegory that contains features and imagery typical of medieval literature, though put to the use of pressuring or questioning – rather than positing or endorsing (as is the case in medieval plays) – certain themes or values. Even the play's title alludes to its medieval form, both because it suggests a metaphorical rather than a literal meaning and because it refers to the archetypal image of the *danse macabre*. The play's setting (a circular tower which used to be a prison, situated on a small island called Little Hell) is

---

[1] *The Dance of Death* is not the only text of its kind; many of Strindberg's post-*Inferno* plays, such as the first *To Damascus*, *Crimes and Crimes* and *A Dream Play*, also have a 'circular rather than linear' form (Robinson 1998: xxii).

also clearly reminiscent of the allegorical medieval morality plays, since it bears patent symbolic connotations (among which is the mirroring of the play's form). Rather than representing an actual place in the world, the stage symbolizes the protagonists' claustrophobic situation, their unrelenting circular struggle and their psychological entrapment. Like the title and setting, the unconventionality of the characters and their dialogue also seems to point to the metaphorical status of the drama's components. However, among these eerie features, the play's circular structure – configured by an exact return to the starting point, absent of any kind of significant development – stands out, in contrast not only to realist or naturalist dramas but also to medieval ones, establishing it as a 'modernist allegory' in its own right (Szalczer 2011: 90).

As a number of critics have observed, more than anything what makes the play different, both from Strindberg's other works and from those of his contemporaries, is precisely its circular form. The pattern of the action subverts the ideological assumptions implicit within the prototypical development of a realist or naturalist drama, whereby the plot gradually unfolds through an exponential linear progression that culminates in either the joyful triumph or tragic failure of its protagonists, reinforcing the progressivist values typical of much nineteenth-century European literature. Metatextually (like most circular narratives), the play also undermines the teleological value of drama through its explicit rejection of a linear progression and a conventional resolution (revealing either a recognition or a reversal).[2] The groundbreaking character of the work's form has been widely acknowledged.[3] Indeed, it was identified by Martin Esslin as a clear precursor to the avant-garde Theatre of the Absurd, where (as we shall see in Chapter 5) the 'rejection of traditional linear plotting in favour of circular plots' or 'spiralling' structures becomes a common feature (1997: 369).

As well as the overall arrangement of the play's plot, many of its other features also share the same circular pattern. The parallelism between the shape of these components and its structure serves to emphasize further the impossibility of progression or escape and to foreshadow the ending while also encouraging the reader/spectator to interpret the play as an allegory. However, as Szalczer notes, unlike in medieval plays it is the protagonists' 'existential predicament rather than a religious doctrine' that is being represented allegorically (2012: 90). If

---

[2] See the analysis of Aristotle's *Poetics* in the Introduction.
[3] The importance of the circular form for the play is also manifest in its 1968 adaptation by the Swiss dramatist Friedrich Dürrenmatt, *Play Strindberg*, which maintains the original's circular structure and transforms the setting into a circular boxing ring.

the circular shape of elements such as the setting downplays its verisimilitude, it also vividly emphasizes the endless and inexorable repetition that constitutes the play's overall movement and overarching theme: the couple's infernal routine. The division of the protagonist's circular room in the granite fort into two different domains, symbolic of their minds (one for each protagonist), is mediated by a neutral space representing a kind of no man's land or battleground where their lethal dance is due to take place.

The dialogue is also a constant reminder of the overall shape of the action and allegorical nature of the drama. It appears to circle endlessly without ever achieving much, unable to make the plot develop. In most cases, the protagonists' interactions seem wholly gratuitous, taking the form of a senseless game devoid of purpose or end. Like the play's setting and title, the dialogue too undermines the realistic or verisimilar qualities of the performance. The opening scene already shows traces of this circular pointlessness. The protagonists appear to be motivated by a will to speak simply for the sake of hearing the sound of their own words, exchanging phrases in a chant-like pattern and rhythm, rather than for the purpose of actual communication:

> CAPTAIN: Won't you play something for me?
> ALICE: What shall I play?
> CAPTAIN: What you like.
> ALICE: You don't like my repertoire.
> CAPTAIN: Nor you mine.
>
> (Strindberg 2008: 113)

Such exchanges give a ritualistic, musical character to the dialogue, as a playful exchange of empty sentences. It leads nowhere and seems to have no purpose apart from the aesthetic pleasure derived from its enunciation, recalling the underlying circular movement of the drama.

This first exchange also introduces the theme of playing, which becomes a leitmotif throughout the play in its several variations (see Szalczer 2011: 91). As well as triggering the conversation that opens the text, the word 'play' characterizes the type of interactions that will take place throughout the rest of the narrative. Unable to make the plot progress as in conventional dramas, the protagonists' actions, like the dialogue, simply become a game they play with no transcendent purpose or consequence. As Strindberg writes in his preface of *Miss Julie*, in this play too the conversation 'wanders, providing itself in the opening scenes with material that is later reworked, taken up, repeated, expanded, and developed, like the theme in a musical composition' (2008: 63). The same may be said about the characters' actions. Causality is undermined through this incessant and repetitive succession of stunts and dialogic duels that consist purely of clichés without any apparent communicative value or purpose.

There are myriad instances where the motif of playing reappears: the protagonists perform certain character roles, take part in games or talk about playing. Alice plays the piano, her husband dances, they both play cards, all in a seeming effort to escape from the dreadful monotony and isolation of their lives. When the games are over and they fail to find alternative ways to amuse themselves, they return to their playful yet tragic dialogue, lamenting the dreadful circular tedium of their relationship in a pantomime that has no discernible end. The action depicted is thus in no way a single or whole one that progresses neatly towards a concrete aim (as in Aristotelian drama). Instead, the plot is made up of many seemingly senseless and disjointed actions that constitute a plural totality of superfluous stunts, which fails to have a single or direct impact on the development of the story. The gratuitous nature of the dialogue also endows the characters with a buffoon-like quality that establishes them as grotesque satirical caricatures. Yet, it also has a magnifying effect that makes their tragic situation all the more perceptible.

The play's allegoric status is further emphasized through the protagonists' limited characterization. Rather than having intricate personalities and complex individual identities, Strindberg presents us with a set of characters that seem to function as broad symbolic entities. They are performative figures, lacking a concrete identity. In other words, the idea of identity as a fixed, innate and perennial construct is undermined. The protagonists do not have unique, intrinsic or permanent psychological qualities or fixed personalities, as in realist or naturalist texts. Rather, their personas are multifaceted and forever changing. They are inherently void entities enacting fleeting roles that they perform and then leave aside only to take on new ones.[4] Identity is thus portrayed as a (Nietzschean) perpetual 'becoming' rather than linked to the idea of an essential, eternal and unalterable (Platonic) state of 'being'. The protagonists are plural characters: they repeatedly change from benign lovers into hateful enemies. They live in the perpetual flux of performing multiple and often wholly

---

[4] Szalczer describes this as 'a direct enactment of plays-within-the-play and roles-within-the-role' (2012: 100).

antagonistic roles. They are multifarious subjects, their 'beings' existing only as a result of their multiple 'becomings'.[5]

The combination of the character's polymorphic identities, the pointlessness of their circular dialogues and games, and, above all, the underlying structure of the play also create a general sense of paralysis.[6] Even Kurt's arrival (the main and perhaps the only genuine event of the narrative), which initially brings about some hope for a development in the situation (at the very least in the form of a tragic denouement), finally results in nothing more than the reinvigoration of the protagonists' quarrel, stressing further their inescapable condition. Kurt becomes the spectator of the couple's unending game of hatred and, as a result, instead of resolving the situation, he unconsciously incites them to perform it with even greater passion. His arrival only highlights further the impossibility of change, which becomes pervasive as the play comes to its circular close. Even if towards the end there appears to have been a slight alteration in the protagonists' minds – Edgar, for instance, momentarily appears to have experienced some sort of spiritual awakening – this is only an ephemeral impression, since, in the end, the couple's relationship remains wholly unchanged. The slender action that takes place only reinforces their inescapable stasis further, since it simply allows the characters to perceive the inevitability of their condition, to understand that playing their 'game' (or dancing their dance) is in fact all there is to their life.

The core events of the plot are therefore utterly incapable of setting in motion the development of the story. Even the ostensible transformations that the protagonists undergo at some points are, given their fleeting nature, insufficient to undermine the overarching sense of paralysis and repetition. Moreover, the play's circular form (mirrored by the setting, dialogue, actions, etc.) makes this paralysis almost unbearable as it materializes before the close of the curtain. The play ends exactly where it started, with the couple sitting face to face in their granite prison, ready to repeat the play, to dance their dance of death once again. Furthermore, the narrative's circular ending also hints at the possibility that other such occurrences (even Kurt's arrival) have taken place in the past, also failing to bring about any real change and accentuating the idea that the

---

[5] In this way, Strindberg seems to be tacitly alluding to the (Nietzschean) notion of the 'being of becoming'.

[6] Although it may seem contradictory that the continuous permutations of protagonists' personas bring about a sense of stasis, they repeatedly return to the same roles in a circular manner, annulling the movement of this incessant flux.

couple is condemned to re-enact this senseless circular routine forever – that no escape or alternative to their situation is possible.[7]

Consequently, we may sum up by stressing that the play presents us with the circular hell of a couple's relationship, an environment characterized by an entrapment that undermines the conventional optimistic resolutions typical of realist marriage plays. The protagonists are forever confined to the asphyxiating isolation of their spherical prison. Any event that initially seems to hint at the possibility of an escape from the incarceration of their relationship only accentuates the senselessness of their acts and shatters all hopes of an alternative. As well as mocking the idea of a conventional resolution and producing a poignant analysis of identity as a polymorphic (rather than stable) construct, Strindberg's play undermines the ideological underpinnings implicit in bourgeois marriage plays by presenting a plural (anti)plot of minimal development consisting of myriad unrelated actions and circumscribed by a circular movement that represents life as a lethal dance, a pointless and perpetual strife.

Gertrude Stein's 'Melanctha' (1909)

Although Gertrude Stein was not a European writer by birth, she undoubtedly became a Parisian after her move to the French capital in 1903. Stein remained in Paris for the rest of her life, making the city of lights her home and becoming, in the space of a few years, a vital figure in the metropolis' cultural life. Thus, despite her North American origins, she was soon immersed in the same intellectual milieu (and therefore influenced by the same stimuli) as her European counterparts. While her relationship with Nietzsche may not have been as obvious as in the case of some of her contemporaries, and especially not as direct as in the case of Strindberg, there are many aspects of her work that display a common ground between the German philosopher's and her own thinking and narrative interests.

It is also reasonable to assume that Stein was familiar with Nietzsche's ideas, since the philosopher was in vogue throughout the world of European letters

---

[7] *The Dance of Death* was followed by a second part (breaking the circularity of its form). However, the 'formal appropriateness' of the original text's ending is, as Robinson argues, 'reason enough for the play to stand alone, unaccompanied by the much shorter and weaker *Dance of Death II*' (2008: xxiii). Besides, Strindberg did not plan to write a second part to the play when he wrote the first (which was conceived as a self-sufficient work) and only decided to compose a sequel at the request of Emil Schering, his German translator, who found the original play too tragic.

even before she had moved to Paris. In one of his letters to Stein, Francis Scott Fitzgerald attests Nietzsche's importance, both in her personal entourage and in the Zeitgeist more generally, when he writes that 'the man of 1901, say, would let Nietche [sic] think for him intellectually' (cited in Pasley 2010: 227). Furthermore, given Stein's studies in philosophy and psychology at Radcliffe College, as well as her passion for reading widely, one may reasonably assume her acquaintance, and even significant familiarity, with Nietzsche's oeuvre.

In any case, if not through the direct impact of Nietzsche's work, Stein would have inherited many of his preoccupations and interests through the unmediated influence of William James, who became her mentor at Radcliffe College from 1893 to 1897, during her early training as an empirical psychologist. James shared with Nietzsche many of his ideas about the nature of language, consciousness and agency, preoccupations that Stein materialized in the form of experimental texts in terms of her use of language, subject matter and formal configuration. These experiments, as groundbreaking at the time as the art of the cubist painters, display a common intellectual concern between the two. If, as Lisa Ruddick claims, 'with the possible exception of Joyce [. . .] no other modernist thought as deeply as Stein did about the implications of formal experimentation' (1991: 255), the inquietude that prompted this interest was a kind of philosophical thinking about the ideological bases underlying certain structurations of reality that was very much in line with that of the German philosopher. Much of Stein's work is a clear effort to 'transvaluate' literature (as well as our understanding of how we experience and interpret reality more generally) by paying close attention to the form of narrative.

The kind of thinking that led Stein to use circular narrative structures begins, as in the case of Nietzsche, with reflections on the nature of language. Stein shared the philosopher's concern regarding language's incapacity to render reality or as she writes in 'Portraits and Repetition' (1935), to make words 'be' that which they are supposed to mean or describe

> the word or words that make what I looked at be itself were always words that to me very exactly related themselves to that thing at which I was looking, but as often as not had as I say nothing whatever to do with what any words would do that described that thing. (Stein 1998: 303)

This question is an abiding one for Stein, who, like Nietzsche, repeatedly asks herself whether language can (and to what extent) represent that to which it refers.

Stein also displays the related (and decidedly Nietzschean) mistrust of the dichotomy between the material and the rational, and especially of the hierarchical distribution of these two notions. She discarded the widely accepted idea at the time that the rational should be taken as a higher faculty in relation to the material world and, as Ruddick notes, exposed all 'supposedly higher faculties' as 'projections caused by the murder of a body' (1991: 257). This kind of thinking about the dualism of mind and body relates to Nietzsche's contention that consciousness is but a falsification of 'the formless unformulable world of the chaos of sensations' and therefore that the mind of a free spirit is 'guided by intuitions rather than by concepts' (1968: 307). In thinking about the mind/matter opposition, Stein, like Nietzsche, was also focused on uncovering the relationship between the privileging of one of the terms and questions of power, violence and sacrifice. Thus, the kind of radical anti-(theo)logical thinking present not only in 'Melanctha' but throughout Stein's oeuvre is evidence of very considerable parallels with that of Nietzsche.[8]

The greatest instance of this parallel is in the notion that life is a 'world of unworded experiences', a 'formless' and 'unformulable' state of constant flux (Nietzsche 1968: 307). This idea, if considered in relation to the body/mind dichotomy, implies an understanding of consciousness as something unstable, shifting and 'bound by temporality above all else' (Ford 2012: 12). It also recalls Strindberg's view of identity as a multi-layered and constantly developing construct, rendered through the portrayal of his characters' multiple and perpetually shifting personalities. In any case, for both authors the idea of consciousness as a stable entity, or the belief that a subject's identity is grounded in an essential and unalterable self, becomes problematic and fictitious, and hence replaced by the depiction of a process of ceaseless becoming.

All of these notions derive from the aforementioned epistemological distrust of the power of language: the awareness of the divide between reality and the concepts which seek to describe it, an idea that came to be known as the 'anthropomorphic error' – that is, the supposition that our conceptualizations of reality reveal the existence of a system or order hidden within it. As Sanford Schwartz argues in *The Matrix of Modernism* (1985), according to this view, reality is instead a 'preconceptual flow of appearances' that cannot be reduced to 'rational formulation', making all conceptualizations

---

[8] 'Ah reason, seriousness, mastery over the affects, the whole somber thing called reflection, all these prerogatives and showpieces of man: how clearly they have been bought! How much blood and cruelty lie at the bottom of all "good things"!' (Nietzsche 2007: 151).

merely instrumental and not the representation of 'a reality beyond the sensory stream' (2014: 19). This 'preconceptual flow' is what Nietzsche calls the 'chaos of sensations', namely, 'the original presentation of reality beneath the instrumental conventions we use to order it' (Schwartz 2014: 20). It is this understanding of reality as a stream of sensations which Stein aims to capture. Or rather, her formal experimentation emerges as a direct reaction against the abstract systems that have been designed to categorize, explain and organize reality, revealing the impact upon her work of the idea of reality as a 'flux' (as proposed by Nietzsche, but also by other philosophers such as Bergson or William James).

As Omri Moses remarks, the philosophies of thinkers such as Nietzsche, Bergson or James encouraged many writers to 're-describe' the ways in which we may account for or explain 'psychic continuity' while at the same time 'giving ethical standing to the self that is suspended in a state of transition' (2014: 19). This seemingly contradictory transitory continuity is what writers such as Stein sought to render in literature. Consequently, although Nietzsche's, Bergson's and James' works contradict each other in many respects, they nevertheless had a common impact upon the modernists concerning the ontological status of reality (as flux) as well as on subsequent understandings of consciousness or the self. Moreover, despite their specific discrepancies regarding ideas such as the aim and value of art, these vitalist philosophers also coincided in encouraging Stein and her contemporaries to reflect upon the nature and possibilities of artistic expression. The interpretation of reality as a flux or chaos inexorably led to certain related questions, such as the possibility of agency if consciousness is in fact determined by a range of external forces, an issue which, as Sara J. Ford notes, led Stein to reflect on 'the ways in which artists can avoid complete determination by conventional ordering principles [such as linearity, teleology, etc.]' (2012: 15).

'Melanctha', one of the three stories that comprise Stein's first published work *Three Lives* (1909), is clearly representative of this effort to give voice to the previous philosophical standpoint. Written a few years after Stein's arrival in Paris, the text was received with considerable curiosity by its first critics on account of its innovative style, which seemed to be paving the way for a new kind of literature. Especially notable was its monotonous, repetitive, simplistic language, very much like that of everyday speech – 'circular, repetitious, boring' (Wagner-Martin in Stein 2000: 14) – as well as the circular shape of its discourse (*syuzhet*), techniques through which Stein seemed to have found a new way of reflecting upon language, the mind-matter opposition, consciousness, identity, agency and so forth.

In 'Melanctha', Stein achieves a profound analysis of the nature of identity by focusing on the portrayal of the repetitive character of our behaviour, the monotony of our daily habits, the constant repetition of which shapes our persona, making us the people we are. It also explores the relation of this frail self to notions such as race, morality and language, producing an unconventional yet meticulous depiction of her protagonists. Although 'Melanctha's' story (*fabula*) is in fact linear (since it follows the protagonist's life from birth to death), its linearity is de-emphasized through the circular structure of its discourse. The protagonist's biography is reconstructed through repeated regressions, taking the form of helical movements. The description develops very slowly; it advances only to return again to certain ideas before it can begin to progress once more. The actual story therefore appears to lack importance or at least seems to be subordinated to the discourse – the text focusing mainly on the depiction of the protagonists' minds, rather than on the events that constitute the plot.

The discourse's circular character is configured through an abandoning of chronology. The narrative begins towards the end of Melanctha's life and circles back to the same point at the closing of the text. The discourse also begins and concludes with the succinct description of the birth and death of Rose Johnson's baby, which is repeated word for word towards the end of the text and which, as Berman points out, is 'narrated more abruptly than the rest of *Three Lives*' and 'without indication of passage of time or development of perspective' (2001: 168). The pattern of the narration thus makes the story appear 'temporally circular', despite the fact that the events narrated are actually chronological, so that, as Vesterman points out, the text lacks an 'end [or middle] in the ordinary Aristotelian sense' (2014: 46). Furthermore (like in the case of Strindberg's *Dance of Death*), as well as the discourse, many other elements of the narrative are also repetitive and circular, such as the loose plot and the dialogues that constitute most of it, emphasizing further the text's overarching movement and giving it the sense of cycles existing within cycles.

'Melanctha' captures what Moses describes as 'the reiterative, slow-moving, and idiosyncratic dimensions of psychological change' (2014: 22) through the somewhat tedious transcription of its protagonists' repetitious descriptions and dialogues. The narrative's style thus mirrors the characters' (changing) psychology – and, more broadly, Stein's understanding of the workings of the human mind. Indeed, as Susan Sontag notes, the story's style renders Stein's particular 'epistemological choice', her understanding of how we perceive, experience and apprehend reality:

> The circular repetitive style of Gertrude Stein's 'Melanctha' expresses her interest in the dilution of immediate awareness by memory and anticipation, what she calls 'association', which is obscured in language by the system of tenses. [. . .] Every style is a means of insisting on something. (2011: 246)

'Melanctha's' style insists on the transitory nature of our subjective ontology and on the repetitive or circular processes that shape our subjectivity (through language). Though initially criticized for its failure to depict reality in a realistic manner, one could argue that the style achieves a rendering of reality that is significantly more verisimilar than that of realist or naturalist linear texts – especially if one sees reality as a perpetual flux which we simplify if we seek to comprehend consciously and rationally through the abstract and limited systematic conceptualizations of our language. For this reason, James Campbell links Stein's style to that of Matisse, claiming that although she may appear to have no 'regard for realistic meaning', the fact is that both artists 'disregard "reality" to create a true form', one that renders life in new and more profound ways (2003: 2). Thus, it may well be that Stein's 'innovatory techniques', such as her use of 'repetitious, insistent, circular sentences', which urge words 'to perform in the way of an artist's line' (Campbell 2003: 2), portray reality more faithfully than the well-rounded phrases of prior literary conventions.

The circular discourse's disrupted structure, which regresses repeatedly as the narrator both tries to relate and is resistant to relating the protagonist's biography (see Berry 1993: 39), creates a tension that mirrors the struggle depicted in the narrative's story, namely, that of Melanctha's refusal to accept the conventional patriarchal values and norms regarding the structure of relationships, marriage and even society more broadly. The protagonist battles against the hierarchical inequalities deriving from race and gender, and society's prevalent (and oppressive) views concerning pleasure, intimacy and sexuality, as voiced by the protagonists' (Jeff and Melanctha's) sustained argument. This struggle also parallels that of the narrative's broader aim, that is, what Ellen Berry describes as the undermining of 'the linear momentum of realist narrative, a momentum that continued to lead to the same conclusion – death of the female and the interdiction of desire' (1993: 39). Stein counteracts these prevalent patriarchal structures, both narrative and sexual, by progressively distancing her texts from the canons of realism and naturalism in an effort to find alternatives to the dominant (and purportedly exclusive) models made ubiquitous by these conventions.

As Linda Wagner-Martin points out, when Stein began writing 'Melanctha' she was having her portrait painted by Picasso, and the stories that one of Picasso's lovers told her during these sittings allowed her to 'gain a new appreciation for the spoken narrative' (cited in Stein 2000: 13). Hence, it may well be that the story's innovative form arose from the combined influence of the avant-garde painters and this new-found interest in oral narrative, as much as from her philosophical interests. Wagner-Martin also notes that in this text Stein's 'use of repetition intensifies' and her syntax grows more 'complex', establishing a connection between 'the qualities of impressionist and modernist painting' and narrative (2000: 13). Language is presented at its rawest, both in the dialogue and in the narrative's discourse. There appears to be no literary mediation. In other words, the text replicates the reiterative, imperfect style of spoken language purportedly without any kind of aestheticization (although this kind of style is itself clearly a kind of aestheticization of the spoken language). This supposed lack of aesthetic refinement is also partly what lends Stein's writing an Impressionistic character, which is why Stephen Ratcliffe contends that she 'gives us not just plot but language, as a Cézanne or Picasso gives us not just the figure on the canvas but paint' (2000: 74).

Given Stein's extensive knowledge about, and importance within, the world of the modernist visual arts, it is no surprise that she would use her combined interest in language, consciousness and agency to produce portraits, a form that would become central to her work throughout the first half of the twentieth century. 'Melanctha' is just such a portrait: both of the eponymous protagonist and of her lover, Jeff. There is no setting; the narrative focuses purely on portraying a set of characters who 'move as if in space, floating free of location, words as disembodied "voices"' (Ratcliffe 2000: 72). Instead of depicting her protagonists by describing their linear biographies, Stein fashions these portraits through multiple circular regressions that gradually outline the profile of each of her characters by superimposing various (yet apparently minimal) descriptive layers bearing slightly different nuances. More importantly, however, the narrative is also a portrait of the protagonists' relationship, which, like the text's discourse, is not linear (neither in the hopeful manner of realist marriage narratives nor in the tragic fashion of fatalist dramas) but circular. As Ratcliffe remarks, Stein renders 'the testing, blossoming, fading, swelling again and then, inevitably, withering of a relationship detailed not as physical action but the endlessly circular conversation' (2000: 72).

The portrayal of Jeff and Melanctha's liaison seems to function at a symbolic, rather than at a representative, level. Instead of presenting us with a detailed account of their story, Stein seems more interested in depicting the stages through which their relationship unfolds (hence the lack of superficial details). As symbolic entities, the protagonists represent the alternative stances of a philosophical (moral and existential) conflict, allowing Stein to explore the intricacies of the bond between two people who desire each other yet are incapable of achieving mutual understanding. Stein's aim is to portray love, yet within a realistic, egalitarian and non-patriarchal relationship, in an attempt to surpass the stereotyped renderings typical of many literary texts. Instead of progressing neatly towards an ideal resolution (symbolizing the triumph of love) or tragic denouement (symbolizing its impossibility), as is common of most realist literature, the relationship depicted in this narrative does not move beyond the couple's 'circular discussions', where Jeff 'extols the middle-class values of "being good and living regular" while Melanctha protests that he is unable – or unwilling – to comprehend the lure of less socially acceptable epistemologies' (Linett 2010: 83). Even in those instances where the couple seems to have reached an understanding, consolidating their bond once and for all (and thus bringing the narrative to a conventional resolution), the protagonists (mainly Jeff) regress into the same conflictual attitudes which they had seemingly overcome, emphasizing the irresolvable nature of their clash once again.

The relationship therefore follows a cyclical pattern of growth and decay. As Duane Simolke points out, it 'slowly blossoms, but then they begin to grow apart, as their failure to communicate goes from a challenge to a source of annoyance' (1999: 13). This circular movement is repeated several times, through alternating phases where there appears to have been a surpassing of the conflict and others where it returns spontaneously, deteriorating the relationship once again:

> Jeff and Melanctha, both learn as much as they can from each other then grow bored. Worse yet, their sense of direction thwarts their connection: his life goes forward while his language goes in circles; Melanctha lives in circles but demands straight forward language. (Simolke 1999: 14)

Jeff and Melanctha's antagonistic perspectives, characterized by Simolke as linear and circular respectively, are irreconcilable. Even if Jeff wishes to believe and trust Melanctha, he is unable to comprehend her circular, wondering nature. His repeated failure to understand his lover is depicted through the insistent repetition of certain expressions, which makes their relationship return to the point of departure again and again, and ever more painfully for Melanctha.

Like the discourse and development of the couple's relationship, the dialogue also adopts a circular shape. Repetitive and at times tedious, it reduplicates the same phrases and expressions time and again – symbolizing the characters' inability to modify or transcend their subjective experience of reality. However, every time a certain phrase is repeated, it is also altered slightly so that each iteration introduces a subtle variation. The variants are produced with such meticulousness that Ratcliffe has characterized the narrative's language as 'mathematical in the way it presents alternatives' (2000: 73). Stein seems to use repetition not only to portray the protagonists' inability to resolve their conflict but to render all the possible alternative ways in which 'thinking and feeling can be "said" (sounded), thereby registering the multiple nuances of perception' (Ratcliffe 2000: 73). Through this excruciating redundancy, Stein draws attention to the arbitrary way in which words categorize perceptions and how minimal phonic variations lead to significant conceptual differences. The text's sentences only change very gradually, so that, as Simolke notes, they 'take many repetitions to become only slightly different', in the same way that 'it takes Jeff and Melanctha many attempts to move only slightly together' (1999: 12). So, despite this certain degree of development the narrative appears static, unchanging. The text continuously defeats the reader's expectations of some sort of improvement in the couple's situation because instead of being centred on the depiction of a story, it foregrounds the exploration of concepts such as identity, consciousness and language over the plot's development.

The circular repetitiveness of the dialogue also corresponds to the struggle reflected in the endless argument between Jeff and Melanctha, which constitutes a great part of the narrative and represents a more general conflict: that of two broad types of thinking or knowing. As mentioned earlier, the first of these 'types of knowing' may be described as 'linear and progressive', and is rendered by the character of Jeff, while the second is 'circular and rhythmic', and represented by Melanctha (Ruddick 1991: 33). These two types of thinking may be linked to the male and female perspectives, and certainly Jeff's world view corresponds to the typical patriarchal codes of the time. However, this may in fact be an oversimplification since Melanctha does not fit in nicely with the feminine stereotype antagonistic to middle-class patriarchy.

The conflict, depicted in so many of the couple's interactions, is not resolved at the level of the story, the text seems to predict the circularity of Melanctha's thinking in its structural configuration. The circular shape of the conflict also has the added effect of continuously taking the narrator through alternating stages of alignment with each of the characters. By entering Melanctha's and Jeff's minds alternately, the narrative voice first seems to favour one and then the other, so that both stances of the conflict are presented equally. This allows Stein to present us with a polyphonic view of the conflict which resists taking one side and emphasizes the irreconcilability of the two perspectives further.

Aside from undermining conventional patriarchal values and structures, empowering Melanctha as a female character, problematizing the conventional depictions of romance in pre-modernist literature and illustrating how identity is constructed through the repetitiveness of experience and habit, the text's circular structure has an added and perhaps even more recognizably Nietzschean purpose: that of situating the story in the apparent 'time-sense of a continuous present' (Vesterman 2014: 45). By adhering to the present tense, Stein insists on what Sontag calls 'the presentness of experience' (2011: 246), a notion that is very much in line with the idea of an 'eternal present' (or eternally recurring 'Moment'), which we saw as one of the culminating implications of Nietzsche's idea of eternal return.[9] This endless or continuous present is constructed by opening the text at the story's conclusion and presenting the entire sequence of events through flashbacks, so that, as William Vesterman notes, 'the time-sense [. . .] never really advances beyond its initial moment until the last few pages' (2014: 45). However, a number of additional techniques are also employed to achieve this temporality: the use of short words and the repetition of the same expressions, the lack of (or very scarce) punctuation and the use of 'a kind of circular syntax, [. . .] loose and repetitive grammar' and 'antanaclasis and polysemous semantics' (2014: 45 Vesterman). The effect of these devices is what Richard Bridgman describes as the 'stretching-out of discourse' and the amalgamation of the protagonists' vital experiences and thoughts into a continuously developing whole (1971: 52). By annulling the division of time in this manner, Stein achieves a 'continuous present', of 'circular, infinitely slow movement, like taffy in the making, always there, always complete' (Bridgman 1971: 52).

---

[9] See Chapter 2.

'Melanctha' thus draws explicit attention to the ideological underpinnings of narrative sequentiality, highlighting the potential of circularity in overthrowing traditional patriarchal values and uncovering the violence caused by the superimposition of masculine linear models upon society as a whole. The text not only links circular time with female subjectivity, it suggests that our experience of reality and identity is in fact constructed gradually through cycles of repetitions that unfold slowly, being transformed through their continued renewal in an endlessly recurring process. By showing the limitations of linearity in describing these processes and perspectives, texts such as 'Melanctha' gradually led to the adoption of the device of circularity by a number of feminist writers,[10] especially in the second half of the twentieth century. This makes Stein the precursor to the development of a new kind of feminist literature that was to blossom in the 1960s, with a succession of works seeking to undertake critical feminist standpoints through the use of a variety of circular narrative structures. These include texts such as Margaret Drabble's *The Waterfall* (1969), Margaret Laurence's *The Diviners* (1974) or Gail Godwin's *The Odd Woman* (1974).[11]

Azorín's *Doña Inés* (1925)

Although best known as a journalist and essayist, José Augusto Trinidad Martínez Ruiz (who wrote under the pen-name Azorín) was also a prolific novelist – even if the classification of many of his texts as novels is challenged by their rupture with the principal conventions of nineteenth-century prose writing. From his first works, *La voluntad* (1902) and *Antonio Azorín* (1903), Martínez Ruiz produced fragmented texts that combine different narrative formats (journal articles, autobiographical descriptions, extracts from other texts, etc.) in order to conform complex portraits of a pseudo-autobiographical protagonist that do not follow a tightly knit story with a single unified action and thus do not adhere to the Aristotelian standard. His works are, instead,

---

[10] Julia Kristeva's essay 'Women's Time' (1981) provides an insightful explanation as to why this might have happened. The essay is 'an attempt to situate the problematic of women in Europe within an inquiry on time: that time which the feminist movement both inherits and modifies' (Kristeva 1989: 15). She argues that female subjectivity 'becomes a problem with respect to a certain conception of time: time as project, teleology, linear and prospective unfolding; time as departure, progression, and arrival – in other words, the time of history'. (1989: 17). Alternatively: 'female subjectivity would seem to provide a specific measure [of time] that essentially retains repetition and eternity from among the multiple modalities of time known through the history of civilizations' (1989: 16).

[11] See Greene (1990).

characterized by fragmentation, perspectivism, episodic descriptions and minimal plots. They have been described as 'lyrical in nature and Impressionistic' (Chandler and Schwartz 1991: 160), given their exemplary tendency to focus on the depiction of the vibrant scenery of the Spanish countryside, cities and towns.

The primary emphasis of Azorín's novels is undoubtedly aesthetic: the meticulous portrayal of his characters' physical appearance and psychological or emotional states, as well as the rendering of stunning exterior sceneries in order to produce complex visual portraits marked by vivid imagery. There is clearly a stronger interest in capturing vibrant landscapes, scenes or impressions of certain moments in a photographic or pictorial manner than in narrating a coherent story. Plot-development is in many cases de-emphasized, annulled or even absent. Rather than relating events or actions and their consequences, Azorín focuses on describing minute details, producing a detailed graphic impression of his narrative world. As Chandler and Schwartz argue, throughout his oeuvre Azorín 'described the countryside extensively, dominated time, and wrote in an exquisite, evocative style [. . .] eschewing narration in the Classical sense' and anticipating the novels of authors such as Alain Robbe-Grillet (1991: 160). This predilection for the aesthetic, and focus on the portrayal of landscapes, has led critics such as Gayana Jurkevich to define his works as having an ekphrastic character.

Azorín's novels consist mostly of fragmented (and somewhat autonomous) descriptive passages, which are only connected by a loose underlying story that is constantly interrupted by these exhaustive narrative images. These ekphrastic passages give a spatial form to the text that seems to counter or suspend its linear sequencing. In other words, with ekphrasis Azorín found a way to suspend or paralyse the ostensible intrinsic sequentiality and temporal movement of writing, producing what Jurkevich describes as 'the illusion of simultaneity and stasis within a normally temporal dynamics' (1999: 20). His descriptions hence arrest language's continuity and freeze the habitual unrelenting pace of the 'temporal unfolding of narrative' by imitating 'the spatial simultaneity' of a visual artwork: 'bend[ing] discursive linearity into the shape of a circular mimesis germane to plastic forms' (Jurkevich 1999: 20). His novels (especially *Doña Inés*) interrupt or stop time (and thus also the story), creating a sense of timelessness where the inherent diachronic movement that we expect in literature is replaced by the synchrony of an ekphratic temporality. Certainly, Jurkevich is right to argue that the movement of literary ekphrasis mirrors that of the 'ouroboros', since it 'converts chronological time into the mythic time of the eternal return' (1999: 20).

Azorín, who characterized himself as a 'little philosopher' (*pequeño filósofo*) in the title of his 1904 novel, had a strong interest in the work of Nietzsche, whom he refers to and cites repeatedly throughout his oeuvre and who clearly constituted one of the philosophical pillars of his thought. Already in his first novel, Azorín openly defined himself as a 'mystic, anarchist, ironic, dogmatic, admirer of Schopenhauer, supporter of Nietzsche' (1969: 152; my translation). This kind of self-characterization is reiterated throughout his writings, with Nietzsche appearing time again as one of his main philosophers of choice. Azorín mentions having read and agreeing with Nietzsche on several occasions and openly displays his influence through the use of Nietzschean terminology, themes and motifs in many of his texts. In *La voluntad*, for instance, he claims that it is necessary to 'break with the old tablet of moral values, as Nietzsche said' (1969: 133). He also reiterates the philosopher's doctrine of the eternal recurrence, characterizing it as 'the indefinite, repeated continuation of the human dance' (1969: 135). In fact, the idea of the eternal return (or at least his personal interpretation of it) becomes, as Jurkevich remarks, one of Azorín's 'favourite thematic hobby-horses' (1999: 20).

Written and published in 1925, *Doña Inés, Historia de amor* is a clear example of an Azorinian text where the idea of eternal recurrence is crucial, both as a motif and as a core structuring principle. The novel is typical of Azorín's effort to compose texts of minimal development where the plot is completely subordinated to the aesthetic rendering of image and sound. The novel is a visual experience in words or, rather, a complete sensory experience in prose. We find many chapters where the action loses focus over other aspects, such as the portrayal of the setting and its atmosphere or the description of the characters. *Doña Inés* thus reworks the popular genre of the romantic novelette to produce a groundbreaking love-story, where the protagonists' romance (which, as the subtitle suggests, supposedly constitutes one of the main elements of the narrative) becomes only a minor aspect of the novel and other features, such as the visual depiction of objects, take the spotlight.

Yet, although little seems to happen (in terms of plot), the text is heaving with meticulous descriptions that submerge the reader into the story-world. Every chapter transports us to a different scene or landscape, the action only developing very subtly in the midst of these images. Rather than being the backdrop to the plot, the decorative elements which normally (in conventional novels) serve merely to complete it (by adding descriptive details that are essentially superfluous to the story's development) here become focal aspects of the narrative, making the plot their backdrop instead. Even when Azorín describes certain events that are supposedly central to the progression of the story (such as those related to the protagonists' romance), he takes more interest in depicting their poetic qualities or symbolic allusions than their consequences or implications for the plot's development. One such event, the kiss depicted in Chapter XXXVII, which is anticipated as one of the central moments of the narrative (being an expected turning point in Inés' love-story), fails to trigger the much-awaited development or acceleration of the story, functioning, instead, mostly as a symbolic element signalling the tale's eternal or transcendent character. The kiss, which mirrors that of Inés' ancestor Doña Beatriz, also sets in motion the circular structure of the narrative by recalling her predecessor's love-story and rendering the whole account as an infinitely recurring episode. Doña Inés' love-story loses its importance as an isolated event, becoming instead a symbol of the growth and decay of love. In this way, the text's circular shape endows the narrative with an atemporal character. By highlighting the episode's recurrence, it becomes universal and eternal: it is not merely Inés' story; it is the infinitely recurring cycle of the blossoming and decadence of love. This idea is made explicit in the narrative's 'unresolved resolution', where Inés, now an old woman, can see that the same pattern will unfold in the next generation.

So, despite the fact that neither the story nor the narrative's discourse are purely circular (most sequences correspond to a chronological progression of time), they are far from linear either. The discourse is fragmented, and the chronological story underlying the narrative is de-emphasized to the point where it seems to lack development (its scarce progression taking place only very gradually) and importance. The story therefore acquires a circular character, not only through the pattern of growth and decay of Inés' relationship (as in Stein's 'Melanctha') but through the eternal status that it acquires by mirroring that of her ancestor and foreshadowing that of the coming generation. The ostensible linearity of both the narrative's discourse and its underlying story are therefore de-emphasized through the permeation of circular structures. To be sure, if, as Darío Villanueva suggests, we were to 'project graphically in the space of our perception' the novel's core shape, we would see two different 'designs' (*diseños*) according to the text's internal development: 'The graph of the temporal split could be a circle or an infinite horizontal line with points that would indicate the repeated incidents' (1983: 135; my translation). Accordingly, even if the narrative's discourse (like Doña Inés' life) is apparently linear, circular features reverberate throughout both, making palpable their dual circular/linear character.

The novel's circularity is further emphasized by the vital significance of the theme of time, which surfaces as a recurring motif in myriad forms throughout the narrative. Temporality was clearly one of Azorín´s fundamental interests, not only in *Doña Inés* but throughout his oeuvre.[12] The text is full of images of time, such as Inés' daguerreotype in Chapter II, the gas lighter in Chapter VI or Don Pablo's dream in Chapter XXXIV. The story opens by situating the action in a specific temporal locus – '1840 [. . .] the first days of June; mid-afternoon' (Azorín 1969: 609; my translation) – and closes by reflecting the passing of time through the description of the movement and decay of daylight as it shines on the buildings of Segovia – recalling Monet's series of paintings of Rouen Cathedral under different lighting conditions during the course of a day. Time also appears in the title of several of the chapters, and Azorín represents antagonistic conceptions of time at various points in the narrative, not only through the ongoing antithesis of linear and circular time but also through the counter-posing of other (related) temporalities, such as historical time and mythical time (Chapter XLI).

This insistence on the theme of time, added to the text's subliminal circularity, allows Azorín to explore and present the reader with antagonistic temporal conceptions (linear and circular) as ultimately in unison with one another. By merging the two notions throughout, Azorín is able to not favour one over the other but draw attention to time's complex, plural nature. The novel emphasizes at once the fleeting passage of time, inevitably linear in that it moves constantly forward without any possibility of regress, and its circular character: eternally repetitious, unrelenting, inexorable. Each notion is portrayed in different ways and serves to underline two antithetical perspectives of reality. Linear time, being an irreversible sequence of singular events or moments which are forever gone, is rendered symbolically through the image of the loss of youth, the depiction of the dimming sunlight as the day comes to an end and the irremediable linearity of Doña Inés' chronology. It emphasizes an anthropomorphic and individualistic perspective of time, the inevitable counterpart of mortality. Circular time, on the other hand, accentuates a non-individualistic perception, a bio-centric or material perspective, supra-individual and thus broader than the

---

[12] In an article entitled 'Clarín and the Intelligence', Azorín asks himself what is the 'condition' that best 'enhances' the literary artist, to which he responds: 'The perception of time and eternity' (2004: 193; my translation).

limited, individualistic scope of linear time (since it transcends any individual subjective perspective, given that the repetition of events takes place in different individuals, settings and historical temporalities).

Although perhaps a Nietzschean vestige, the kind of eternal return depicted in Azorín's narrative is a simplification of Nietzsche's idea, since it relates to the notion of recurrence purely at a communal level, as a repetitive history across generations, and not to its repercussions for an individual. Azorín focuses purely on showing how the circular patterns that are concealed within a subject's chronological experience of time may shine through this assumed linear perception. It hence emphasizes a continuity across generations that makes our isolated individual subjectivity a subliminal plural totality. As a result, this Azorinian version of eternal recurrence does not preclude the idea of linear time. Eternal recurrence works as a structuring principle but only obliquely: the reader is encouraged to assume that Inés' story will repeat itself, but this is not stated explicitly in the narrative. Although the notion of circular time reappears constantly throughout the novel it only does so fleetingly, constituting at once a clear yet veiled thematic pillar of the text. Moreover, its depiction serves purely aesthetic ends: the idea is an underlying force endowing the text with an eternal character, as a pattern that may be appreciated in nature, showcasing the complexities of our supposedly simple reality, rather than as an ontological reality (although this idea is not overthrown either). As a result, the novel's synthesis of the two antagonistic modalities of time highlights both points of reference, the individual and the supra-individual, as a harmonic unity.

The text's temporality is consequently neither exclusively linear nor circular. By combining sequentiality and simultaneity in an overarching, absolute time (instead of replacing or privileging one over the other) Azorín makes the central elements depicted throughout the narrative (objects, settings and characters, as opposed to action) representative of this duality. These elements function as *loci* where linear time (as past, present and future) and circular time (as repetition) meet. In the cities, villages, countryside landscapes and protagonists depicted in the story, the division of time as past, present and future at once materializes and breaks down, undoing, as Inman Fox claims, 'the destructive force of linear time' and unveiling 'a new reality determined by shared rhythms and sensibilities' (1988: 154). Doña Inés is the most obvious representative example of this meeting place, being herself the central element driving the narrative forward (in a linear fashion), yet at the same time symbolizing the past (through her parallelism with Doña Beatriz)[13] and foreshadowing a recurring future (through her observations about the schoolchildren at the closing of the text).

Inés is also said to experience the duality of time within herself on several occasions in the narrative. She reflects on the nature of time repeatedly, wondering whether it actually exists, and feels a past consciousness blending with her present self at certain key moments of the narrative:

> Doña Inés, thoughtful, absorbed, experienced again, with more intensity, the strange, indefinable sensation that she experienced days earlier when she laid her hand on the statue of Doña Beatriz. Does time exist? Who was she, Inés or Beatriz? (Azorín 1969: 647; my translation)

Inés confuses herself with her ancestor in Chapter XXXVI, their two timelines conflating into an eternal or timeless present. This conflation (of past and present and – as revealed at the end of the novel – implicitly also future) into an atemporal moment is epitomized in Chapter XXXVII, as she suffers the hallucinatory experience of the loss of her identity and her fusing with her predecessor.

The same is apparent in the character of Don Pablo, who is said to experience the three-part division of time (as a linear past, present and future) as much as its circular repetitiveness, becoming another locus where the two temporalities are conflated: an embodiment of time's plural unity. There are many occasions where Don Pablo reflects on the complex character of this multiple, absolute or overarching temporality, and Azorín even dedicates an entire chapter (Chapter XVI, 'Uncle Pablo and Time') specifically to this character's experience and understanding of its complex nature. In it, the narrator tells us that 'Don Pablo lived as much in the past as in the present', that 'any incident whatsoever made the gentleman experience with prodigious exactitude, with anguishing exactitude, the same sensation that he had experienced fifteen, twenty or thirty years before' and that 'in the present he saw the future' (Azorín 1969: 625; my translation). This establishes him as a clear nexus between linear and circular time.

Aside from the protagonists, many of the other central elements depicted in the narrative also function as these multi-temporal *topoi*. This is true of most of the text's settings (the cities of Segovia and Madrid, the house in Segovia, Eufemia's house, the church in Chapter XXV, etc.) and objects (the

---

[13] Her parallelism is rendered visually through her physical similarity with her ancestor – as reflected in the ekphrastic descriptions of Doña Beatriz's portrait and statue.

daguerreotype, the letter in Chapter III, the gas lighter, Doña Beatriz's painting and her and her husband's statues, etc.). So, as the narrative progresses it also becomes increasingly clear that one of Azorín's fundamental aims is precisely the depiction of this complex absolute temporality through the portrayal of a range of different elements.

The main way in which these elements become symbolic of the conflation of different temporalities is through their ekphrastic nature. However, even if the ekphrastic passage inherently arrests the progression of time, Azorín is only able to achieve a synthesis of suspension, progression and past–present simultaneity by placing these descriptions within the fragmented yet overarching concurrently linear and circular framework of his narrative. He also makes these elements the object of digressive reflections on the nature of time, the keyhole to past and future temporalities, establishing them as eternal (timeless) objects. Hence, his ekphrastic descriptions not only have the desired effect of arresting the linear sequentially of narrative by annulling or at least delaying its progression, or, as Jurkevich puts it, of 'recreating within the parameter of language art forms the synchronic and spatio-visual qualities of the plastic arts' (1999: 88); they also endow certain scenes, characters or objects with the paradoxical temporality of the eternal return owing to the nature of the narrative structure that contains them. Azorín's use of ekphrasis is therefore motivated by an philosophical as well as an aesthetic reason. Aside from aspiring to give his writing a pictorial character, he saw the potential of exploring the complexities of temporality through this narrative technique.

Overall, in *Doña Inés* Azorín displays an insistent desire to undermine or destabilize linearity with the intention of salvaging, as José Ortega y Gasset puts it, 'the restless world that hurls onward toward its own destruction' by 'suspending the movement of things so that the attitude in which he surprises them is made eternal' (cited in Jurkevich 1999: 88). In other words, the effect is not only to halt time through a writing style that recalls that of impressionist painting but to underscore its versatile nature through a fragmented narrative that blurs the pace and nature of its unfolding. *Doña Inés* thus renders Azorín's famous formulation of Nietzsche's idea, 'to live is to return' (*vivir es volver*), through the combination of the unique temporal qualities of the ekphrastic passage with those of the eternal return. The novel's special treatment of time allows its thematic and structural nuclei to resonate in an effort to show its complex dual nature (as both linear and circular). In this manner, Azorín does away with the supposedly intrinsic linear sequencing and structure of narrative, replacing it, if not by an absolute and inexorable circularity, then by a helical configuration containing both possibilities in unison.

* * *

Consequently, although in very different ways, the three works studied earlier use circularity in order to produce radical critiques of many of the prototypical values postulated by the representative trends from which they arise, undermining the very philosophical standpoint implicit in the use of the linear narrative model. Instead of positing certain ideals through teleological resolutions that reveal either the triumph or failure of their protagonists, these narratives undermine such a structure, inviting us to consider what kind of world view is being affirmed by those kinds of texts: whether it is truly representative of reality or, rather, motivated by a specific ideological interest.

Strindberg presents us with a subversion of the bourgeois marriage play, where a circular movement underscores the protagonists' inability to change or put an end to their disputes. Circular patterns also underlie the couple's actions and dialogues, establishing them as performative characters, devoid of essential attributes, and rendering identity as a fluctuating construct, wholly dependent on a person's context and actions. Gertrude Stein also dwells upon the shifting nature of our subjectivity, drawing attention to the forces that shape it violently by subjecting individuals to pre-established customs, values and norms. The circular form allows her to show the dynamics of psychological change, the way in which consciousness is affected by language, and to counterpoise two alternative world views or ways to structure reality: a stereotypically male perspective and a female one. Her text thus conflates linearity and circularity by de-emphasizing the linear trajectory of her *fabula* through the circular structure of its discourse, and vice versa. On the other hand, Azorín presents us with a meditation on the nature of time through a fragmented text that focuses on the detailed descriptions of a series of scenic landscapes, picturesque buildings, objects and snippets from the protagonists' lives where various temporalities collide. The faint plot emerges ever so slowly in the midst of these descriptions, but rather than following the protagonists' lives, it becomes the portrayal of an eternal story, beyond a specific historical moment or generation. Although time passes, its pace is vague and at times even completely annulled by the peculiar effects of the descriptive passages, which not only suspend its course but impose a peculiar temporality upon the text: that of the eternal recurrence.

4

'Vivir es volver'

Queneau, Nabokov and Kharms

If the texts analysed in the previous chapter are some of the first evidences of a growing preoccupation with the structure of narrative, those examined in this chapter are evidence of the crystallization and acceleration of this tendency. While many of the first circular texts arise out of an effort to find new and improved ways to give voice to old problems (those of past conventions)[1] – inexorably surpassing them, albeit in some cases inadvertently – increasingly it is an effort to give a new voice to new problems that motivates the use of circular forms. Many authors began to grasp the ideological implications of the structures they were using, encouraging them to find new ways to organize their texts.

In the interwar years, Raymond Queneau, Vladimir Nabokov and Daniil Kharms move beyond the initial undertakings of their predecessors prompted by an acute awareness about the vested character of form: a cognizance that emerges as a by-product of the assimilation of the idea of the 'death of God'. The absence of an absolute or transcendental frame of reference from which to value or explain existence encouraged many European writers to rethink their prevailing assumptions regarding the ways in which we conceptualize, systematize and structure reality, and thus narrative too. The circular form is therefore representative of an incipient crisis of values that would become ever more present as the century progressed. These texts arise out of that crisis: they reflect and respond to it, engaging with the fundamental problem from which the conversation on nihilism derives. As we shall see, this effort becomes ever more patent in the works studied in the following chapters, achieving a peak towards mid-century. Accordingly, if the kind of circular structures that we find

---

[1] As discussed in the previous chapter, Strindberg's play, for instance, is in many respects both naturalist and post-naturalist.

in the earlier texts are subtle, in terms of both how they construct their circularity and how they display the limitations and implications of the linear form, the texts analysed here and in the following chapters exhibit an ever-growing level of explicitness in both respects.

Raymond Queneau's *The Bark Tree* (1933)

Raymond Queneau was a ferocious reader and innate man of letters. He had a remarkable passion for literature from a very early age, was already reading Nietzsche at sixteen (see Sturrock 1999: 180) and developed a fervent interest in philosophy that he cultivated throughout his lifetime. Having received his *baccalauréat* at Le Havre (his native town), Queneau moved to Paris to study philosophy at the Sorbonne from 1921 to 1923. Nietzsche was undoubtedly one of the thinkers who impacted on him most vividly during his adolescence, an interest which did not decline as he grew older. Repeated references to the philosopher can be found in several of Queneau's essays – notably in his collection *Letters, Numbers, Forms* (1950) – displaying the extent to which Nietzsche remained a crucial stimulus for him throughout his life.

As well as having strong interests in linguistics, poetry and philosophy, Queneau also developed a passion for mathematics which is worth mentioning due to the impact it had upon the formal composition of his works. While he became associated with the Surrealists in 1924, and his works have been described as presenting existentialist features or as pertaining to the *nouveau roman* (see Taylor 2006: 326), Queneau defied all of these labels by both adhering to and deviating from these intellectual and artistic trends in various respects. His distinctiveness from any single artistic movement soon encouraged him to distance himself from the Surrealists, breaking his ties with the group in 1929. His philosophical interests were also multifarious. Despite his appreciation for Nietzsche, Queneau became a student to Alexandre Kojève, attending his lectures on Hegel from 1934 to 1939 alongside André Breton, Pierre Klossowski, Jacques Lacan, Merleau-Ponty and Georges Bataille, and even editing and publishing them (as *Introduction to the Reading of Hegel*) in 1947. However, the circularity of his texts displays a surpassing of Hegel's idea of a helical dialectic progression, pointing to his reluctance to commit to a single philosophical system.

Overall, Queneau's works are, as Calvino argues, 'unique in their own genre', given his insistent desire to strive 'against the grain of the dominant tendencies of his age and of French culture in particular' through 'an endless need to invent and to test possibilities' (2014: 246–7). Queneau aimed to overthrow many of the preconceptions and generalized assumptions of his time, making him (like Nietzsche) stand out as an eccentric figure. Yet, his 'eccentricities' were not the result of a gratuitous desire to provoke or shock the intellectual community or society more broadly. Rather, they respond to three fundamental questions which are indicative of a specific philosophical outlook and representative of the concerns motivating Queneau's formal experimentation: What is the nature and function of artistic creation? How does language enable us to grasp reality? And how veracious or truthful is the knowledge that it allows us to construct? These questions led Queneau to address two overarching themes, which, as Beno Weiss notes, become key throughout his literary career: 'the importance of artistic creation and the human value of knowledge' (1993: 92).

Queneau expounds these and other preoccupations in his 1938 essay 'What Is Art?', where he arrives at the conclusion that literature is important, among other things, because it expresses *and* transforms 'natural realities (cosmic, universal) and social realities (anthropological, human)' (2007: 37). These ideas draw a close parallelism between Queneau and Nietzsche in their analogous understandings of the nature and value of science, art and knowledge. In 'The Place of Mathematics' (1923), Queneau argues that since science is purely a 'human activity, a social and historic phenomenon', it performs the same functions as art (that of expressing and transforming natural and social realities), highlighting the affinity between both disciplines and underscoring that if one is to be considered as 'a kind of knowledge' so should the other (2007: 99). Nevertheless, he implies that neither should in fact be taken as such. Instead of seeing science as a more transcendental activity through which one can unveil the truth about reality, Queneau equates the two, establishing them as techniques or methods that can be used to render, but also to change, the natural world. Accordingly, Calvino stresses that Queneau's 'practice' finds itself simultaneously 'on two contemporary dimensions': that 'of art (as technique) and play, against the backdrop of his radical epistemological pessimism' (2014: 253), a paradigm which he sees fit for literature as much as for science.

Also like Nietzsche, Queneau sets out from the idea that 'all reality is chaos' and uses art to counterpoise it: to 'introduce a little order, a little logic, in a universe which is totally the opposite' (Calvino in Weiss 1993: 94). Innovation is seen as the only way of imposing a personal symmetry upon the turmoil of existence. Unwilling to succumb to the normalizing forces of convention, Queneau strives to find a new way of portraying reality, so as to impose his particular order and voice on its pandemonium. As a result, his aim is to challenge this meaningless, chaotic world by depicting it through the mediating filter of his subjective perception. It is this perspectivist gaze which characterizes his art, both at a thematic and at a structural level. Indeed, as Esslin claims, Queneau's texts are 'devoted to the destruction of ossified forms and the dazzling of the eye by phonetic spelling and authentic Chinook-type syntax' in an attempt to avoid the laxity of his contemporaries who followed the conventions of the time blindly and to find an individual voice to impose a personal 'meaning and measured order to the formless universe' (cited in Calvino 2014: 248).

We may thus sum up Queneau's views on literature very broadly by citing John Sturrock's observation that for Queneau writing 'was not politics but play' (1999: 180). This does not mean, however, that he saw his art as a simple game. The driving force behind his formal experimentations was a desire to express reality through the voice of his individual subjectivity, which, to a certain extent, may be defined as anti-ideological. For this reason, Queneau's oeuvre is particularly hard to classify. It is, as Carol Sanders suggests, '*transgénérique*, transgressive' in its attempt to shake norms, modes and traditions (1994: 5). Yet, the reappearance of certain themes (language, subjectivity, consciousness, duality, etc.), the continued focus on form and the insistence on finding a personal voice for his subjective experience of reality indicate a prevalent concern that suggests a specific philosophical stance: a post-death-of-God world view. This is already apparent in his first novel *The Bark Tree* (1933) (or *Witch Grass*; *Le Chiendent*), a half-comic, half-philosophical narrative that aims to render the veiled beauty of the mundane struggle of everyday life. The work has been described (by Weiss et al.) as an 'antinovel' because it is 'replete with events, situations, characters, and plots' that are 'held together' by a seemingly arbitrary circular structure' (1993: 91), rather than by causality or logical necessity. It depicts the intriguing and awe-inspiring nature of the chaotic randomness of the everyday, but this depiction is, as Sam Slote argues, 'overlaid by a rigid scheme perceptible only to the most attentive of readers' (2004: 387). The paradoxical portrayal of life's frenzied haphazardness through a tightly knit structure obliquely signals the dual nature of existence as both immensely chaotic and potentially ordered. This duality is also perceptible in the novel's style, which Karen L. Taylor describes as combining 'mathematical rigor with humor and a spirit of innovation' (2006: 325).

Although most critics point out that *The Bark Tree* draws most heavily from Cartesian dualism (since Queneau's initial intention was to 'translate' or transcribe Descartes' *Discourse on Method* into the more down-to-earth discourse of spoken language) the fact is that the novel's philosophical backdrop is far more complex, bearing, as it does, several other (post-Cartesian) influences. Queneau's dismissal of his original idea (to transcribe Descartes' text) in order to write a work of fiction (see 'Conversation') is representative of how the ideas that he wished to examine in the novel extended far beyond the confines of Cartesianism. Hence, despite the prevailing tendency to characterize the work as a literary re-writing of Descartes' text, critics have also signalled a number of additional philosophical 'sources'.[2] Calvino's insightful description of the novel reveals this heterogeneous philosophical and technical melting pot out of which it emerges:

> written in 1933 after the formative experience of Joyce's *Ulysses*, [*The Bark Tree*] was intended to be not only a linguistic and structural tour-de force (based on a structure that was numerological and symmetrical, as well as on a catalogue of narrative genres), but also a definition of existence and thought, nothing less than a novelised commentary on Descartes' *Discourse on Method*. The novel's action spotlights those things which are thought but not real, but which have influenced the reality of the world: a world which in itself is totally devoid of meaning. (2014: 248)

The final sentence of this passage situates the novel not only in a Cartesian world but also in a post-Nietzschean one: meaninglessness is accepted as a given, and Cartesianism, if at all, can only function within the boundaries imposed by such an awareness.

In an effort to establish some distance between the philosophical questions explored in *The Bark Tree* and the basic premises of Cartesian dualism, Queneau himself noted at a later date (see 'Errata') that it had been 'a certain John Dunne, the author of a philosophical treatise on the nature of time' rather than Descartes, who had inspired the writing of his first novel (Stump 1998: 45). The novel engages with, and restates, several key notions of Descartes' text, though only to depart from his quest for a principle of certain knowledge,

---

[2] Marc Lowenthal deems *The Bark Tree* to be 'a Heideggerian rewriting of Plato's *The Sophist*, recognizing the fact that "being is determined by nonbeing"' (2000: 149). Slote stresses that it 'works in structural allusions to Plato' as well as Descartes 'in a manner similar to Joyce's use of Homer' (2004: 388). Weiss characterizes the novel as a 'commentary on Descartes', although it also 'deals with the Platonic, Cartesian, and Pirandellian question about what is real beyond appearances' (1993: 91).

since the protagonists' search for meaning (symbolized by Taupe's door) is, as Jordan Stump argues, 'founded on error, and each logical step in the characters' reasoning engenders other errors and leads others into error, as inexorably as each truth leads to another truth in Descartes' model' (1998: 47). Consequently, the novel seems to propose what Stump calls a 'pessimistic Cartesianism' (1998: 47), since Descartes' inductive reasoning leads to the opposite of what is expected: erroneous assumptions, flawed reasonings and so on. Logical deduction is presented as an illusory attempt to see a supposedly 'true' reality beyond its appearance, which is repeatedly proven to be a fantasy. Every attempt to interpret existence through the lens of reason leads the protagonists to a false conclusion, or a dead end. Moreover, Cartesianism is also undermined explicitly in the novel through the character of Ernestine, who defies the reductive dualism it proposes:

> Imagining yourself just like you are, only not having any eyes, or arms, or legs- doesn't make sense. On account of I've realized that what you are, it's not just a little voice that talks in your head, but it's your whole body, too, that you can feel is alive, and everything you can do with it. (Queneau 1971: 196)

Ernestine stresses that our subjectivity is inseperable from our material body and environment within which it is ecapsulated and through which it is constructed.

More importantly, the novel undermines Cartesianism in favour of a Nietzschean scepticism and epistemological critique by exploring the relationship between the notions of knowledge, appearance and reality through the theme of language. The next logical step after Descartes' *cogito ergo sum* is to name oneself, in order to distinguish the 'I' that thinks (and thus *is*) from all the other thinking subjects that exist alongside it. It is here that language comes into play. The importance of reflecting upon its workings, then, becomes evident, since it is only through language that we can make the world knowable. Queneau plays out these reflections and invites meditation on the same by reproducing certain expressions or words particular to spoken discourse, that is, through the transcription of what he termed 'neo-français'. This is accomplished through the loss of certain consonants or vowels, the agglutination of words and the transcription of other distinctive features typical of the Parisian dialect.[3] As well as these phonological peculiarities, Queneau also uses certain terms of the Parisian street jargon, indulges in continuous orthographical innovations,

---

[3] The loss of certain consonants or vowels, assimilations, palatalizations and so on (see Sanders 1994: 10).

adopts a conspicuous grammar and has some words change grammatical field with bizarre effects (see Sanders 1994: 10–12). The *effet de surprise* (since the transcriptions are not systematized) caused by the contrast of the two registers (spoken and written) encourages the reader to reflect upon their differences: to consider how and why they differ, how they each function and why they coexist. Their simultaneous rendering allows Queneau to show how each kind of expression enables a different (yet equally valuable) manner to depict and shape reality, and hence, to exemplify how there may be several contrasting yet analogous referents for the same signified: how two (seemingly antagonistic) kinds of knowledge may describe the same reality.

So, rather than transcribing 'neo-français' for the sake of verisimilitude, Queneau's aim is to highlight the division between these two discourses in order to show the great divide existing between a language's (quasi-Platonic) written form and its spoken reality, mirroring the gap between a language's ability to describe reality and that reality itself. In this way, Queneau not only underscores the divide between writing (a virtual system of closed possibilities) and the more tangible language of speech (which is fluid, ever-changing and therefore more closely in line with the flux of reality), he also stresses (like Stein in 'Melanctha') the distance between our concepts and the reality they seek to represent: the anthropomorphic error.[4] Furthermore, these linguistic experiments also emphasize that reality is itself constructed and shaped by language, since it is through words that we assemble and impose our world view. Language filters reality and we adapt it in accordance with this filter. Exploring the workings of linguistic reasoning thus becomes crucial for Queneau, since it is the sole way to properly comprehend how our knowledge of the world and our individual subjectivity are configured.

Equally important to his choice of language, the organization of his text also becomes crucial in the expression of his philosophical outlook. In *Entretiens avec Georges Charbonier* (1962: 47), Queneau stresses his belief that the structure of narrative is of particular importance. He repeatedly directed criticisms both at the Surrealists and at the general history of the novel precisely for their lack of attentiveness to this matter. In contrast, his texts display a rigorous attention to form, where the overall arrangement of the components follows a specific, logical and preconceived shape. This has led critics such as Sanders to stress that

---

[4] See Chapter 4.

content and form are intimately linked in his narratives, as much as in his poems (see 1994: 7).

Queneau's general views on form are detailed in the essay 'Technique of the Novel', in *Letters, Numbers, Forms* (1950), an account of the ways in which he managed to overcome his contemporaries' structural slovenliness and impose a specific order and shape to his writing. The essay begins by indicating that novels appear to lack the need for a specific formal configuration:

> the novel has eluded every form of law for as long as it has existed. Anyone can drive an indeterminate number of seemingly lifelike characters along before him, like a flock of geese, across an empty plain measuring some indeterminate number of pages or chapters. No matter what, the result will always be a novel. (Queneau 2007: 26)

Although Queneau does not dwell upon the reasons for this formal slackness, he seems to be suggesting that the principal cause lies in the assumption that narratives automatically become meaningful teleologically. In any case, the effort to overcome this '*laisser-aller*' becomes an imperative task for him. Rather than leaving the formal configuration of his texts to the implicit linear sequencing of language or the arbitrariness of chance, he sought to devise structures that had their own internal coherence and character. Taking the lead from authors such as Joyce, Queneau stressed that there should be no essential differences between the formal composition of novels (at least of the kind that he intended to write) and poems (see 2014: 43). Yet, with such comments he did not seek to impose these ideas upon his contemporaries or lead to the emergence of a new literary trend but merely to describe what he called a 'conscious technique' for the novel.

Queneau expounds this technique by referring to his first three published novels, *The Bark Tree*, *Gob of Stone* (1934) and *The Last Days* (1936), noting that all three texts 'express one single theme, or rather variants of one theme, and, consequently, have the same structure: circular' (2007: 27). However, he also points out that the kind of circularity found in these three texts differs significantly. The latter two contain pseudo-circular forms, since in *Gob of Stone* 'the circular movement returns not to its starting point but to a homologous place, and so forms a helicoidal arc', and in *The Last Days* 'the cycle is simply a seasonal one, recurring until the eventual disappearance of all seasons: the circle is broken by a catastrophe' (2007: 27). The structure of *The Bark Tree*, in contrast, is that of a perfect circle: 'the circle closes on itself and returns to its point of departure, which is suggested, perhaps heavy-handedly, by the fact that the last sentence is identical to the first' (Queneau 2007: 27). Accordingly, Queneau describes the novel metaphorically as 'a man who after a long walk finds himself back where he started' (2007: 28). This analogy captures the spirit of the novel perfectly even in its vagueness and is particularly telling of its anti-teleological nature. The path of the narrative leads nowhere and has no end.

The Bark Tree is therefore, as Christopher Shorley observes, 'doubtless the most striking as well as the explicit example' of narrative circularity within Queneau's works (1985: 60). The verbatim repetition of the opening sentence – 'the silhouette of a man appeared in profile; so, simultaneously, did thousands' (Queneau 1971: 7, 280) – at the closing of the text throws the reader back to its first scene, annulling the storyline or at least de-emphasizing its significance. The circular shape of the narrative affects the text on two different levels. At the level of the story, it 'negates the impetus of the text as the reader has read it' and, as Shorley contends, 'severely compromises the possibility of any new beginnings' (1985: 61), generating a general sense of entrapment and banality. In the absence of a resolution the idea of a narrative *telos* disintegrates. The circular return also shocks the reader, undermining his general expectations about narrative[5] and calling for a renewed perception of the entire sequence of events – and thus of the novel form itself.

At an overarching level, the structure establishes the text as an autonomous, self-contained unit, auto-referential and self-conscious of its status as literature, evincing its poetic essence and, above all, its aestheticism. The circular form also emphasizes that there is no end to the story, no resolution that posits certain underlying values or gives a particular sense to the narrative as a whole. It highlights, instead, the playful character of the text, which seems motivated only by a desire to aestheticize life: to render a set of characters and events in a disinterested manner, producing a multifarious portrait that illustrates the chaotic interconnectedness of modern urban life. The circular return also stresses that the author's control extends over every single aspect of the narrative. He is not limited by coherence, logic, causality, teleology, the expectations and assumptions set up by certain literary conventions or even by the confines imposed by the laws of the natural world. So, although many of Queneau's other texts (including *The Sunday of Life* (1951) and *Zazie in the Metro* (1959)) also have pseudo-circular or cyclical structures, as Shorley points out, in no case

---

[5] 'The whole notion of irreversible events, and the possibility of permanent change – generally seen as essential to narrative – are thrown into doubt' (Shorley 1985: 61).

does their circularity 'negate linear progress as unequivocally as in *Le Chiendent*' (1985: 61).

As well as delineating the overall shape of the narrative, and as in the works studied in the previous chapter, circularity also reverberates internally throughout the text. There are a number of instances in the novel which foreshadow the circular return and its 'abolition of the intervening time' (Shorley 1985: 60). Examples of these echoes include the linking of death and birth through the description of Père Taupe's desire to withdraw himself from the outside world as an '*idéal de foetus*'; Saturnin's comment about the potential readers of his book, which clearly foreshadows the fate of the protagonists: 'May they be burned and be reborn from their ashes! Let them be shredded and reborn from their debris! May they decompose and be reborn from their putrefaction!' (1971: 159); and, most explicitly, the final dialogue regarding the possibility of a return ab initio, which expresses the remaining protagonists' desire to 'suppress that episode literally cross it all out' and 'start all over again', anticipating (or rather setting in motion) the repetition of the story (1971: 279–80). These hints also accentuate the text's fictionality, literary status and aestheticist nature, problematizing its referentiality and signification.[6]

A shared fascination with precursors such as Joyce, numbers become extremely important as structuring principles in Queneau's novels (see 'Technique of the Novel'). He explains that *The Bark Tree* is made up of ninety-one sections (seven chapters of thirteen parts each) because ninety-one is 'the sum of the first thirteen numbers and its own "sum" being 1', which is both 'the number of the death of living things and of their return to existence' (2007: 27). Far from arbitrary, the choice of ninety-one segments signals the text's circular form as a number of death but also of recurrence. Queneau further discusses the complexity of the novel's structure by claiming that he is unable to 'explain the scheme for *Le Chiendent* without relying on the tables which could well incorrectly give the illusion of a game of chess' (Queneau in Slote 2004: 388). So, although the novel focuses on depicting the randomness of the everyday, it also adheres to a rigid numerological scheme, even if this is not immediately perceptible. The seemingly chaotic cosmos of the novel, which, as Slote notes, 'revolves around coincidences, interlaced plots, doublings,

---

[6] Parts of the following section on Queneau, as well as the sections on Beckett, Arrabal and Robbe-Grillet, were modified and expanded into an article entitled 'On a Circular Road: Queneau, Beckett, Arrabal and Robbe-Grillet', published in the collection of essays *W drodze/On the Road – Perspektywy badawcze* (2019), Wydawnictwo Naukowe Mazowieckiej Uczelni Publicznej w Płocku.

deceptions, divagations, suppressed information, dream sequences, outright fantasy, and, ultimately, return' (2004: 388), also conceals a firm structure that endows the narrative with an underlying sense of symmetry and order. This numerological basis is one of the major factors allowing the novel to become a sort of poem, since, among other features, it provides the work with a formal rigidity very much in line with that of the poetic metre.

Queneau offers additional evidence of his text's formal rigour by emphasizing the autonomy of each of the sections into which it is divided. He describes the ninety-one segments that constitute the text (with the justified exception of two or three) as being 'one': single, individual and complete. Queneau claims that every part is an autonomous whole 'first of all, as a tragedy is, which is to say that it observes the three unities. It is one not only in terms of time, place and action' but also in terms of genre:

> pure narrative, narrative interspersed with reported speech, pure conversation (which bears a certain resemblance to theatrical dialogue), first-person internal monologue, reported monologue (as if the author could read the character's minds), or spoken monologue (another theatrical mode), letters (of which some wonderful novels are entirely composed), journals (not diaries, but account books or excerpts from daily newspapers) or dream accounts (to be used sparingly, so hackneyed has that genre become of late). (Queneau 2007: 28)

Of these sections, every thirteenth is 'situated *outside* of that chapter, in another direction or dimension' (2007: 28), constituting a pause in the narrative and thus composed in monologue form. Section 24 does not follow this rule since it functions as the pseudo-resolution 'to end it all' (2014: 19; my translation).

All in all, then, the novel's circular structure (and the repeated allusions to it referred to earlier) emphasizes, as both Shorley and Simonnet contend, that 'Queneau's first literary priority is an aesthetic one' (1985: 59). Indeed, the text's aestheticism and the role of its structure in endowing it with such a status become clear, not only from Queneau's remarks about the importance of structural rigour or his claims about wanting to compose his novels in the manner of poems but from the effects that the form bestows upon the narrative as a whole. The text's circular shape de-emphasizes the importance and value of its story, since its significance is subverted with the final return. As a result, the basic quality and function of the narrative become the aesthetic rendering of its characters, their relationships and environment, as well as the undermining of the assumption that the story has an underlying meaning (due to be revealed in the denouement). This subversion of the plot's value and aim has the correlative effect of emphasizing the importance of other elements, since the destabilization of the story causes those features that are merely a surplus in conventional linear narratives (style, characterization, description, etc.) to occupy the central vacant position left by the circular structure's undermining of the plot.

Moreover, as mentioned earlier, the circular structure also encapsulates the narrative, stressing its autonomous, self-referential status. It evinces that the text does not actually wish to describe or refer to the 'real world'; it is, rather, wholly detached from it, existing independently and under its own (poetic) rules. The lack of a resolution turns the story into an aesthetic game that has no underlying direction or *telos*. It establishes the narrative as a sheer aesthetic object (without a mimetic, representative, didactic or other kind of teleological role). However, as Sanders notes, we would be wrong to think that it is a '*jeu gratuit*', since the structure allows Queneau to convey a number of important ideas (see 1994: 29) – such as the untenability of teleology. The form also allows Queneau to express a range of allusions contained within the image of the circle, which go from the perfection of the Omega (representing union, complete harmony, absolute knowledge, etc.) to zero (nothingness or the infinite) (see Sanders 1994: 31). These tacit symbolic references endow the novel with an '*épaisseur mythologique*' by placing the facts of everyday life in a cosmological context (Sanders 1994: 31), a hypothesis which Queneau himself sustained in relation to *The Last Days* – but which is also clearly in line with *The Bark Tree*, especially the last part (the war against the Etruscans). In this way, the idea of circularity functions thematically as well as structurally, revealing Queneau's belief that by melding content and form into one 'the form expresse[s] what the content believed it was disguising' (2007: 27).

To conclude, it is worth citing Queneau's essay 'The Place of Mathematics in the Classification of the Sciences' (1943), given that it contains some of the essential tenets of his philosophy, implicit in his desire for formal rigour and therefore motivating *The Bark Tree*'s circular structure. The passage, which describes Queneau's general views on science, is important because it shows how his conception of science mirrors his understanding of art, given their common paradigm:

> Is science a knowledge, does it allow us to know? what do we know in mathematics? Precisely nothing. And there's nothing *to* know. We no more know the point, the number, the group, the set, the function than we 'know'

the electron, life, human behaviour everything we know is a method accepted (agreed) as true by the scientific community, a method which has *also* the advantage of being linked to manufacturing techniques.

But this method is also a game, or more precisely what is called a *jeu d'esprit*. Hence the whole of science, in its most complete form, presents itself to us both as technique and as a game. That is to say no more and no less than the way the *other* human activity presents itself: Art. (Cited in Calvino 2014: 253)

The extract not only accentuates the similarities between the 'death of God' logic and Queneau's philosophical point of departure, it also stresses that art, being at the same time a technique and a game, must be both methodical and playful, which is exactly the case with *The Bark Tree*. Additionally, the possibility of knowledge is here undermined. The essay recalls Nietzsche's 'On Truth and Lies in a Nonmoral Sense' in its implicit reference to the idea that truth is a matter of convention. Queneau does away with the notion of a transcendental point of reference (be it theological or otherwise) and dismisses the possibility of capturing, describing or knowing life's ontological reality – a belief upon which the idea of science rests. Thus, the passage is representative of Queneau's more general approach: the radical sceptical epistemology underlying his world view and the subsequent understanding of science and art as methods or techniques through which to counter the inherent meaninglessness of existence and impose a personal order on the world's chaos.

Vladimir Nabokov's 'The Circle' (1934)

Born in St Petersburg at the turn of the century into an aristocratic family, Vladimir Nabokov spent most of his life in exile. Following the outbreak of the October Revolution, the Nabokov family was forced to flee their hometown, first to the city of Livadia in Crimea and then to England where Nabokov enrolled at Trinity College, Cambridge. Attesting to his wide-ranging interests and commitment to his intellectual development, Brian Boyd observes that at the age of nineteen Nabokov prepared himself for university by drawing up 'his own idiosyncratic reading list from the Yalta library', which included 'entomology, duels, naturalist-explorers' and Nietzsche (2016: 150). Nabokov spent fifteen years living in Berlin before moving to France and finally to the United States in 1940, in order to escape from the war. These constant displacements complicate his status as an exclusively Russian writer, making him, instead, a truly European author. This is accentuated by the fact that he learned to read and write in English even before he had mastered his native tongue.[7]

Nabokov was a particularly well-rounded author, writing poems, short stories, novels, plays, works of criticism, autobiographical texts and even lepidopteral studies. Despite this diversity, his literary work shows a recurring interest in the themes of memory and autobiography. This is apparent throughout his oeuvre: from his first novel *Mary* (1926) to later works such as *Speak, Memory* (1967) or even in his final novel, *Look at the Harlequins!* (1974). Alongside these primal narrative interests, and starting in his early texts of the 1930s, there is also a clear focus on narrative form – this having been emphasized by critics from early on. The influential Russian scholar Vladislav Khodasevich, for instance, highlights Nabokov's concern with form unequivocally in the introductory remarks of his 1937 essay 'On Sirin' (Sirin being Nabokov's pen-name), when he states that 'Art cannot be reduced to form, but without form it has no existence and, consequently, no meaning', suggesting that if 'the analysis of a work of art is unthinkable without an analysis of form' it is especially so in the case of Nabokov (cited in Page 2013: 61).

Sirin saw the formal configuration of his works as a fundamental aspect of their composition. Khodasevich further stresses this aspect by arguing that the structural configuration of Nabokov's texts is so 'cumbersome and complicated' that he only sees himself fit to advance 'certain observations' in this respect, finding 'a true and complete analysis' of his form 'impossible' (2013: 61). Of these, the key observation he provides is that Sirin is an 'artist of form, of the writer's device', not only because 'the formal aspect of his writing is distinguished by exceptional diversity, complexity, brilliance and novelty' (Khodasevich in Page 2013: 61) but also because he places his formal elements at the forefront of the narrative, setting them above other features of the text (such as plot or narrative telos). Khodasevich also argues that Nabokov's manoeuvres 'catch the eye' of the reader above all because, rather than hiding his devices (as other writers do), he 'places them in full view like a magician who, having amazed his audience, reveals on the very spot the laboratory of his miracles' (2013: 61).

Accordingly, the primary purpose of Nabokov's focus on form is not aesthetic but metalinguistic. One of his 'major tasks' is, as Khodasevich claims, precisely

---

[7] Although Nabokov's first published texts were written in Russian (many of them were later self-translated into English, sometimes with the help of his son Dimitri Nabokov) it is with his English works that he would achieve his greatest literary recognition.

'to show how the devices live and work' (2013: 62). His insistence on form is in itself essentially a commentary on narrative: an insistence on its importance, and an elucidation of its design and effects. By placing his devices at the forefront of the narrative, Nabokov wishes to unveil the way in which narratives structure events into unified sequences that seek to express a specific underlying idea or value, or are internally organized under a specific nucleus of signification. In doing so, he subliminally reflects on how memory (a special kind of inner or personal narrative) comes to be and how it unfolds within a subject. As a result, his preoccupation with narrative form acquires a thematic focus as well as a metalinguistic one. The specific way in which Nabokov structures his texts allows him to dwell upon the nature of certain notions (such as memory) subtly, through the implicit significance that the text acquires on account of the way it is organized. As we shall see, it is precisely through this meticulous attentiveness to the structural configuration of his narratives that Nabokov is able to fully explore and express his various thematic interests.

Even Sirin's detractors, or rather, his most critical commentators, point out the same facet of his work, namely the importance (perhaps somewhat excessive) that he places on his text's form. This is reflected, for instance, in Sartre's 1939 critique (published on June 15 in the literary journal *Europe*), where he describes Nabokov's narratives as consisting of 'Longwinded introductions after which – when we have been duly prepared – nothing happens; excellent thumbnail-sketches; charming portraits; literary essays' (cited in Page 2013: 66), in short, as series of devices structured into a single (yet apparently arbitrary) whole. Thus, Sartre asks, 'Where is the novel?' (cited in Page 2013: 66). The superimposition of devices over the narrative's story, the subversion of this traditional narrative hierarchy (the subordination of all elements to plot), encourages Sartre to claim that there is no novel because 'It has dissolved in its own venom' (2013: 66). However, what Sartre's critique seems to be missing, or rather, the very thing that he appears to dislike about Nabokov's texts, is precisely what makes them unique: that what matters is not so much *what* happens (which is perhaps why Sartre finds that 'nothing happens' at all) but *how* it happens.[8]

Even Nabokov's notorious teaching style highlights this preference. In an article published on 22 March 2013 in the *New York Review of Books*, one of

---

[8] Interestingly, other authors of circular narratives were also condemned on account of writing stories where 'nothing happens'; perhaps most famously this was the case with Beckett's *Waiting for Godot* (1953).

Sirin's former students, Edward Jay Epstein, bears witness to the way in which his narrative interests shone forth in his lectures:

> He [Nabokov] said we did not need to know anything about their historical context, and that we should under no circumstance identify with any of the characters in them, since novels are works of pure invention. The authors, he continued, had one and only one purpose: to enchant the reader. (2013: n.p.)

Epstein also recalls how Nabokov was uninterested in the plot of texts in his classes and how in an examination on *Anna Karenina*, he asked only one question: 'Describe the train station in which Anna first met Vronsky' (2013: n.p.). Such details display a clear disinterest in the conventional reading of texts and hence also in those features that were traditionally considered as the most important aspects of narrative, a predilection which becomes blatantly apparent in his writing.

This is why critics such as Boyd argue that Nabokov's genius resides in his ability to find 'the formal and fictional inventiveness to express all the problems his philosophy poses' (2016: 292). His preoccupation with narrative form responds to a desire to seek out new ways through which to play out his reflections, without falling into the trap of the latent ideological underpinnings of conventional models. Formal experimentation thus becomes intimately linked with a desire to explore the workings of memory and its relationship with consciousness, subjectivity and identity. At the same time, Nabokov also strives to present the reader with a new vision of the everyday, one that turns what we take for granted in life into something that will reawaken our curiosity and renew our sense of wonder (see Boyd 2016: 292). Sirin condemns common sense, or 'the practical side of life' which looks so 'singularly unreal in the starlight' (cited in Boyd 2016: 292), counter-posing art to its annihilating mundanity. Still, Nabokov did not feel that art was more valuable, real, necessary or important than any other human activity, nor did he see it as an exercise of escapism from the tedium of everyday life. Rather, he understood art as the ability to find beauty in the dull, the unamusing or even in the repulsive, which this is precisely what his texts aim to show.[9]

In order to recognize and extract such beauty from the apparent insipidness of the mundane, Nabokov became enthralled by the different ways in which we seek to comprehend reality and register the outside world. He showed a mesmerizing

---

[9] Boyd describes this facet of Nabokov's writing vividly as 'the spirit that could see beauty in a butcher's carcasses' (2016: 293).

fascination for our ability to grasp elements either individually or as combinations (with other objects, subjects, moments or events). His desire was to show both that the world is full of patterns that are easily dismissed and that those patterns, some of which we believe are essential or intrinsic to the physical world (our understanding of time, space, etc.), are in fact contingent on the predominant ideologies of a given society. As a result, and closely resembling Nietzsche in his meticulousness, Sirin loathed generalizations, which he counteracted through radical associations. He sought to draw attention to the exception, the improbable or the unexpected. As Boyd puts it, he insistently sought that which is 'still to be discovered at a new level of specificity [and] could always explode the prison of classifications, determinisms, general rules', so as to 'view the moment in its openness', cherishing what is unconstrained in the mind and searching 'for some more complete liberation of the soul from the cell of personality' and 'the jail block of time', among other limitations (2016: 293). Nabokov found his own voice by experimenting with radical combinations, bringing into line elements of apparently disparate orders (subjects, objects, ideas, moments, events, signs, words, senses, etc.) so as to draw implicit parallelisms and explore the complex relationships between these different spheres of signification.

Already we can see a clear parallelism between the kind of reasoning motivating Nabokov's focus on form and Nietzsche's 'death of God' logic. In the absence of an absolute frame of reference (of a way to penetrate 'the thing in itself'), the world not only becomes inherently meaningless but immensely meaningful in the heterogeneous plurality of potential possibilities for subjective meaning-making. It is for this reason that Nabokov sees the need to reflect upon the functioning of our consciousness, the processes through which these meanings become fixed and assembled into what we call our world view. The awareness that there is no way to experience reality other than through the mediation of our subjective perception urges Nabokov (like Nietzsche) to show his readers the 'truth' of perspectivism. Sirin does this by depicting the mechanisms of our subjectivity – by illustrating the ways in which our consciousness interprets and systematizes reality through the structuration of our experiences.[10]

Nabokov sees consciousness as both 'the only real thing in the world and the greatest mystery of all' (cited in Boyd 2016: 293). Yet, he did not believe

---

[10] Boyd's description of Nabokov is also clearly reminiscent of Nietzsche: 'His skepticism is ruthless, he shucks off the intellectually untenable and the emotionally indulgent, and he offers answers not as firm conclusions but as philosophical possibilities that force us to reopen doors we thought had reason to shut' (2016: 295).

that consciousness is all that exists. He accepted the ontological status of reality but understood that the only way to access it is through the both immensely powerful and inevitably limited mediation of our subjectivity. Accordingly, the different layers that shape and constrain consciousness – such as personality, time or knowledge – become key narrative interests and recurring motifs in his writing. Affected by (or interrelated with) these three layers, and constituting a fourth, is the aforementioned focus on the theme of memory – one of his key obsessions, perhaps owing to its interdependence with consciousness and its role in bestowing us with our understanding of time, knowledge of the world and subjective identity.

As we shall see through the analysis of his short story 'The Circle' (1934), Nabokov depicts the workings of consciousness by finding a formal configuration that mimics the way in which our mind structures past events into the relatively stable narratives which make up our biographical memory. Indeed, it is by finding a structure that reflects the complex process of memory that Nabokov is able to portray its functionings in that text. Thus, his formal choices reveal two overarching notions: the vital importance of a narrative's structure in alluding to certain values tacitly (which in some cases constitutes the most effective way of expressing certain ideas) and his mindfulness regarding the antagonistic connotations that an account may acquire, depending on whether it has a linear, spiral, circular or other type of form.

Aside from memory, as a kind of personal narrative that constitutes the basis of our consciousness, Nabokov's primary narrative interests were consciousness, as the structuring of our memories and experiences; temporality, as the way in which we organize said structures; and narrative form, as its literary equivalent. While these themes align his work with that of writers such as Bergson or Marcel Proust,[11] the deep-seated sceptical epistemology that constitutes the basic premise upon which Nabokov's entire world view seems to rest aligns him more closely to thinkers such as Nietzsche. Indeed, as Vladimir Alexandrov points out, in 1925 Nabokov was actually 'avoiding Proust in favour of figures like Pushkin or Nietzsche' (2014: 472), showcasing a gradual distancing from the former's lyricism in favour of a growing inclination towards the latters' inquisitiveness and radical scepticism. So, even if critics such as John Burt Foster Jr contend that these two writers highlight 'some very different tendencies within

---

[11] Boyd mentions his parallelisms with Bergson and his indebtedness to Hegel (see 2016: 295), while Alexandrov et al. refer to Proust's influence, as well as Bergson's.

the modernist movement' (such as their antagonistic views regarding 'myth or depth psychology'), and that it is only during the first stages of his literary career that Nabokov had 'contact with Nietzschean modernism', it is equally true that he furthers and even exceeds some of Nietzsche's intellectual aspirations in some respects (such as his 'commitment to individuality and the literary image') (1993: xii).

Like Nietzsche, Nabokov's 'initial encounter with the modern' takes the shape of what Forster Jr describes as a 'jolting temporal break' that ultimately leads to 'a complex, many-layered sense of time' (1993: 44). Rather than perceiving and reconstructing the past (both historical and personal) as a unified, continuous and consistent whole, both thinkers look back at it purely to retrieve certain instances, details, events or experiences, the total combination of which is all that makes up such a past. For Nabokov, the past is a collection of scattered moments that, although once thought trivial, re-emerge repeatedly in one's present, constituting a kind of eternal recurrence of the self (within one's self). This perspective of the past, and of the related notion of recurrence within a personal rather than a collective (national, continental, etc.) sphere, is particularly manifest in 'The Circle'.

Originally written in Russian in February 1934 and characterized as a 'small satellite' of his 1938 novel *The Gift* (Nabokov in Boyd 2016: 405), 'The Circle' is one of the clearest examples of the author's attempts to reflect upon and render his views on memory and consciousness through the use of an innovative structural configuration. As Nabokov himself explains in an oft-quoted passage, the story 'separated itself from the main body of the novel and started to revolve around it' as he was working on its last chapter, taking a life of its own and constituting an interconnected yet wholly independent world, with its 'own orbit and colored fire' (1973: 254). Accordingly, the story has been repeatedly deemed by critics a 'preparatory sketch' for the novel (Toker 1989: 19). Alexandrov, for instance, stresses that it tests several significant devices used throughout Nabokov's oeuvre, such as 'the almost invariable use of first-person narration and the curved, sometimes even circular, composition' (2014: 104). Nevertheless, it also stands as a wholly autonomous text that does not depend on the novel to complete its meaning. Despite its undeniable connection to *The Gift*, Nabokov stressed that 'A knowledge of the novel is not required for [its] enjoyment' (1973: 254). Besides, regardless of whether it was in fact written as a test piece for his later work or as an independent creation, its autonomy becomes explicit through the effects of its circular structure, which encapsulates the narrative as a 'speck of time' recurring inexorably in the mind of its protagonist.

Nabokov explains 'The Circle' by stating that it describes the Gudonov family (the protagonists of *The Gift*) through the perspective of 'an outsider' (1973: 254). However, what seems to be most important in the text is not the story it recounts (the narrator's thoughts about the ins and outs of the Gudonov family, his relationship with them or his love for Tanya), but rather the implications that the tale acquires due to its form. If Toker is right in asserting that 'Like all his subsequent writing, Nabokov's first novel describes a circle' (1989: 38), then his derivative story, 'The Circle', is, as the title suggests, possibly the most explicit example of circularity in his oeuvre.[12] As Sirin himself states, 'Technically' the story describes a circle since the discourse loops back to its point of departure through the enumeration which the protagonist starts at the text's close, making the final sentence exist 'implicitly before its first one' (1973: 254). This endows the narrative with several fundamental effects, ranging from the inciting of a second reading to the self-encapsulation of the narrative as an autonomous object, as in Queneau's *The Bark Tree*, though with particular repercussions.

Above all, the text speaks through its form rather than its content. It is the specific significance that the content acquires through its circular shape that allows it to express its full spectrum of meaning. Content and form become melded so that even if the reader is presented with a sequence of events and implicitly encouraged to decipher their significance for the protagonist, the story only becomes meaningful after the structure makes its presence felt. The text's ending places the events in a second plane, foreshadowing their status as divagations within the mind of the narrator and thus pointing tacitly to their speculative, unstable (and superfluous) nature. The narrator's descriptions lose importance individually, becoming meaningful only as the reflection of a recurring thought within his mind. It is how they shape his identity and how their memory becomes a traumatic burden for the narrator that becomes most important.

If at the level of the story what matters most is not what happens with the Gudonov family but how the narrator perceives such events, at an overarching

---

[12] Nabokov emphasizes the circular character of his story, aligning it to the work of Joyce by stating that it 'belongs to the same serpent-biting-its-tail type as the circular structure of [...] *Finnegans Wake*, which it preceded' (1973: 254). Even so, certain scholars (see Toker 1989: 158–63) have deemed it an infinite spiral rather than a circle. They take their cue from Nabokov's definition of a spiral as a 'spiritualised circle': 'In the spiral form, the circle uncoiled, unwound, has ceased to be vicious; it has been set free' (cited in Boyd 2001: 10). However, this does not seem to apply to this short story.

level the narrative's structure serves to mirror the process of memory. Being, in its entirety, a recollection of the narrator, the text's form emulates the internal structure of a memory. Rather than describing how the process of memory unfolds, Nabokov presents us with a direct rendering of it, an 'ideo-visual' image of the memory. In this way, the notion that memory is a kind of internal, personal narrative is subliminally expressed, suggesting that narrative, memory and identity are in fact very similar processes consisting essentially in the structuring of reality through the filter of our subjective experience. Nabokov shows how recollections (like art) shape the heterogeneity of phenomena that make up our experience of the world into feasible normalizing totalities – assembled through the filtering and patterned selection of certain phenomena.

The circular structure also encourages a second reading of the story. It compels the reader to look for additional details that may elucidate the picture drawn by the narrator. In the same way that the protagonist revisits his memories to find clues about his present self, the circular form incites the reader to go back to the text a second time with the intention of shedding further light on the character of the narrator or on the nature of his recurring memory. The text's style also alludes to this aspect. Like the circular form, Nabokov's meticulous descriptions also seem to suggest that a small detail, no matter how seemingly trivial, is susceptible to becoming immensely significant. The repetitious nature of the memory accentuates what Dana Dragunoiu argues is Innokentiy's central epiphany: that 'nothing is lost, nothing whatever, memory accumulates treasures' (Nabokov 2011: 384).[13] The narrative stresses how certain apparently superficial moments or particulars of our past may become crucial in the development of our character, the configuration of our identity or subjectivity and the shaping of our world view, even if we initially fail to realize their importance when they take place or fail to grasp them at all (affecting us – or even defining us – unconsciously).

As well as showing how the reminiscences of our past engage with our present self, the structure also highlights that memory is not a linear process, that its movement is never-ending, unrelenting. The circular form mimics the specific way in which memory plays out within our consciousness to shape our subjectivity. As a result, the narrative also acquires a circular character at the level of the story (despite the fact that it describes a linear set of events), since the discourse's shape captures the utter repetitiousness of the events within the

---

[13] See Dragunoiu (2011: 79).

protagonist's mind. Past becomes present as the memory replays insistently within the narrator, turning the text's temporality into a kind of eternal present. Besides, the structure has two further temporal effects. First, as Márta Pellérdi argues, it deploys 'the metaphor of the demonic or magic circle' to illustrate 'consciousness entrapped in time' (2010: 38), so that it is not only the past which becomes present: the narrator's present also becomes trapped in the past. Second, the circular structure bestows an atemporal character on the narrative, since, within the protagonist's mind, the events cease to belong exclusively to the past, present or future; their concrete outset, development and resolution become blurred. Nabokov himself described this effect in discussing the process of literary composition during one of his university lectures, claiming that 'the past and the present *and* the future come together in a sudden flash', so that 'the entire circle of time is perceived, which is another way of saying that time ceases to exist' (cited in Pellérdi 2010: 38).

This idea also parallels Sirin's understanding of inspiration, which he defined as 'the combined sensation of having the whole universe entering you and of yourself wholly dissolving in the universe surrounding you' or as 'the prison wall of the ego suddenly crumbling away with the non-ego rushing in from the outside to save the prisoner – who is already dancing in the open' (cited in Pellérdi 2010: 38). The protagonist's memory becomes a moment of insight (or inspiration) that is crystalized through the words of the narrator. Furthermore, as Alexandrov claims, the circular form also suggests that the narrator's consciousness has 'absolute power over textual space and time' (2014: 162). By unveiling that the enumeration which initiates the narrative begins at the closing of the text, Nabokov stresses its 'virtual' status, as a thought that is self-contained within the narrator's mind, making the relationship between the protagonist, the narrative voice and the author manifest. The story's reference to the outside world becomes dubious, if not wholly irrelevant. It is the narrator's consciousness that contains the whole cosmos of the narration instead. The events and characters to which the narrative refers stand as disembodied entities that live on only within the narrator's psyche, not real people but memories, interpretations or partial views, taking on a new life through the subjectivity of the narrative voice. Rather than being the representation of an outside world (real or fictive), the narrative refers to an immaterial world of ideas. It is only through the text's form that the reader becomes aware of this.

Circular structures reappear throughout Nabokov's works, though in no case is their circularity as categorical as in 'The Circle'. These are mostly achieved through the *mise en abyme* technique, since Sirin frequently concludes his texts by having his protagonists express their intention of writing a book recounting precisely what these texts themselves describe. The *mise en abyme* device will be analysed in detail further in relation to the work of Daniil Kharms, since he presents a more explicit (if not radical) version of this kind of circularity. All the same, the structure of 'The Circle' surpasses the effects of other instances of circularity in Nabokov's oeuvre by breaking down, subverting or de-emphasizing the importance or need for a narrative plot. Indeed, it is not a plot or story which 'The Circle' presents, but rather a mental portrait of the narrator's mind or, more concretely, of his memory and the way that it affects his consciousness and present self. If, as we saw in the analysis of *Doña Inés*, the circular form of Azorín's text bestows it with an ekphrastic quality, the structure of Nabokov's short story transforms the narrative into a portrait of the narrator's mind, a kind of psychological ekphrasis, what one might call a 'psy-phrastic' narrative.

Daniil Kharms' *Elizabeth Bam* (1928), 'A Tale' and 'How the Old Woman Tried to Buy Ink' (1935)

To put it as bluntly as one of his own stories, Daniil Ivanovich Yuvachov was born in St Petersburg in 1905, where he was to live throughout most of his life, achieving very little recognition as an avant-garde writer and a limited reputation as an author of children stories. He was arrested in 1941 for being an 'anti-Soviet' writer, simulated insanity to avoid execution and died a year later from starvation. Educated in German and English at the prestigious Peterschule, Yuvachov began to write at a very early age (his first preserved manuscripts date from 1919). He made a name for himself as an author in 1925 by giving readings of his poems in Leningrad, adopting the pseudonym 'Kharms' and becoming friends with Alexander Vvedensky, a relationship that turned out to be crucial in his development as a writer. Together with Vvedensky, and the established poet Nikolai Zabolotsky, Kharms founded the OBERIU (Union or Society of Real Art), a collective of artists that Neil Cornwell defines as a blend of 'Futurist art forms and Formalist aesthetics' (1991: 6).[14]

---

[14] Both the Futurist and Formalist movements were strongly influenced by Nietzsche. On Nietzsche and Futurism, see Gunter Berghaus (1996: 23); on Nietzsche and Formalism, see Kujundzic (1997).

The OBERIU sought to create a kind of art that would do away with mimesis and break with the conventions of the time by combining words, characters, objects and actions in strange and pioneering ways. Focusing on poetry and drama, the aim was to free words from the constraints of syntax and grammar, as well as of their conventional uses, merging them in imaginative combinations that disregarded the coherence, cohesiveness and logic of traditional literature. Nevertheless, their apparent incongruities were in many instances also direct and ferocious critiques of the world. Although most of the OBERIU's works have not survived, the impact achieved by their performances was to remain in the collective memory of their city for years. Indeed, it is thanks to the events organized by this group that Kharms was able to make a name for himself in Leningrad.

The OBERIU erupted in the Petersburg literary scene with the publication of their declaration in January 1928, together with a theatrical evening entitled 'Three Left Hours'. The evening consisted of several readings, the presentation of Kharms' play *Elizabeth Bam*, a meditation on cinema and the projection of the montage *The Mineer*. The declaration read at this opening evening proclaimed the group's activities in literature, theatre, cinema, music and the fine arts.[15] Regarding narrative (theatrical and cinematic), one of the OBERIU's central aims was, as Cornwell points out, to move away 'from the traditional spotlight on plot, to allow other, more disparate, factors to come into play' (1991: 6). Rejecting conventional literary drama ('a tale told by people about something that happened'), where the plot is the basic element that structures the text and where every other component strives 'to explain the meaning and the course of the events more clearly, more comprehensibly, and in a more life-like way', the group sought instead to present its audience with absurdist scenes full of subversive yet implicit (or allegorical) significances: 'separate moments' with no apparent causal link structured into a unified whole through the (sometimes seemingly arbitrary) arrangement of the producer or playwright (Kharms in Cornwell 1991: 200).

The kind of anti-literary plot that emerged from this type of drama was called a 'scenic plot' and in various ways was radically different from the plots of traditional plays, having its own particular mode of expression and meaning:

---

[15] Meilakh notes that the text is an article, not a manifesto, although it has often been 'erroneously referred to' as the latter (cited in Cornwell 1991: 2001).

This is a plot which only the theatre can present. The plot of a theatrical representation is theatrical, just as the plot of a musical work is musical. They each represent one thing – the world of phenomena, though, depending on the material, they each express it in its own way...

[. . .] our aim is to present the world of concrete objects on the stage in their mutual interaction and confrontations. This is what we have been aiming at in our production of *Elizaveta Bam*. The *dramatic* plot of the play is shattered by many seemingly irrelevant themes which isolate the object as a separately existing whole, without any connections with the rest; so the viewer will not see a clearly delineated *dramatic* plot, for it as it were flickers behind the back of the action. In its place is the scenic plot, which emerges spontaneously from all the elements of our show. (Kharms in Cornwell 1991: 201)

Differentiating between dramatic and scenic plots, and favouring the latter over the former, the OBERIU sought to revolutionize literature by making a kind of scenic aestheticism (rather than mimesis) the primordial function of drama. The aim was to challenge logic and appearance through a pervasive distrust of conventional explanations and representations of reality. It is this distrust which led them to the development of their new literary language.

As well as their readings, theatrical evenings and other avant-garde events, another fundamental aspect of the group's activities was the transformation of the artists' private lives and personal images into artistic stunts and objects: to make life art. The aim was, as Tatiana Nikolskaia notes, to emphasize the theatricality of life, though 'not so much to shock as to perplex the public by the alogicality of what was happening' so as to 'give a twist in the public's consciousness to normal causal-investigatory notions, having exposed reality in all its illogicality' (cited in Cornwell 1991: 195). Indeed, the members of the OBERIU saw life and art as one and the same thing, and aimed to emphasize this one-to-one correspondence at all times. Lakov Druskin records that by end of the 1920s Vvedensky was claiming that 'Kharms does not create art, but is himself art' and that even Kharms himself, 'at the end of the 1930s, used to say that the important thing for him was not art, but life: to make his life like art' (cited in Cornwell 1991: 6). This draws a strong parallelism between the OBERIU's efforts and Nietzsche's own literary endeavours, which, if Alexander Nehamas' central thesis in *Nietzsche: Life as Literature* (1985) is correct, were directed at (re)creating himself as a character in his own works throughout his career.

However, this is not the only common ground between Nietzsche and Kharms. The impact of Russian Futurism, especially of its leading figure Velimir Khlebnikov, also bears witness to this point of encounter, since Khlebnikov was a strong influence on Kharms and Nietzsche's work had been a major reference for Khlebnikov.[16] Besides, Kharms participated in the Druskin school of philosophy: a group of philosophers and poets that Cornwell characterizes as sharing 'a concern for the (in)adequacy of language as a means of communication, which runs from Plato, through the romantics, to the extreme linguistic relativism' of the twentieth century, very much in line with Nietzsche's 'conclusions about the relativity of truth according to different perspectives' (1991:14).[17] Furthermore, other features also draw Nietzsche and Kharms together. As Branislav Jakovljevic remarks, if Nietzsche philosophized with a hammer – 'an aggressive mode of critical thinking' (Deleuze 1983: 3) – then Kharms' texts were also hammered, given the aggressive style of his prose (see 2009: 269). Certainly, despite their obvious differences in terms of style, content and form, both authors achieve a thrashing effect through their short, witty texts that shock and perplex in an insistent struggle to think beyond logic and common sense, showing the unexpected within the expected, the bizarre chaos or absurdity of the everyday.

With the composition of *Elizabeth Bam*, Kharms began a productive stage of formal innovation in his writing that was to last (developing through several divergent stages) until his death. During this time he also became a regular contributor in two children's magazines: *Ezh* (*The Hedgehog*) and *Chizh* (*The Siskin*), writing stories, doing editorial work and translating for them from German into Russian from their inception until his arrest in 1941.[18] While contributing to these magazines Kharms also published nine children books, which he signed under different pseudonyms. The short stories that will be discussed further are examples of this work as a children's author; however, they are also relevant for a mature readership since it is precisely their simple style that allows them to play out a metatextual critique. Kharms' most important texts were written during the prolific decade of 1927–37. These encompass his activities with the OBERIU and his late prose. Of them, *Elizabeth Bam* is one

---

[16] See Baran in Rosenthal (1994: 59).
[17] Cornwell further notes how, alongside 'such epistemological nihilism', Kharms also displays a kind of Camusian existential nihilism (1991: 14), which is nevertheless also paradigmatic of Nietzsche.
[18] Children's literature became the last resort for many of the Russian avant-garde writers of the 1930s, who were later persecuted and killed under Stalinism.

of the few preserved works representative of the kind of experimental narrative that he was writing in the earlier years.

As Alice Nakhimovsky points out, the key to the play lies in the discussion about plot found in the OBERIU declaration (cited earlier), being that it was written 'at the request of the theatre section of OBERIU', especially for the 'Three Left Hours' evening (1982: 2). The text is clearly representative of the collective's aims in narrative. In it, the traditional elements of drama are presented only to be removed or subverted, in the same way that the expectations of the audience or reader are set only to be continuously undermined (Elizabeth does not know why she is being accused and is accused of killing the accuser; her mother seems to appear as a symbol of protection but indicts her, etc.). The play's incongruity achieves such extremes that a description of its plot would not only be reductive but do no justice to it at all, since the storyline's summary cannot begin to render, even remotely, what takes place throughout the spectacle, given that it consists mostly of illogical games or stunts:

> Elizabeth's turning the two prosecutors against each other and playing tricks on them, the disjointed bickering, the storytelling, the skits and vaudeville scenes, the fluctuating identity of the characters, the songs, dances, fights, medieval jousting, and other helter-skelter activity. (Gibian 1997: 39)

Adding to the overall sense of incongruity, and bringing the dramatic plot back to focus yet only to destroy it once and for all (to annul its value), the circular shape of the action consummates the absurd display, throwing the audience back again to the opening scene and thus implicitly undermining the entire sequence of events.

As announced in the OBERIU declaration, Kharms' work aimed to shatter the audience's expectation of a dramatic plot, even as its first scenes clearly suggest its presence: as the play opens, the audience is encouraged to ponder what Elizabeth has done in order to be pursued by her accusers, anticipating or suggesting the ensuing development of a plot. However, contrary to such expectations, the awaited dramatic storyline increasingly fades away behind the succession of senseless stunts, giving way to a full-blown scenic plot that arises from the radical combination of the spectacle's components, taking its place as the central element of the drama. So, as Nakhimovsky claims, 'Actions are not motivated [. . .] there is no progression toward a goal', teleology is crushed; the 'elements of the spectacle [. . .] live their separate lives without subordinating themselves to the ticking of the theatrical metronome', they are 'autonomous' in their 'significance' and 'independent' of the plot's 'will' (1982: 26). Led by the conviction that the action-oriented plot of traditional drama 'is not at all what the theatre is' (Kharms in Drain 2002: 48), *Elizabeth Bam* demonstrates that another type of theatre is possible: that meaning can be constructed differently, without any need for a succession of causally connected events or a coherent dialogue that pushes the action forward towards a resolution. Instead of expressing a specific message, the play operates according to the principle that drama can convey a plurality of (scenic) senses.

Although it is uncertain whether *Elizabeth Bam* was composed as an attempt to illustrate or give a concrete shape to the poetics expressed in the OBERIU declaration, or whether this declaration was written later in an effort to explain the play, it is clear that the two go hand in hand. *Elizabeth Bam* does not present us with the typical sequence of logical connections that we expect to see in drama and which conventional dramas presuppose also exist in life. Instead, by doing away with such causal connections entirely, the play subliminally (yet also quite clearly) stresses that these logical relations may in fact be a delusion or an idealist fantasy and that life actually resembles more closely the illogicality or absurdity of this spectacle. The play has no one explanation – it does not attempt to express a single underlying message or posit any values through its story – it simply 'render[s] the world of concrete objects on the stage in their interrelationships and collisions' (Kharms in Drain 2002: 49). The viewer is forced to experience the performance without the possibility of elucidating it. By showing how 'an object and a phenomenon transported from life to the stage lose their lifelike sequence of connections and acquire another – a theatrical one' (Kharms in Drain 2002: 49), the play suggests that every event when rationalized becomes transformed (through its act of supplementation), betraying the reality which it supposedly represents. So, although one could argue that *Elizabeth Bam* refers to the outside world (to the sociopolitical context from which it emerges) and provide a historical explanation for its inception (by claiming that it emerges from the climate of incertitude and fear caused by the Stalinist arrests and purges, for instance), the fact is that it consciously blurs these connections, forcing its audience to make sense of it in different ways.

As well as the subversion of the dramatic plot and the undermining of many prototypical features of conventional dramas, what stands out among the play's 'eccentricities' is its structure. *Elizabeth Bam* is divided into nineteen sections, each of which appears to stand as an independent, autonomous segment, written in a wholly different style and containing radical changes in characterization, mood, tempo and so forth. The repetition of the first scene towards the play's closing (in the penultimate section) endows it (if only momentarily) with a circular structure, bringing the action back to its point of origin. With the recurrence of this opening scene, the play circles back to the moment where the dramatic plot had begun to disintegrate, accentuating the illogicality of all subsequent events – or annulling them as if part of a delirium or dream – but also emphasizing further the subversion of the dramatic plot, which seems to re-emerge only to be downplayed. Consequently, although the storyline resurfaces towards the ending, the final duel over the protagonists' life shatters once and for all any expectations of a logical resolution as the scene returns to its original state of affairs, dictated by the stage direction '*Scene is as at the beginning*' (Kharms in Cornwell 1991: 239).

Nevertheless, this circular structure is also annulled, and Kharms concludes the drama by providing a pseudo-linear denouement, as Elizabeth is finally arrested and taken away. This climax has the effect of reducing the dramatic plot to three concrete moments: the appearance of the police officers, their confrontation with Elizabeth and her family, and her final arrest. Yet, set against the incongruous actions that take up the majority of the spectacle, this synthetic and already inconsistent plot (since Elizabeth is arrested on account of murdering the person arresting her) appears merely as another of its incongruities. Thus, even if it is not exclusively circular, circularity plays a central role in the play. It encapsulates the different bizarre stunts and draws a margin between these 'scenic' events and the miniature dramatic plot, which seems to function solely as a frame for the anti-narrative. To be sure, if one was to remove the linear ending one would find an infinitely recurring incongruous spectacle, a playful dance where the little evidence of a dramatic plot only serves the purpose of setting the game in motion. *Elizabeth Bam* illustrates, quite literally, Kharms' claim that 'every snout of reasonable style' provokes in him 'unpleasant feelings' (cited in Jakovljevic 2009: 159). Indeed, the production not only aspires to incongruity, it does away with all that is reasonable. If it contains certain glimpses at coherence or logic, it does so only to destabilize them, as is the case with the miniature dramatic plot. The work presents an outright rejection and radical subversion of reasonableness, of all that is sensible, consistent and rational, in terms of style, form and content.

Aside from a children's puppet show entitled *Circus Shardam* (1935), *Elizabeth Bam* was the only play that Kharms was able to stage during his lifetime. It was, as George Gibian claims, 'one of the high points of Kharms's literary achievement' (1997: 39). The scandal it provoked infuriated the official press and caused so much controversy that the OBERIU was forced to cease its activities within two years of its foundation. This encouraged Kharms to turn to a clearer and more concise prose, so that, as Nakhimovsky notes, the 'cacophony of words and objects that characterized their early work' was replaced by 'an atmosphere of unusual sparseness' achieved through a contraction of his 'vision to the tiny details of the ordinary world around him' (1982: 2). Even if these later works are no more rational than their predecessors, there is a clear change in style.[19] Although we find many similarities in terms of the features that make up these narratives and the earlier works, the end to which they are used varies significantly. In the late texts most violations of logic, distortions of reality and senseless uses of language are put to specific uses. The texts' incongruities produce a grotesque climate that accentuates the absurd nature of certain aspects of everyday life. Among these bizarre elements, the circular structure is also reappraised, this time fully, rigorously and with various concrete ends.

The first example of this 'purer' circularity is found in a variant of an untitled story which Jean-Philippe Jaccard relates to Henri Michaux's 'Plume at the Restaurant' (see Cornwell 1991: 51). In it, a waiter refuses to serve a man called Petya and threatens to throw him out of the restaurant. However, in Kharms' variant (which Jaccard also links to Michaux's text)

> the waiter does not understand the order and repeats incessantly and imperturbably 'What do you wish to order?'. When he finally manages to repeat the strange words ('bet-bui'), he leaves the dining room perplexed and a new waiter brings the menu, thus repeating the opening scene. (Jaccard in Cornwell 1991: 67)

The story's circularity recalls that of *Elizaveta Bam*, but in this case Kharms does away with the resolution, underlining the futility of the protagonist's efforts and the absurdity of the entire experience. The circular form also flouts the reader's expectations, both of a coherent resolution and of an underlying meaning, reinforcing the spectacle's senselessness instead. The repetition of the waiter's question 'What do you wish to order?' also shapes the dialogue into a circular game, echoing the overall shape of the structure but also creating an internal sense of circularity: circles existing within circles, with no apparent purpose or resolution. Additionally, the circular form aestheticizes the event. Isolated,

---

[19] Nakhimovsky describes this transition as a move from 'something like dada' into 'the absurd' (1982: 13).

lacking a plot and seemingly removed from any functional end, it acquires an autonomous, intrinsic one. The structure eradicates the idea of a narrative *telos*. Rather than providing us with a specific comment about the waiter or his client, their relationship or society as a whole, the repetitive narrative captures and underscores the covert beauty and bizarre splendour of the mundane event.

In 'A Tale' (1935), one of the many stories that Kharms published in the children's magazine *Chizh*, the device of circularity is again reappraised, yet this time with the added effect of producing a multi-layered metalinguistic commentary. The play's circular structure is constructed through a *mise en abyme*, a device which we find in several of Kharms' texts. The *mise en abyme* fashions the narrative into a circle through the shape of its discourse, since the ending of the text reveals that the story actually refers to itself. As Jakovljevic argues, by revealing that the whole narrative 'revolves in on itself and ends in its own beginning', the '*mise en abyme*' device has the effect of representing 'language detached from "things"', it suggests that language refers to itself rather than to reality, in the same way that 'The causes that make Vanya try to write the story are the same ones that force him to read it' (2009: 166). The parallelism between the auto-referential nature of the narrative and that of language is implicit in the story's resolution. Moreover, the tale also encloses three stories, each of which also displays its own circular pattern: the first two mirror the structure of *Elizabeth Bam*, where the circular movement is followed by a concluding denouement, while the last (which tells the story of a hammer) is purely circular, since the hammer's head starts and ends in the same place, so that its movement appears to represent that of the overall trajectory of the narrative. This internal circularity trivializes the three meta-stories while inviting the reader to consider a crucial question, namely: What is a story? And, what is its purpose? With these three failed attempts Kharms encourages reflection on the nature of narrative, its components, structure, function and aims.

The *mise en abyme* device is also used in another of Kharms' texts, 'How the Old Woman Tried to Buy Ink'. However, in this case it revolves around the figure of the protagonist rather than the author. As a result, instead of implying the same metalinguistic notions as the aforementioned text, the appearance of the author at the end of the narrative, yet only as a minor figure within the story, makes the *mise en abyme* acquire a different effect (one which is nevertheless also alluded to in 'A Tale'). The circular return emphasizes the autonomy of art, both of the creative act and of the created object. The return suggested by the final scene encapsulates the text within the confines of its own story, stressing its auto-referential status. The referential connection to an outside reality collapses, as the reference becomes the referenced. The story is revealed as its own *supplement*.[20] What is more, this auto-referentiality endows the narrative with a peculiar temporality. The protagonist's present becomes the narrated past, as does the author's future intention to write the text, since the story has already been written. Furthermore, like in 'The Tale', the idea of circularity is also hinted at within the main body of the narrative through the continuous repetition of the question 'Have you fallen down from the moon?' bestowing the text, once again, with the inherent purposelessness and aesthetic playfulness of a carousel.

* * *

Taken together, Queneau's, Nabokov's and Kharms' circular works represent a step beyond the efforts of their predecessors in terms of both a greater self-awareness about the importance of narrative form (given the inherent implications existent in every framework) and a more explicit circularity. Queneau presents us with an infinite recurrence at the level of the discourse (through the reduplication of the first and final line of the text), which has the effect of subverting the linear progression of the story, the idea of a narrative *telos*, the referential function of the narrative and thus the reader's expectations about its underlying meaning or significance, highlighting its aesthetic qualities in turn. Nabokov also constructs his circularity purely at the level of discourse, ostensibly safeguarding the inherent linear character of his story. Nevertheless, the narrative's form lends the sequence of events that make up the narrative a peculiar temporality as an eternal present, where the past-present-future division appears to lose its sense. Furthermore, by only revealing the text's circular structure at its ending, Nabokov de-emphasizes the importance of the plot, stressing instead the multiple significances that the narrative acquires at once – as a portrait of a memory. Finally, Kharms uses circularity to shatter his texts. His shocking stories undermine our expectations about what a narrative is and what it should do (as well as how it should end), inviting reflection on the same. His circularity not only encapsulates his fictions as auto-referential objects, aestheticist renderings of an absurd world; it also establishes them as 'anti-narratives' that challenge our assumptions about the nature of language, meaning and literature.

[20] I use this term in Jacques Derrida's sense (see *Of Grammatology* (1967)).

5

Circulus vitiosus litterae

Joyce, Borges and the Theatre of the Absurd

With the heterogeneous modernist movement at its peak,[1] the writers of the interwar period had long lost their respect for the literary conventions of the nineteenth century. Expressionism, Dada, Surrealism and the succession of subsequent avant-garde movements made experimentation, both formal and thematic, the norm. Though linearity continued to be the paradigmatic structure of narrative, circular texts and other experimental forms became increasingly common. If the radical avant-gardist innovations of the turn of the century were initially the extravaganzas of a minority, and their artwork seemingly to the taste of but a few, following the First World War their practices became endorsed throughout the continent by writers and readers alike. Furthermore, with the rise of fascism and the outbreak of the Second World War, modernist art appears to become an ethical imperative. Although scholars such as Mark Antliff have recently problematized the assumption that 'fascism and modernism were mutually exclusive' (2007: 17), the 1937 exhibition *Entartete Kunst* (Degenerate Art) was a categorical call to arms to many modernist artists.

The increasing success of the movement achieved such heights that it soon became a part of 'mainstream culture', maintaining this wider popularity throughout most of the century. Thus, while some critics (Clement Greenberg et al.) argue that modernism culminates in the 1930s, and though the debate about where (and whether) modernism ends and postmodernism starts appears to be without any clear resolution, what is certain is that formal experimentation continued to be an ambition of both late modernists and early postmodernists alike. Beckett is perhaps one of the best figures to exemplify this: deemed a later

---

[1] One of the underlying arguments of this is that modernism was not a single movement and other categories (such as structural ones) may be used to examine and establish connections tying its diverse works together. The circular trend is one of many examples of such an effort.

modernist by critics such as Morris Dickstein and Anthony Cronin (see 2009) and a postmodernist by others (see Hassan 1975 or Slade 2007), his work is clearly representative of a striving to create a new kind of narrative language, both in prose and in drama. In fact, the related (and perhaps equally problematic) dramatic movement which writers such as Beckett and Ionesco are said to inaugurate – the so-called Theatre of the Absurd – is also representative of this effort, as well as of the allegedly 'discontinuous continuity' between modernism and postmodernism.

So, regardless of how we wish to classify the experimental literature of the post-1930s, what is certain is that narratives display an increasing complexity and inventiveness, particularly in their structures. The radicalness of the modernist experiments grows ever more extreme, seemingly heading towards pure aestheticism, in some cases almost to the extent of incomprehensibility. This is perhaps the result of an attempt to distance literature from consumer society, but conceivably also the outcome of a general habituation to experimentation. As modernism becomes increasingly established as a literary movement, the circular form is also progressively consolidated as an alternative to linearity. Clearly representative of this development, the texts analysed in this chapter are some of the most explicit examples of narrative circularity. In many cases, the loose linear plot discernible in some of the prior circular texts is now completely abandoned. The subversion of the notion of plot is accomplished outrightly; the defiance of teleology is consummated. The circular structure, now a literary form in its own right, becomes a sort of 'anti-conventional convention', achieving its epitome, in both prose and drama, with texts such as Joyce's *Finnegans Wake* (1939) or Beckett's *Waiting for Godot* (1953).

James Joyce's *Finnegans Wake* (1939)

Having published *Dubliners* (1914) and *Portrait of the Artist as a Young Man* (1916), on the one hand a rather conventional collection of naturalist short stories and on the other a less conventional form of the *Bildungsroman*, Joyce moved beyond the restrictive grasp of past and contemporary trends, venturing to experiment both in style and in structure with his groundbreaking *Ulysses* (1922). Bearing a cyclical structure – mimicking, as it does, the *Odyssey* in terms of both form and content by enacting the classical *nostos*, or return home – *Ulysses* was soon recognized as 'the preeminent modern accomplishment, an epitome of the classical modernist narrative', as well as 'a provocative seedbed of theoretical issues' (Lutzkanova-Vassileva 1999: 183). Still, it is with *Finnegans Wake* that Joyce undertakes full-blown formal experimentation as his central aim: venturing into uncharted literary landscapes and producing one of the most innovative yet also complex (and probably unread) classics of English literature.

Joyce's two final works stand apart from his earlier ones. If *Ulysses* raised the bar in terms of formal and stylistic experimentation, *Finnegans Wake* went far beyond any of its contemporaries (and even many of its successors) in testing innovative modes of expression and the limits of narrative. Christopher Butler attributes Joyce's 'relativist opposition to the beliefs of the past' and engagement with 'radically new ideas, current in that period, concerning consciousness, time, and the nature of knowledge' to the influence of writers such as 'Bergson, Freud, Einstein, Croce, [and] Weber', but also Nietzsche (cited in Attridge 2004: 68). To be sure, Joyce's texts stem from a reaction against the values of modernity that recall the modernist mantra ('make it new!') like no others, revealing a clear desire to 'transvaluate all values', at least in literature, suggesting that Joyce was arguably a modernist at least to the extent that he was a Nietzschean. In fact, his relationship with the German philosopher was far greater and more significant than most critics have traditionally wanted to admit.

Although Richard Ellmann dates Joyce's discovery of Nietzsche's writing to 1903, Neil R. Davison points out that already 'by 1902 Nietzsche's ideas had become ubiquitous in the intellectual world of Dublin, especially through the influence of W. B. Yeats' (1998: 112), meaning that it is not only plausible but very likely that Joyce had already come into contact with Nietzsche's work by that date. Moreover, as Davison also notes, Joyce had certainly 'read a fair amount of Nietzsche' even before he left Ireland 'for the Continent' in 1904 (1998: 112). So, despite the traditional scholarly disinclination to describe Joyce as a Nietzschean and to emphasize, instead, that he was 'sceptical about this sort of enthusiasm' (Butler in Attridge 2004: 67), this claim has been increasingly hard to sustain under the weight of copious evidence. Furthermore, critics are forced to avow that Joyce indisputably considered himself a Nietzschean by 1904, since on July 13 of that year he signs off a letter to his friend George Roberts with the pseudonym 'James Overman'. This gesture should be seen not only as 'the flashing of some cultural capital' by referencing 'the most dangerous and disreputable figure in contemporary European letters', as Patrick Bixby claims (2017: 47), but also as unquestionable evidence of the importance of this relationship.[2]

Joyce found in Nietzsche a lucid articulation of the anti-Christian views that he himself was contemplating at the time, which together with the philosopher's aristocratic radicalism and notion of the *Übermensch* provided Joyce with an aid to surpass the bourgeois, nationalist and Catholic values of his youth, as well as to forge the ideals of a 'race' as demanded by Ireland's complex cultural and sociopolitical situation at the time. However, Joyce's interest in Nietzsche was not a mere fancy of his youth or merely fuelled by a desire to revitalize the Irish spirit, as several scholars suggest. Davison emphasizes how his '"hyperborean" behaviour after his return from Paris also indicates a Nietzschean influence, which was aided by way of his relationship with Gogarty, who was an avid reader of the philosopher' (1998: 112). Additionally, we also know that Joyce owned translations of *The Birth of Tragedy*, *The Gay Science* and the two works on Wagner, which were not published until 1909 and 1911.

Besides, references to Nietzsche appear repeatedly throughout Joyce's works. In *Dubliners*, Duffy, the protagonist of 'A Painful Case', owns copies of *Zarathustra* and *The Gay Science*, a detail which is all the more telling if we consider Stanislaus Joyce's remark that his brother 'lent Mr. Duffy some traits of his own, [such as] the interest in Nietzsche' (cited in Davidson 1998: 112). Stephen Daedalus (in the posthumous *Stephen Hero* (1944)) claims that 'it is a mark of the modern spirit to be shy in the presence of all absolute statements' and that he is 'fond of saying that the Absolute is dead', statements that are clearly Nietzschean vestiges. Thomas S. Hibbs further notes that there are 'striking similarities' between Joyce's *Portrait* and Nietzsche's *Birth of Tragedy*;[3] and both Buck Mulligan in *Ulysses* and Shem the Penman in *Finnegans Wake* have been

---

[2] In an outstanding recent essay that traces a number of Nietzsche's ideas through Joyce's texts (slave morality, bad conscience, the death of God and the *Übermensch*), Bixby analyses the peculiar 1904 signature, explaining that although the gesture has been mostly disregarded as a joke by critics and biographers alike (since it appears in a comic letter where Joyce is asking for money), its significance should not be taken lightly. Nietzsche's work had been recently translated into English and thus was a popular topic of discussion among intellectuals. Moreover, Bixby stresses that Joyce shared Nietzsche's preoccupations with 'the elevation of the exceptional individual [. . .] the promises of the artistic vocation, the significance of classical culture [. . .] the perspectival nature of human knowledge, and the emergence of certain affective orientations and their associated values' (2017: 48). Bixby also reminds us that at the time of his 'polemical' signature, Joyce was also signing some of his correspondence as Stephen Daedalus, 'indicating the proximity in his imagination between Nietzsche's *Übermensch* and the protagonist of his own recently commenced autobiographical novel' (2017: 47).

[3] He points these out in his Nietzschean reading of Joyce's text (in Ramos 2000).

identified as Nietzschean characters.⁴ Thus, under the weight of such abundant evidence, the claim that Joyce merely experienced a passing infatuation with Nietzsche collapses. Indeed, Nietzsche is still present in Joyce's library in the 1920s, when he was finishing *Ulysses* and beginning work on the *Wake*.

Consequently, the efforts to dismiss Joyce's Nietzschean heritage may be taken more as an attempt to distance him from such a notorious figure as Nietzsche than at face value, since their affinities are hard to dispute. In fact, studies elucidating this relationship have become gradually more commonplace in recent years.⁵ Of these, it is worth highlighting Thomas J. J. Altizer's *History as Apocalypse* (1985), which surpasses similar endeavours by characterizing Joyce as a 'priest of the anti-Christ', identifying Nietzsche as his direct precursor and arguing that the eternal return is both a preparation for and an anticipation of Joyce's novels (1985: 228). Furthermore, Altizer suggests a parallelism between Joyce's connection with Nietzsche and that of Dante with Aquinas, arguing that it is actually irrelevant whether Joyce ever read Nietzsche seriously, since he was 'closer to the integral center of Nietzsche's thinking than Dante as a poet was to the center of Aquinas theological thinking' (1985: 228).

Aside from the aforementioned affinities, additional aspects of Joyce's writing can be traced back to Nietzsche. Among these, perhaps the most obvious is his fierce scepticism regarding the institutions, facts, dogmas and customs inherited from tradition.⁶ This scepticism manifests itself as a meticulous adhesion to fact and, like some of the authors discussed in the previous chapters (Strindberg, Stein, etc.), as a desire to see and represent things 'as they really are', aspiring to a realism that 'perpetually combats larger ideological commitments' (Butler in Attridge 2004: 68). The stylistic diversity of *Ulysses* is itself a stance against the authority of certain means of expression,⁷ such as the linear, teleological model of the nineteenth-century realist novel:

> In realism you get down to facts on which the world is based; that sudden reality which smashes romanticism into a pulp. [...] idealism is the ruin of man, and if we lived down to fact, as primitive man had to do, we would be better off. That

---

⁴ The latter in particular has been described by Margot Norris as a dramatizing of 'Nietzsche's attention to the lack of innocence in the historicizing act [...] as violent transgression of empirical historical practice' (Norris 1996).
⁵ See Valente (1987), Slote (2013) and Davinson (1998).
⁶ Butler and Battaglia agree that this was indebted to the Nietzsche.
⁷ Joyce's stylistic diversity shows that there are myriad contrasting ways to experience and order or depict reality, or, as Karen Lawrence puts it, he uses 'a series of rhetorical masks' in order to make the reader 'doubt the authority of any particular style' and aware of the 'different but not definitive ways of filtering and ordering experience' (cited in Attridge 2004: 69).

is what we were made for. Nature is quite unromantic. It is we who put romance into her, which is a false attitude, an egoism, absurd like all egotism. In *Ulysses* I tried to keep close to fact. (Joyce in Attridge 2004: 68)

Joyce's purportedly unrealistic style is hence a result of striving for a more realistic realism. Indeed, the protagonist of *Stephen Hero* captures this idea well when he describes the modern as an anti-traditional way of seeing things as they really are. This concern with accuracy drives Joyce to utilize diverse 'stylistic frameworks, which are all relative to each other, and which often disrupt the conventions of word formation and syntax', inaugurating what Butler calls a 'revolution of the word' (cited in Attridge 2004: 69) that culminates in his last work.

Finnegans Wake accomplishes this 'revolution' by fusing content, style and form until they become indistinguishable. Anthony Burgess deems it 'the first big technical breakthrough of twentieth-century prose writing', a text stressing the premise already present in *Ulysses*: 'to every phase of the soul its own special language' (cited in Attridge 2004: 73). Yet the work also seems to respond to one of Nietzsche's imaginative claims, namely, that 'we are not rid of God because we still have faith in grammar' (2003: 483). The *Wake* is a post-death-of-God work whose inventiveness undermines and surpasses such faith quite explicitly. The text is characterized by a complex creativity that challenges comprehensibility through the blending of morphemes and the creation of new words. It is a narrative which does not allow for a summary since it conflates form and content, dissolves the boundaries of character and problematizes the one-to-one correspondence between signifier and signified upon which language rests. As an early critic of the novel remarked, asking what the book is about is perhaps 'a question which Mr Joyce would not admit', since the text 'is nothing apart from its form, and one might as easily describe in words the theme of a Beethoven symphony' (cited in Deming 1970: 678).[8]

If, as Vivian Heller points out, in *Ulysses* Joyce holds 'the mirror up to narration' and dramatizes 'the relativism of literary style, treating individual styles as moments within a circular history' and dissolving 'the boundaries of character', in *Finnegans Wake* he reduplicates and furthers these endeavours by creating a 'new kind of narrative', a '"present tense integument" [...] whose every cell repeats the history of the human race' (1995: 162). The *Wake* undermines and forces us to question our assumptions about narrative by subverting our expectations about a consistent plot, a setting or a set of characters, simultaneously

[8] In a review for the *Guardian*, published on 12 May 1929.

allowing a variety of contrasting readings. So, despite the bounteous critical material attempting to elucidate it, there are still many fundamental areas of disagreement and uncharted aspects awaiting exegesis. Nevertheless, for all the text's complexity, one aspect remains clear: its circular structure.[9]

While scholars such as John Harty are right in noting that 'Joyce gave us little help in deciphering *Finnegans Wake*, misleading the reader as often as not' possibly owing to his desire "'to keep the professors busy for centuries'" (2015: 23), he did give us the basic key to its form by pointing out that the work 'ends in the middle of a sentence and begins in the middle of the same sentence' (cited in Fargnoli and Gillespie 2014: 246). Besides, we find further support for exergesis in the famous edited volume that proceeded its publication (owing to the publisher's fear of a total lack of readership), *Our Exagmination Round His Factification for Incamination of 'Work in Progress'* (1929), a collection that still stands as one of the *Wake*'s most enlightening commentaries. The key contributions discussing the novel's form are Beckett's, Marcel Brion's and Elliot Paul's essays, all of which dwell upon the circular nature of the text. 'Dante . . . Bruno. Vico . . . Joyce' is perhaps the most well-known and celebrated essay in the volume, providing the conventional and unchallenged key to the work:

> Here form *is* content, content *is* form. You complain that this stuff is not written in English. It is not written at all. It is not to be read – or rather it is not only to be read. It is to be looked at and listened to. His writing is not *about* something; *it is that something itself*. (Beckett 1974: 14)

The essay also offers the most conventional explanation of the text's structure, which links it to Giambattista Vico's circular theory of history.

Beckett tells us that Vico postulates a cyclical history consisting of three ages: a Theocratic, a Heroic and a Human (or civilized) age, a process driven by 'Divine providence', which, however, is not a transcendental force but 'immanent and the stuff itself of human life, working by natural means' (1974: 7). This process is said to recur endlessly, with each stage having the correlative value of 'rise', 'development' and 'peak' (followed by a recursive decline). Having outlined Vico's theory, Beckett goes on to align the novel's parts with Vico's stages:

---

[9] The notion of circularity is already explored in Joyce's earlier works, albeit more subtly. Heller notes that the 'Oxen of the Sun' and 'Circe' sections in *Ulysses* have a circular plot and that the former 'conforms to Stephen's circular theory of art', in that the succession of styles found in the chapter mirrors the way in which 'literary history depends on one style being supplanted by another; creation depends on negation' with literary history becoming 'a metaphor for the history of the human race, a metaphor which Joyce pushes farther in *Finnegans Wake*' (1995: 90).

Part I. is a mass of past shadow, corresponding therefore to Vico's first human institution, Religion, or to his Theocratic age, or simply to an abstraction – Birth. Part 2 is the lovegame of the children, corresponding to the second institution, Marriage, or to the Heroic age, or to an abstraction – Maturity. Part. 3 is passed in sleep, corresponding to the third institution, Burial, or to the Human age, or to an abstraction – Corruption. Part 4 is the day beginning again, and corresponds to Vico's Providence, or to the transition from the Human to the Theocratic, or to an abstraction – Generation. Mr. Joyce does not take birth for granted, as Vico seems to have done. So much for the dry bones. (1974: 8)

Beckett then highlights several references to Vico's 'insistence on the inevitable character of every progression – or retrogression' found within the text (1974: 22). The analysis thus demonstrates how Vico's ideas, although not determinative of the book as a whole or indicative of Joyce's agreement with the historian, are clearly analogous to several of its central aspects, including many of its motifs (which hence have a threefold character) and its overall structure. The essay concludes with the description of the *Wake* as a 'spherical' purgatory which 'excludes culmination', where there 'is no ascent' only 'flux – progression or retrogression, and an apparent consummation', a 'movement' that is 'non-directional – or multi-directional', since 'a step forward is, by definition a step back' (1974: 21–2), a description which applies to *Finnegans Wake* as much as to Nietzsche's idea of eternal recurrence.

However, the text's circular structure is not only fashioned through a mirroring of Vico's theory. As Brion notes, Joyce also 'creates its own time, as he creates his vocabulary and characters' by doing away with chronology, so that 'characters most widely separated in time find themselves unexpectedly cast side by side' (1974: 32), making it not always possible to discern the exact moment in which the episode narrated is temporally located:

When we are made to pass, without any transition other than an extremely subtle association of ideas [. . .] from the Garden of Eden to the Waterloo battlefield we have the impression of crossing a quantity of intermediary planes at full speed. Sometimes it even seems that the planes exist simultaneously in the same place and are multiplied like so many 'overimpressions'. These planes, which are separated, become remote and are suddenly reunited and sometimes evoke a sort of accordion where they are fitted exactly, one into another like the parts of a telescope. (Brion 1974: 32)

This conflation of different times is circular both because Joyce unites characters and events that should be separated by time and space, and because these persons and moments reappear repeatedly throughout the text. This endows some scenes with what Brion calls 'a strange transparence', since 'we perceive their principal element across four or five various evocations, all corresponding to the same idea but presenting varied faces in different lightings and movements' (1974: 32).

A number of other aspects also contribute to fashioning the work's circular form. Frances L. Restuccia notes how certain passages in the book's beginning mirror or 'complement' parts of its ending (see 1985: 443–5). Fargnoli and Gillespie highlight the emphasis placed upon the cyclical nature of human experience, which is rendered as 'patterned and recurrent, in particular, the experiences of birth, guilt, judgement, sexuality, family, social ritual and death' (2014: 91) – a process through which the archetypal 'characters' also emerge. Elliot Paul also emphasizes this aspect, noting how characters pertaining to different times are fused together owing to their common features and according to the circular design. He also draws attention to the fact that the 'elements' of the plot 'are not strung out, one after the other', as in conventional narratives, but 'organized in such a way that any phrase may serve as a part of more than one of them', citing as examples the fall of man and the tale of Noah's ark, which 'recurs again and again' throughout the text (Paul 1974: 136). Joyce's treatment of plot is, like his treatment of character and language, polyphonic in nature, since his ideas do not succeed one another in a regular sequence or at a constant pace. What is more, many of the narrative's topographic elements, such as the city of Dublin or the River Liffey, also echo the work's structure, adding a visual dimension to its circular character.

It is important to note that although all three essays dealing with the text's form in *Our Exagmination* (Beckett's, Brion's and Elliot's) refer to Vico's theory in order to account for its circularity, and while the three parts of the novel may certainly be aligned with Vico's stages (with the fourth part functioning as a 'return'), the *Wake*'s structure is not purely Viconian and the significance of Nietzsche's ideas in this respect must not be overlooked. Both Altizer and Andrew John Mitchell agree that 'there is no thinker, including Vico, who offers a fuller way into the night language of *Finnegans Wake* than does Nietzsche', since his notions of the death of God and the eternal recurrence are crucial in 'opening up' *Finnegans Wake* (1985: 228). Nietzsche's discussion of nihilism anticipates the 'coming of the language and the world' of the work, highlighting, as Mitchel remarks, the two writers' 'similarity of concern', since while 'Nietzsche helps to elucidate what is at stake in Joyce's text, the *Wake* itself enacts Nietzsche's thought, more powerfully perhaps than Nietzsche himself ever attempted to do' (2002: 419).

The obscurity provoked by a language which problematizes the idea of an unequivocal referentiality, or even of conventional polysemy, is illuminated by Nietzsche's proclamation of the 'death of God'. The *Wake*'s language and form are consequential of the event: the text challenges the idea of God at a syntactic level through its polyphonic conflation of referents and at a structural one through its relentless returning which forever precludes the possibility of a resolution (or teleology). Instead of expounding these ideas through the conventional coherence of a philosophical discourse (as Nietzsche does), Joyce 'surrenders his text to the event and its aftermath' (Mitchel 2002: 419), making the book an emblem of the outcome of God's death. Furthermore, the reader's response to the text's baffling style is also very much like the experience of coming to terms with Nietzsche's event: a potential anxiety regarding the possibility of enduring and making sense of the world – or the work (see Mitchell 2002: 420).

Finnegans Wake also re-enacts some of Nietzsche's ideas through the allegorical significance of its 'characters' and the 'events' of its 'plot' (if we may use these terms as vaguely as the text requires us to). HCE and ALP embody the dichotomy of being and becoming, God and Dionysus:

> ALP is the Dionysian moment of becoming to HCE's being, and Joyce creates a tension between the solidity of HCE as a spatial constant, interred in the landscape, or even a building [. . .] and the looseness or flow of ALP, identified with the river Liffey. (Mitchell 2002: 428)

The rigorous manner in which the assembled company follows the procedure of HCE's burial is also reminiscent of the way in which 'we still idolise God's shadow, after his death' (Aphorism 108 in *The Gay Science*); and the constant repetition of HCE's fall, condemnation and crucifixion symbolizes, as Mitchell observes, that 'God's death cannot be regarded a *fait accompli*, because He dies only to reappear again', with 'each appearance announcing a subsequent death' (2002: 423). Joyce's aim is therefore to make the question of God's death appear in its sharpest focus and thus compel the reader to consider whether the event is in fact not a ruse: whether 'the human' can be 'construed independently of God', whether 'finitude' can be thought of 'apart from the infinite' (Mitchell 2002: 423).

More importantly, however, the necessary verdict demanded by the eternal recurrence, that of deciding between God and Dionysus or being and becoming, also recurs throughout Joyce's text as in no other. It appears explicitly in chapter 1.6, a section which, according to Roland McHugh, Harty and Mitchell, 'deals directly with the structure' of the work, associating it with 'contemplation and temporality' (2002: 425). The fragment paraphrases Nietzsche's first formulation of the idea (in *The Gay Science*) very closely, articulating the thought as a question, like in the demon's aphorism. However, unlike Nietzsche, Joyce provides us with a portmanteau answer: 'A collideorscape!', which, as Mitchell observes, 'only emphasizes the decision to be made', since 'At this collision of so many oppositions' the refusal to 'escape from one's abysmal possibilities into the purported stability of God' in favour of 'the "kaleidoscope"', that is, 'continually shifting appearances of dancing color and light, a play that is justified only aesthetically' merely 'accentuates the struggle here, withholding resolution' (2002: 428). Hence, the work literalizes the eternal recurrence's imperative. By rendering a single event through multiple perspectives, Joyce emphasizes the importance of every detail, writing the tension of the eternal return into the fabric of his work. Consequently, to read the text is, as Mitchell concludes, a process whereby one must abandon 'the will to mastery, a finite way of reading', give up 'the wish to be God – or the author' so that, as readers, 'we too must kill God' (2002: 431).

All in all, the text's form proposes a Viconian conception of history and emphasizes the circular character of life and experience (as Stephen Daedalus puts it, 'Every life is many days, day after day'), but also literalizes the idea of the 'death of God' entraping both text and reader within the relentless movement of the eternal recurrence. Yet, at a more superficial level, the circular structure also forces the reader into a subsequent reading (what Philip F. Herring calls a 'heuristic ending'), necessary to decipher an additional layer of this circular conundrum. The recursive ending makes the interpretation of the text also a circular process by undermining the idea of a resolution (even an eventual one, say, after second reading), encouraging an eternal rereading that will forever bring new meanings to the surface that were initially overlooked. This is why Herring argues that Joyce's texts (the *Wake* in particular) seem as though 'they cannot be read, but only reread' (2014: 170).

Jorge Luis Borges' 'The Circular Ruins' (1940)

In one of the many interviews recorded for television, Jorge Luis Borges says, 'I love Buenos Aires a lot but I have other motherlands. I can think of Adrogue, of

Montevideo, of Austin, of Geneva above all. I hope to have as many homelands as cities I have visited' (1995: 129; my translation). This remark, though playful, certainly holds some truth regarding his status as a writer. Although an Argentinian by birth, Borges was also very much a European author.[10] He bore English, Portuguese and Spanish origins, which he was proud to highlight in interviews, received a 'European education' as a child (being raised bilingual in Spanish and English and home-schooled by a British governess from the age of six) and encouraged to read the European classics (from Plato to Stevenson and from *Don Quixote* to *Faust*) by his father, whose library he famously described as 'the biggest event of his life'. Moreover, at the age of fifteen, Borges also found a new home in Europe, when his father decided to take his family to Geneva in search of a cure for his failing eyesight.

Amy Sickels describes Borges' move to Europe as 'an important catalyst in his development as a writer'.[11] Indeed, it was in Switzerland that Borges would learn French, German and Latin and become for the first time accepted and praised for his intellectual faculties by his fellow classmates. In Switzerland he also discovered French literature, as well as some of the writers who would become most influential throughout his life, including Schopenhauer, Carlyle and Nietzsche. Borges also commenced his literary career in Europe, more specifically in Spain, where he wrote two unpublished books, took part in the Ultraist movement (which he would later export to Argentina), published his first poem and became acquainted with a number of notable writers (such as Gómez de la Serna, Valle Inclán and Guillermo de la Torre). So, despite being the Argentinian (if not Latin American) storyteller par excellence of the twentieth century, his early education and relationship with Europe situate him within the framework of European literature. Borges was not only a clear heir to the literature of the continent, he was also very much responsible for bringing Argentina (its *gauchos* and *arrabales*) to the European world of letters.

Borges knew Nietzsche's work well. Although he did not have a specialized education in philosophy, he was stimulated to read it by his father, who was very interested in idealism and encouraged him to venture into the world of metaphysics. As Clive Griffin notes, Borges 'returned time and again to the same thinkers – Heraclitus, Zeno, Plato, Spinoza, Berkeley, Hume,

---

[10] Borges himself refers to this European heritage, as well as to the problem of categorizing him as an exclusively Argentinian writer, in his essay 'The Argentine Writer and Tradition' (1951).
[11] See her 'Biography of Jorge Luis Borges' in Bloom (2004: 4).

Schopenhauer and Nietzsche' – and displayed a persistent fascination with a number of metaphysical problems: 'substance (matter or reality), time, identity, the limits of human understanding, language, infinity, eternity, death, causality, determinism and chance, and the question of the design of the universe' (cited in Williamson 2013: 5), all of which bear clear ties to Nietzsche's work. Borges also wrote repeatedly about Nietzsche in the 1940s, displaying his extensive knowledge of the philosopher's work. In 'Some of Nietzsche's Views' (1940), he denounces the immoral readings of the philosopher's work: those decontextualized interpretations serving ulterior political motives (such as identifying him as a precursor of Nazism) so in vogue in the 1930s. The defence suggests not only a wide familiarity with Nietzsche's ideas (also displayed in his 1940 essay 'Nietzsche: The Purpose of Zarathustra') but a sense of closeness – in striving, as he did, to cleanse the philosopher's name from political appropriation.

Many of Nietzsche's major themes are present in Borges' own writings. One need only think of his mistrust of the notion of the subject – which he deemed a 'grammatical illusion' (stressing the multiplicity of the self instead) – his perspectivism or his views on language. Numerous scholars have discussed these parallelisms: Silvia G. Dapía, for instance, claims that in many texts Borges responds to Nietzsche's 'ways of philosophizing' (2015: 8); Alfonso de Toro points out that both share 'the conviction that all the visible and existent is a product of language', insisting on the playfulness of philosophy's deconstructive power and on the plurality of possible interpretations for any event (2012: 37); and Rosemary Arrojo argues that 'Borges's non-essentialist conceptions of language and translation [...] share a great deal with Nietzsche's radical critique of Platonic notions of truth and representation', citing 'On Truth and Lies in a Nonmoral Sense' as the potential source for his ideas' (2017: 68).[12] Yet, of all the Nietzschean motifs found in Borges' work, and probably due to his profound interest in the concept of time,[13] he seems to have become particularly enthralled by the idea of eternal recurrence.

---

[12] Arrojo even goes as far as to claim that the short story 'Funes the Memorious' could be read as a 'creative translation' of *Zarathustra*.

[13] In a passage that shows both his familiarity with Nietzsche and his philosophical interest in the notion of time, Borges writes: 'I tend to be always thinking of time, not of space. When I hear the words "time" and "space" used together, I feel as Nietzsche felt when he heard people talking about Goethe and Schiller – a kind of blasphemy. I think that the central riddle, the central problem of metaphysics – let us call it thinking – is time' (cited in Merrell 1991: 114).

As Floyd Merrell observes, the idea of the eternal return 'never ceased to fascinate Borges' (1991: 113). He refers to it in many of his works, dedicating several essays to its discussion, but also using it as a theme or structuring principle in some of his texts (in both prose and poetry). His first explicit discussion of the idea is found in his 1934 essay 'The Doctrine of Cycles', where he seeks to refute Nietzsche's idea as a cosmological principle, arguing that Cantor's set theory disproves the hypothesis. Nevertheless, despite rejecting the idea in the first half of the essay Borges also recognized the notion's value, as well as the valour of Nietzsche's effort in proclaiming it, praising the philosopher's endeavour by stressing that 'he disinterred the intolerable Greek hypothesis of eternal repetition' in order to 'make this mental nightmare an occasion for jubilation' (1999: 120).

Borges used Nietzsche's concept in order to refute the notions of time and self, a belief that he upheld and developed throughout the 1940s, notably in 'A New Refutation of Time' (1946). Although he perceived time, reality and identity as illusions, Borges also understood that we are unable to comprehend our existence in the world without them since they are our only way of grounding our experiences and representations of reality. Similarly, while he dismisses the eternal return as a cosmological principle, he sees recurrence and repetitions as inevitable features of our experience. Thus, even if he rejects Nietzsche's idea in his 1934 essay, Borges seems unable to free himself from its grasp. In *A History of Eternity* (1936), he claims that he tends 'to return eternally to the eternal return' (Borges 1999: 91), and certainly, despite his disbelief, the notion re-emerges as a frequent motif in his fictions published during the first half of the twentieth century.

The eternal return first appears in Borges' literary works as the underlying theme of the poem 'The Cyclical Night' (1940), which also has a circular structure since it opens and closes with the repetition of the same verse. While the repetition of a poem's first line in the closing verse might not seem particularly worthy of attention (since many poems begin and end in this fashion), the title, content and specific manner in which Borges reiterates this first line all emphasize the circular character of the work. The final verse is not a mere reduplication of the first in the style of a refrain, for it is bracketed as a hint at the repetition of the entire poem. Moreover, the poem is full of references to the idea of circular time.

In 1940, Borges also wrote 'Tlön, Uqbar, Orbis Tertius', where, although the idea of eternal recurrence is not mentioned explicitly, there are a number of allusions to it in the depicted civilization's understanding of time and art, in particular to a historical kind of circularity reminiscent of Vico's theory of history. The theme appears again in 'The Garden of Forking Paths' (1941), within a beautiful passage where Borges reflects on the idea of circularity in relation to literature while pondering the ways in which a book might be eternal:

> I kept asking myself how a book could be infinite. I could not imagine any other than a cyclic volume, circular. A volume whose last page would be the same as the first and so have the possibility of continuing indefinitely. (1962: 67)

The passage also refers to the *Arabian Nights*, pointing out that in one of its tales Shaharazad begins recounting the frame story, running the risk of returning to the night in question and thus of repeating the story infinitely. Finally, the same passage also discusses the idea of a 'Platonic' book, passed on from generation to generation and written eternally in this manner. It is perhaps out of these reflections that Borges would find the encouragement to venture into the use of circularity as a structural device in the composition of his own fictions.

The philosophical discussion of the idea of eternal recurrence is taken up once again in the 1943 essay 'Circular Time'. However, in this case, rather than arguing against Nietzsche's 'greatest thought', Borges formulates his own version of the idea: an eternal recurrence of the different rather than of the same. The essay contains two broad assertions that make up his particular conception of the eternal return and which were later incorporated as the central theme of several of his short stories. First, he describes 'universal history as the history of one man' (Merrell 1991: 116), recalling one of the key aspects of Joyce's conception of circularity – his conflation of different historical characters within archetypal acronymic protagonists. This idea can also be conceived conversely: the history of one man as the combined lives of all men – the multiplicity of the self, the being of becoming. Second, Borges argues in favour of the Heraclitan or Schopenhauerian idea of the present as an ever-flowing continuum – a notion which, despite Borges' rejection of Nietzsche's idea of recurrence, clearly recalls Zarathustra's description of the 'Moment portal'.[14] Borges' eternal return therefore evokes what is possibly the most famous line of Ecclesiastes: 'What has been will be again, what has been done will be done again; there is nothing new under the sun' (1.9).

Moreover, Borges' formulation is also clearly reminiscent of Deleuze's reading of Nietzsche's notion:

---

[14] See Chapter 2.

We misinterpret the expression 'eternal return' if we understand it as 'return of the same'. It is not being that returns but rather the returning itself that constitutes being insofar as it is affirmed of becoming and of that which passes. It is not some one thing which returns but rather returning itself is the one thing which is affirmed of diversity or multiplicity. In other words, identity in the eternal return does not describe the nature of that which returns but, on the contrary, the fact of returning for that which differs. (1983: 48)

Borges, like Deleuze, sees eternal recurrence as a return of the diverse: a wheel 'endowed with centrifugal powers that drives away the entire negative' and owing to which 'Being imposes itself on becoming', since 'it expels from itself everything that contradicts affirmation' (Deleuze 1983: 48). This formulation also recalls the description of eternity in 'A History of Eternity', where Borges discusses the idea of homogeneous facts, referring to the singing of a bird and the chirping of the crickets as timeless sounds, since he argues that such experiences are not merely identical to those of past times, they are 'without superficial resemblances or repetitions, the same' (1936: 138).

Circularity also reappears as a motif in some of Borges' later short stories: 'The Theme of the Traitor and the Hero' (1944), 'The Immortal' (1949) and 'The Plot' (1957). In the first, the eternal return is again rejected, this time by depicting it as a misapprehension resulting from a conspiracy and thus underlying its illusory or deceptive nature. However, in 'The Immortal', a story which Ronald J. Christ deems 'the culmination of Borges' art' (1969: 192), the idea appears as a central theme, though it is his particular understanding of the 'return of the similar' and his conception of history as the history of one man that features in the text. The idea is reiterated once again in 'The Plot', where the event depicted in 'The Theme of the Traitor and the Hero' is reappraised but with the converse purpose of emphasizing its reality (again as the eternal recurrence of the different rather than of the same). Still, aside from his 1940 poem, none of these texts are in fact circular narratives; the discussion of circularity in these works follows in every case a rather conventional linear form.

Borges' first use of a circular narrative structure in prose appears in his 1940 short story 'The Circular Ruins'. A number of critics have aligned the text with Heraclitus' ideas, since the dual nature of time (at the same time static and in flux) found both in this story and in 'The Cyclical Night' recalls Heraclitus' concept of a unified state. Other scholars point out that the story is in fact a literary rendering of the ideas on time expressed in his essays. However, the type of eternal return found in this narrative is more in line with a Nietzschean recurrence of the same than with Borges' (or Deleuze's) recurrence of the similar. This would support Annette U. Flynn's argument that many of his short stories 'can be seen as organic explorations of essayistic themes', yet with 'the added freedom of the imagination and fewer constraints of reality and rationality' so that 'the medium' of fiction is used 'as a creative plane to enact the *as if* (2011: 12). While Borges disregards Nietzsche's idea in his essays, he turns it into reality in his imagined world and in this case into the structuring principle of the text too.

Nevertheless, the form of 'The Circular Ruins' is not immediately perceptible to the reader, nor made explicit in the text, either through the repetition of the text's opening at its closing or through a Joycean unfinished sentence circling back to the beginning of the work. Instead, Borges endows his tale with a circular structure by alluding to the idea of circularity repeatedly throughout the course of the narrative, as well as through the protagonist's final revelation at the story's resolution. Beginning with the ruins themselves, there are a number of elements that hint at the idea of circularity, foreshadowing the text's recursive structure. We find, for instance, references to the protagonist waiting 'until the moon's disk was perfect' (alluding to its cycle), images that recall the symbology found in Nietzsche's *Zarathustra* and even more explicit allusions, such as the protagonist's reflection ('At times, he was troubled by the impression that all this had happened before') or his premonitory remark that 'what was happening had happened many centuries ago. The ruins of the fire god's sanctuary were destroyed by fire' (Borges 1962: 55).

Yet, the text's circular form is not disclosed until its ending and even there it is done in a tacit manner: as the dreamer becomes aware that he himself has been dreamt, just as he dreams his subject into existence. The circular effect produced by such a realization is stressed further by the implication that beyond the fictive world of the story, the narrator (Borges) is that other (third) dreamer who dreams the protagonist. Furthermore, beyond that third dreamer, we may find the reader who dreams Borges dreaming his dreamer, and beyond that, Borges dreaming the reader who dreams him in turn, thus immersing author, reader and story in an inescapable circular world of dreams. In this sense, Borges' story seems to allude to the kind of *mise en abyme* found in Kharms' works – yet here the idea that we are reading the text being written is not made explicit, it merely looms over the narrative as an absent presence. Moreover, this would be a doubly circular *mise en abyme*, since it would also contain the reader. Consequently, despite the fantastic setting of the story, the idea of circularity acquires a very real allegorical significance, as a symbol of the relationship between text, author and reader, signalled implicitly by the circular ending.

The final exposure of the narrated cosmos as a superimposition of several layers of appearances (or dreams) can also be read as a commentary on the problem of the referentiality of language and concepts – and how these create the fictions of being and identity. As Lisa Block de Behar argues, the story evidences 'the referential fracture, the inevitability of breakdown through the phenomenon of signification' (2014: 16). The protagonist's final realization exposes his own 'supplemental' nature, and thus of all that exists (or that the dreamer perceives that exists), as well as of all that he creates by dreaming:

> Representation as the point where the abyss opens: the sign is the origin of other signs, said Peirce, recognizing the il-limitation of semiosis as the path that, by way of the breakdown, precipitates the infinite. (Block 2014: 31)

The process of dreaming (of the dreamer's creation) becomes symbolic of the mechanism of signification. The protagonist's final realization symbolizes the discovery of this abyss: his own nature as a representation, as a supplement of a supplement.

More importantly, the circular structure has yet another allegorical significance related to the previous notions. Owing to its circular form, the story can also be interpreted as an allusion to the smaller self-reflective cycle of subjectivity and, more specifically, to that of the author creating himself as author. The desire of the dreamer to dream an entity that is a reduplication of himself recalls that of the author recreating himself within his own writings. Nevertheless, the final realization of the creator's own nature as someone else's dream compromises the assumed unidirectional rapport between creator and created, implying that such a procedure is in fact a circular process by which the creation recreates the subject in turn. What is more, since the protagonist realizes that it is an 'other' who was dreaming him, the allegory becomes symbolic of several possibilities. This 'other' may in fact be himself as other (to his creation), in which case the story represents the circular process of self-creation described earlier. However, this 'other' may also refer to the deterministic quality of our subjectivity – as a configuration imposed by exterior forces (genetic, historical, cultural, linguistic, etc.). Lastly, a subsequent, albeit more subtle, allusion also emerges from the allegory. The narrator's revelation may also be read, more broadly, as a critique of theology (God revealed as some 'other's' dream), with the precise moment of the protagonists' revelation representing the modernist devaluation of the highest values. According to this interpretation, the dreamer's discovery of his nature as a dream would equate to the madman's announcement of the death of God.

Hence, an unanswered question remains regarding who the 'other' that dreams the protagonist is and whether that 'other' is not, once again, someone else's dream (the implication being that he is).

As a result, Nietzsche's notion of the *Übermensch* also looms over the text, albeit negatively, since the denouement's circular turn acts as a subversion of this idea. By characterizing his protagonist's identity as a creation of some unknown 'other', Borges suggests that far from having the possibility of becoming 'overmen' who recreate themselves consciously and continuously (affirming the process of becoming), we are 'dreamed by someone else'. Accordingly, Borges offers us his terrifying variation of the view of life as art: as an artwork created by an unknown other, an obscure artist who dreams us. The story's circular structure thus evidences that, to use Klossowski's phrase, 'all is mask'. Yet, rather than an affirmation of the process of mask-making and mask-wearing (à la Nietzsche's *Übermensch*), Borges posits a somewhat gloomy self-less process, where we are but an other's dream (a series of grand narratives, perhaps) and therefore the mask is put on us. This characterization of the process of becoming as a self-reflective construction, added to the dreamer's circular realization, corresponds to Klossowski's notion that there is no true essence, no actual face behind the mask. There is no origin and no end, no first nor final cause, only effects: the face covered by the mask is (always already) a mask itself.

In this sense, Borges' story represents an eternal recurrence of the other: an infinitely recurring process of creation, both of recreating ourselves as an exterior 'other' and of being created by some 'other' – who in turn is created by a third 'other', and so on, infinitely. It is an endless process of continuous creation and recreation. The 'other' here is not a concrete subject but a focal point at which a series of effects converge. The subject is always defined by this otherness and therefore always exists as an 'other' to itself. This 'eternal recurrence of the other' destabilizes the assumed order of cause and effect, exposing it as an illusion, the deceptive trickery of the act of representation, which in reality is nothing more than an infinite game of supplementation.

The Theatre of the Absurd: Ionesco, Adamov and Beckett

When Eugène Ionesco's *The Bald Soprano* premiered at the Théâtre des Noctambules, on the evening of 11 May 1950, few could have foreseen that this play would mark the birth of a new type of theatre that was to develop in Paris in the years following the Second World War. Taking the baton from authors such as Strindberg and Alfred Jarry, Ionesco's self-proclaimed 'anti-pièce' aimed to confront and reject the realistic or representational trend that had dominated drama since the mid-nineteenth century. The first production of Ionesco's play, staged by Nicholas Bataille, was not favourably received initially: it 'angered its audiences' (Londré 1999: 440), performed to almost empty houses and, due to its poor reception, lasted but a month on stage. However, by as early as 1957 *The Bold Soprano* was being played on a daily basis at the small Left Bank Théâtre de la Huchette (where it is still performed to this day), catapulting its author from anonymity to one of the leading playwrights of his time in the space of only seven years.

A similar fate was in queue for Samuel Beckett's *Waiting for Godot* (1953). Originally staged by Roger Blin at the Théâtre de Babylone, *Godot* sought (or so Esslin claims) to challenge 'the accepted conventions of the theatre of [the] day', and though poorly received at first, it soon became 'one of the greatest successes of the post-war theatre' (1968: 39). Hence, regardless of whether Ionesco and Beckett were aware that by going against the grain of representational theatre they were laying the foundations of a new dramatic trend, and in spite of the fact that the Cuban Virgilio Piñera had already written a work deserving the 'Absurdist' title some time before the publication of Ionesco's text,[15] *The Bald Soprano* and *Waiting for Godot* were deemed the plays that inspired a new theatrical movement: a succession of groundbreaking pieces that shook the literary scene, startling audience and critics alike.

In *The Theatre of the Absurd* (1961), Esslin identified the numerous plays that were gradually appearing in the small theatres of the Parisian Quartier Latin as 'part of a new, and still developing stage convention that ha[d] not yet been generally understood and ha[d] hardly ever been defined' (1968: 21). The study enjoyed considerable success. Even if a number of the alleged 'Absurdists' rejected the label and some scholars are reluctant to speak of an absurdist trend,[16] Esslin's work quickly became a landmark study, so successful that John Calder describes it as 'the most influential theatrical text of the 1960s' (2001: 23). Even Michael Y. Bennett, who disagrees with Esslin's classification, is forced to

---

[15] *False Alarm* (1948).
[16] Coinciding with the fiftieth anniversary of the publication of Esslin's study, Michael Y. Bennett published *Reassessing the Theatre of the Absurd* (2011), in which he dismissed Esslin's ideas by arguing that the characterization of these plays as absurdist works had been based upon a misreading of Camus' essay. However, even if critics such as Worth or Bennett question Esslin's classification, it is hard to dismiss the similarities between these plays.

avow that since its publication the plays it analysed 'have been pigeonholed as absurdist texts by the general public and academia alike' (2001: 2). To be sure, by delineating the stage convention, elucidating the significance of these polemical works and providing new criteria through which to evaluate and judge them Esslin in effect created a literary movement, using Albert Camus' *The Myth of Sisyphus* (1942) – an essay which is clearly indebted to a reading of Nietzsche's discussion of nihilism – as the theoretical cornerstone under which to categorize and collect such diverse works.

So, while it is clear (especially seeing how Piñera wrote an 'absurdist' text before the so-called Absurdists) that these plays respond to a specific historical moment: that of a loss of faith and disillusionment triggering the devaluation of values, foreseen by Nietzsche decades earlier but made a reality by the various atrocities that took place during the first half of the century, it is also true that (for this same reason) the works bear a common philosophical basis that is strongly related to Nietzsche, through Camus. Esslin rightly saw these plays as mise en scènes of the absurd cosmos depicted in Camus' essay:[17] the situation of mankind when faced with the realization that life has no underlying meaning or purpose. Certainly, if not earlier, God had died once and for all in Auschwitz, taking with him any other residual metaphysical values that may have been left behind. Thus, in *The Myth of Sisyphus* Camus describes the aftermath of the event: deeming the situation of the individual faced with the predicament of living a meaningful life in a meaningless world an absurd one. The famous line that Esslin takes from Camus to draw his definition of absurdity is the following:

> A world that can be explained even with bad reasons is a familiar world. But, on the other hand, in a universe suddenly divested of illusions and lights, man feels an alien, a stranger. His exile is without remedy since he is deprived of the memory of a lost home or the hope of a promised land. This divorce between man and this life, the actor and his setting, is properly the feeling of absurdity. (Camus 2012: 6)

In other words, Camus sees Nietzsche's affirmation of life as an acceptance of its absurdity and like Nietzsche proclaims this embracement.

Sisyphus becomes Camus' absurd hero because he is able to bring together 'the sense of alienation and the yearning for unity' (Sagi 2002: 2), in a paradoxical

---

[17] In contrast to a number of the absurdists' contemporaries, who expressed similar philosophical ideas through a type of narrative which resembled that of past dramatic conventions (Sartre, Camus, etc.), these works aimed to present existence's absurdity by matching the thematic content of their works to their form and aesthetics.

internal harmony which constitutes his happiness. Accordingly, Camus stresses that, regardless of the senselessness of his endless task, we must think of Sisyphus as a happy man since his daily struggle constitutes an essential path towards self-realization. Thus, Sisyphus is an active nihilist in the Nietzschean sense as much as he is an absurd hero:

> He is, as much through his passions as through his torture. His scorn of the gods, his hatred of death, and his passion for life won him that unspeakable penalty in which the whole being is exerted toward accomplishing nothing. (Camus 2012: 28)

The plays of the Theatre of the Absurd recreate Sisyphus' cosmos, even if in many cases Sisyphus himself is absent. In constructing this world, the circular form becomes crucial. The structures of many of these texts re-enact the logic of Sisyphus' punishment, the unbearable burden of the eternal return: infinitely recurring meaninglessness. Circularity is 'absurd' because it makes all possibility of progress impossible; it problematizes the idea of meaning and confronts us with meaninglessness. Sisyphus' myth illustrates this clearly – it depicts the idea of pointless action. This brings into focus the question of nihilism and therein lies the connection to Nietzsche's work. Camus is therefore the crucial mediator of Nietzschean ideas for many of the so-called absurdists; Beckett, for instance, who we know thought highly of *The Myth of Sisyphus*.

Yet, aside from (or owing to) their common philosophical backdrop, the absurdist plays share other important traits: the limited psychological characterization of the protagonists, the frequent use of incongruous dialogue, the rejection of realism and the embracing of fantasy in order to construct plays that resemble dreams (see Esslin 1968: 24), and in many cases, the abandonment of the classical Aristotelian dramatic structure in favour of circular forms. Indeed, plays such as Ionesco's *The Bald Soprano* and *The Lesson* (1951), Beckett's *Godot*, *Act without Words II* (1956), *Endgame* (1957), *Play* (1963) and *Not I* (1972), Arthur Adamov's *The Paody* (1950) and *All Against All* (1953), Jean Genet's *The Blacks* (1958), Edward Albee's *The Zoo Story* (1958), Harold Pinter's *A Slight Ache* (1959) and Fernando Arrabal's *The Architect and the Emperor of Assyria* (1967), to list but a few, all deploy circular structures with various purposes and results. In what follows we will focus on some of the most interesting examples of circularity in the absurdist trend.

Both of Ionesco's first two plays make use of circular structures, although the way in which they are constructed and the effects they have are significantly different. In *The Bald Soprano*, the circular form is configured purely through the inclusion of a final stage direction indicating the re-enactment of the first scene, but also suggesting the repetition of the entire representation:

> The words cease abruptly. Again, the lights come on. Mr. and Mrs. Martin are seated like the Smiths at the beginning of the play. The play begins again with the Martins who say exactly the same lines as the Smiths in the first scene, while the curtain softly falls. (Ionesco 2015: 42)

This reiteration undermines the overall sense and purpose of the representation, already challenged by the preponderance of bizarre conversations. While the repetition is not exact (since the Smiths have been substituted by the Martins) this difference only emphasizes their interchangeability – reinforcing their status as vague performative entities by denying them a concrete identity beyond their fluctuating roles (as in Strindberg's *The Dance of Death*) or superficial social masks. The circular structure also subverts the value of the (pseudo-) plot's development, accentuating the overall sense of incongruity and bestowing the play with a ritualistic aura. As in the case of other circular narratives, the spectacle seems to become a senseless game that the protagonists engage in for no apparent reason, almost giving the impression that they are self-consciously performing a play within a play. As we shall see, this kind of circularity (devised through a final revelation undermining the 'events' that have taken place) and its overall effects (the undermining of teleology, the critique of certain ideals – in this case, of bourgeois values – and the transformation of the play into a kind of ritual or meta-representation) is common to many absurdist texts, albeit with some important variations.

Described as a '*drame comique*', Ionesco's second play, *The Lesson*, presents us with a similar type of circular structure. Like in *The Bald Soprano*, the story's recursive nature is only exposed in the denouement, though instead of being disclosed explicitly through a stage direction it is merely alluded to in the plot's resolution. The final revelation that it is the fortieth time that the professor has committed the same crime that day, added to the arrival of a new student, suggests the eternal repetition of the dreadful act. Robert O'Neal describes the play's form as a 'symbol of futility' (1980: 115), but the structure has a number of additional effects. *The Lesson* is a play about language. The preponderance of senseless dialogues highlights (as in *The Bald Soprano*) the impossibility of true communication, more specifically the isolation caused by such impossibility. This idea is reinforced through the professor's lecture on the neo-Spanish tongues and his failure to teach anything to his student, but more importantly, through the maid's repeated inability to prevent him from committing the crime. The value and effectiveness of logic and reason are also undermined, echoing Nietzsche's assertion that it is not the universe which is meaningless but the faith in reason that has led modern society to see it as such. If the professor's philology class highlights the inefficacy of language (to represent reality and to communicate), the arithmetic class is analogous with regard to the inefficacy of logic.

The Lesson is also a play about authority and power relations. The professor's class is in fact a struggle for dominance between himself and his pupil, depicting the repressive nature of dogmatism and the violence of patriarchy. The initial hierarchy existing between both characters is quickly subverted as the professor loses his initial timidity, imposes his authority and forces his knowledge upon the student. The professor undertakes the role of a totalitarian tyrant who, using language as his 'instrument of power', imposes his will and dominates the pupil by becoming the 'arbitrary prescriber of meanings' (Esslin 1968: 143). The repeated appearance of the maid foreshadows the inevitability of the professor's crime (even if the audience is only able to appreciate this in hindsight). She undertakes the role of a peculiar mother figure since her sporadic appearances infantilize the professor while also accentuating the predictability of the dramatic outcome. The professor is forever unable to learn from his lesson, self-control is out of his reach, his brutal game of domination and violence must continue indeterminately. Given the peculiar nature of the performance, all these events might even seem comical (despite their dreadfulness) if they happened just once, but the circular structure makes them unbearable. So the play's form symbolizes not only futility but the impossibility of true communication or knowledge, the inalterability of the human condition, the unfeasibility of progress or change and the inescapability of violence and suffering.

Rather than having the centrifugal cleansing effect of Deleuze's eternal recurrence, Ionesco's circular world emphasizes the permanent nature of the tragedies exposed within it. Furthermore, the combination of the play's underlying circular movement with a superimposed linear progression implicit in the passing of time has the effect of accentuating the sense of stasis further. As Kenneth Wishnia stresses, this twofold treatment of time produces a 'nightmarish' effect, since although time is moving forward the characters are condemned to 'repeat endlessly the same actions', inevitably leading 'to a dead end' (1999: 124). The professor's conscious willingness to re-enact the lesson, to experience (once again) the circular shift from subdual to tyranny, and to reiterate the assassination makes the representation acquire (as in *The Bald Soprano*) a ritualistic character: as an absurd pantomime depicting the tragic recurrence of abuse and violence.

A contrasting type of circular structure appears in Adamov's *All Against All*, yet with somewhat similar effects to those found in Ionesco's plays. In this case, the text's circularity is configured through a series of internal cycles that depict the persecution of a population of refugees whose situation changes drastically and repeatedly as the 'wheel of political fortune turns and the persecutors become the persecuted' (Esslin 1968: 107), time and again. Hence, circularity here exists only as an underlying element within the plot. The cycle of change is not an intrinsic attribute of the protagonists' universe but the consequence of the authoritarian forces that function within it, the impositions of a totalitarian government. Consequently, while the play may be roughly divided according to the classical Aristotelian three-part structure, a cyclical motion also underlies time's arrow.

The plot's circular developments are unveiled through bodiless voices retransmitted through the radio, whose corporeal absence symbolizes an extra-human quality. It is the omnipotent voice of the totalitarian state, able to know and see everything, and to impose its will by means of its all-embracing power. The absence of concrete references situating these disembodied voices within a specific context allows them to represent power in its absolute form. Their 'neutral' and 'impersonal' character (Adamov 1965: 15) reflects the idea that 'beyond the control and comprehension of man are forces which can compel him to bend their will' (Moss 1980: 68). Although the play's resolution partly puts a stop to its circular movement, through the protagonist's decision to hide his true identity and hand himself in to the authorities, this final act only serves to further underpin the omnipotence of the underlying forces that set the cycle of power in motion.

Overall, the plot's circular trajectory undermines dialectical conceptions of history (Hegelian, Marxist, etc.) by showing how political systems are overthrown only to be replaced by equivalent ones, recalling the French proverb '*Plus ça change, plus c'est la même chose*'. As Susan Moss argues, the play depicts political struggles as 'a potentially indefinite cycle of powers succeeding one another without progression' (1980: 63). The impossibility of bringing the conflict to an end suggests, as in Ionesco's *The Lesson*, that all political systems must inevitably fail due to the nature of power (or of the 'will to power'). Political authority is not only incapable of resolving the conflict, it is the force igniting the hatred between social classes. By subverting the figures of the hero and villain, suppressing the initial characterization of the refugees as victims and emphasizing the exchangeability of the roles of oppressor and oppressed, Adamov exposes political adversaries as two sides of the same coin. The play's circular shifts also show how power ostensibly legitimates a particular moral stance, through the perspectival nature of alterity, thus underlining the relativity of morality. The protagonists' interchangeable identities also stress what several of the characters repeatedly exclaim throughout the play: that regardless of their apparent differences, humans are 'all the same!' (Adamov 1965: 209; my translation).

In any case, perhaps the best example of how the circular absurdist form dramatizes the world of Camus' Sisyphus is Beckett's *Waiting for Godot*, a work that, in own Beckett's words, 'is striving to avoid definition' (cited in Kennedy 1991: 32). Precisely because, as Simon Critchley observes, the play seems 'particularly, perhaps uniquely, resistant to philosophical interpretation', it has been described in a range of contrasting ways:

> whether it is the sub-Cartesian interpretation where Beckett is allegedly concerned with the 'inexpressible nature of the self whose figurings people the landscape of post-Cartesian modernity', or the sub-Heideggerian interpretation where Beckett strives to attain 'the existential authenticity of being prior to language or of being *as* language', or the sub-Pascalian absurdist interpretation where Beckett expresses 'the quintessential and pessimistic tragic fate of modern man'; or whatever. (2009: 166)

Granted that it is a work that strives to remain elusive, it is evident that it is also about waiting, since Godot never arrives, the experience of waiting becomes, as Sanford Sternlicht argues, 'the being and the end in itself, the only process' (1998: 106).

The play's circular form underscores the static nature of the plot, the absence of progression and the apparent purposelessness of the characters' perpetual task. The protagonists are trapped in a never-ending present: days repeated on end, always slightly different yet always essentially the same; they are condemned to the repetition of a senseless routine and destined to the absence of change. A number of diverse elements function to construct this immutable universe where 'Nothing happens, nobody comes, nobody goes' (Beckett 1966: 57–8). These include the virtual erasing of the protagonists' past through their failing memories, the lack of the conventional crisis of Aristotelian drama and the predominance of non sequiturs in the dialogues, which make it seem as though not only is nothing happening but nothing is being said either. This unbearable sense of paralysis and purposelessness is unconceivable without the recursive structure.[18]

Beckett combines the devices used by Ionesco and Adamov in order to reveal the circular nature of the 'plot' (if one can call it that). He includes implicit references to its recurrence (as in *The Lesson* and *All Against All*) and reduplicates the initial scene (as in *The Bald Soprano*). However, circularity is also devised through the division of the play into two separate acts, designed in a parallel or symmetrical fashion, each following the course of a single day. *Godot*'s structure emphasizes mythical or ancient time: the cycle of the day, the year and the seasons, inscribed in nature's movements (the planets, stars, etc.). It challenges the validity of linearity as the accepted structural model of modernity by undermining ideas such as certainty and progress, rejecting the value of the forms proposed by Aristotelian and representational drama (where linearity is inscribed) so that many of its elements, such as the theme of waiting or the dialogue (interrelated by means of their reliance on the idea of teleology), are denied their inherent coherence and significance. The rejection of linearity also allows and encourages Beckett's reductive process of ambiguation – see his *Proust* (1931) – since in rejecting a structural model founded on intention, direction and purpose, in abandoning plot, Beckett shifts theatre's focus to the depiction of that which remains after his excavatory process.

Godot's circularity has been discussed extensively by critics. Collin Duckworth, for instance, describes the action as 'circular and almost static', arguing that the plot is created through 'visual occurrences' that 'succeed one another with an underlying pattern of repetition' (cited in Beckett 1966: lxxxiv). Plot therefore is reduced to the creation of circularity, so that it is not that the play has a circular plot, but rather that the plot is nothing but a circle. The elements that make up this 'pseudo-plot' are the same in both acts, precisely to conform this circular structure: one of the protagonists (Estragon in Act 1 and Vladimir in Act 2) standing alone at the opening of the act, an initial reference to the boots, the entering of the other protagonist, the talk of Estragon being beaten during the night, the arrival of Pozzo and Lucky, the appearance of the boy, the sudden falling of night and rising of the moon and the final comment, 'Let's go',

---

[18] Parts of the following section on Beckett were modified and expanded into an essay entitled 'What Goes Around Comes Around: Godot's Circularity and World Literature', published as a chapter of Thirthankar Chakraborty and Juan Luis Toribio's *Samuel Beckett as World Literature* (2020).

antagonized by the stage direction '*They do not move*' (Beckett 1966: 85). Thus, as several commentators point out, the famous comment on *Godot* as a play where 'nothing happens, twice' works as an accurate description of its structure.

Furthermore, like in Ionesco's pieces the 'basic structural unit of the play' becomes, as Lawrence Graver maintains, 'a self-contained routine or ritual' (2004: 32), given the many secondary (ritualistic) internal instances of circularity:

> Vladimir's repetitious pantomime, taking off his hat and knocking out an invisible foreign object; Estragon's repeated fussing with his boots; Lucky's recurrent acts of picking up and putting down the luggage; the hat-exchanging routine; Vladimir's endlessly repeatable round-song [. . . and] the repeated line 'On attend Godot'. (Graver 2004: 32)

To which we may add Didi and Gogo's circular exchanges:

> ESTRAGON: All the dead voices
> VLADIMIR: They make a noise like wings
> ESTRAGON: Like leaves
> VLADIMIR: Like sand
> ESTRAGON: Like leaves.
>
> (Beckett 1966: 150)

The redoubling replies that close the protagonists' enumerations – thrusting them into what Lois Gordon calls 'the circular miasma of thought-frustration-rationalization' (2008: 63) – follow a circular movement similar to their psychological states (as in Strindberg's play),[19] which shift constantly from happiness to sorrow in a cyclical fashion, beautifully described by Pozzo at the sight of Gogo's sobbing: 'The tears of the world are a constant quantity. For each one who begins to weep, somewhere else another stops. The same is true of the laugh' (Beckett 1966: 100).

The play's circular form undermines the little action that does take place, subverting its role as dramatic action and producing an unbearable stasis by eradicating progression and levelling down all action to an eternal moment of waiting. In so doing, the circular structure destroys the plot as plot (depiction of action), generating an anti-plot in which the dialogue is free (not subjected to plot) or anti-functional. The inescapabilty of the characters' situation is intensified by a deterioration (both psychological and physical), which is the only perceptible change between the two acts. Yet, this deterioration does not

---

[19] See Chapter 3.

imply an end, since the protagonists even fail in committing suicide. Rather, it intensifies the circular movement, emphasizing their immobility still further. Additionally, this stasis results in a highlighting of the present moment, since the removal of progression and purpose revalorizes it as an eternal one (Nietzsche's 'Moment portal').[20] Their daily routine becomes infinite; time ceases to exit, as Pozzo laments after becoming blind.

This stasis also produces a revalorization of the play's anti-dramatic dialogue as poetry. The protagonists' exchanges acquire a different quality to that of conventional drama, as their thoughts are uttered rhythmically and without an apparent purpose or *telos*. The dialogue becomes a synthesis of *noein* and *poiesis* through its lack of functionality. Speech becomes poetic as the characters' aphoristic interventions fail to lead anywhere yet constantly allude to an evasive meaning whose expectations are never met. They suggest a concrete sense only to repeatedly undermine it, like a succession of questions accepting no single answer. Uncertainty underlies the very meaning of the utterances as they are spoken, of the references as they are set. The characters are always saying too little and thus saying too much. In this way, every statement becomes an attempt to fill the void with the lyricism of thought – to appreciate or impose beauty upon every single instant, by constructing a meaning that collapses immediately within the moment that repeats itself eternally. The dialogue becomes a central aspect of the play not for its performative function but for its aesthetic value. In drama, where almost all is dialogue, and almost all dialogue is plot, Beckett creates a dialogue that becomes poetic in its rejection of plot. Revalued in this process (through its multi-referentiality), the plot's chief function becomes aesthetic (as opposed to teleological). As a result, the play produces a reversal of the traditional dramatic hierarchy, where the aesthetic is subordinated to plot and mostly expressed through form, setting, costume and gesture. If in conventional drama *what* happens is more important than *how* (content over form), in *Godot* this is subverted: form becomes content (*how* becomes *what*).

Although various critics have contested the circular nature of *Godot*'s form,[21] its many adaptations are a clear testament to its importance. Thus,

---

[20] See Chapter 2.
[21] Steven Connor argues that there are two forms of repetition in the play: 'on the one hand [a] circular model [. . .] but on the other a linear [one], whereby some of the repetitions that we perceive [. . .] seem to indicate not endless reduplication but entropic decline (1988: 121). Graver points out the divergence of the second act in 'texture, tone, and implication', stating that although Act 2 is a repetition, it is 'repetition with a difference', since 'within the circle there has been a precipitous decline' (2004: 54). Weller deems it 'an asymptote, with the point of tangency [. . .] occurring only at infinity' (2005: 129). Mehta claims that *Godot* (as well as 'all of Beckett's theatre') is not circular but

in an adaptation that Anne C. Murch calls one of the play's most 'radical "tampering[s]"', *Ils allaient obscurs sous la nuit solitaire* (1979), while setting, scenography, characters and dialogue all underwent significant variations, its 'circular structure' was 'retained' and 'underlined in powerful visual terms in the finale' (1993: 189). This highlights the importance of the circular structure as one of the play's central components, safeguarded in such a bizarre and eclectic adaptation. Moreover, circular or cyclical structures can also be found throughout Beckett's later oeuvre, in works such as *Endgame, Act without Words II, Play, Not I* and *Quad*. So, despite the aforementioned reservations, it is hard to deny that Beckett's plays have become representative of what S. E. Wilmer describes as 'a kind of purgatorial non-space of endless time where the characters are stuck in repetition of the same phrases and sequences' (cited in Carvalho and Homem 2008: 162).

Among *Godot*'s many 'sequels' or 'spin-offs' we also find circular plays. Visniec's *The Last Godot* (1998) depicts a conversation between Beckett and Godot himself in which 'the last scene [echoes] the first: [opening] with Godot asking Beckett "Ils t'on frappé?", [and ending] with Beckett saying: "Demande-moi s'ils m'ont cassé la gueule"' (Astbury 2008: 196). And later playwrights such as Paula Vogel have not only avowed the influence of Beckett's circularity but gone as far as to affirm that *Godot*'s anti-Aristotelian 'circular approach to narrative', which removes linearity's traditional focus 'on the conflict between male characters leading towards a dramatic conclusion', 'opened out theatre to women writers in the 1970s and 80s' (2008: 168). However, even if some of these plays are direct descendants of *Godot*, the Absurdist use of circular structures is clearly not only a result of Beckett's influence.

There are both earlier and later examples of absurdist circularity, some of which may be aligned with Beckett but not all. In fact, in many cases their use of circularity differs considerably from Beckett's. In Arrabal's *Fando and Lis* (1955), for instance, it is the stage rather than the plot that becomes a circle, as the characters exit from one side only to re-enter from the other, incapable of arriving anywhere. The pseudo-action within this circle is again one of degradation with ultimately dreadful consequences. In Pinter's *A Slight Ache*, the stasis experienced by the protagonists achieves its height when the circular

helical, emphasizing that the second act is significantly different to the first, accelerated among other variances, and that the repetitions are not exact (the first act being humorous and charming and the second grave and turbulent), proposing a descending spiral model (2010: 372). Even Duckworth, who clearly identifies the structure of each act as 'circular', defines the overall structure of the play as following a 'gradual downward linear movement [...] towards disintegration' (1966: lxxxv).

nature of the plot is revealed and the roles of the characters interchanged, as in Ionesco's and Adamov's plays. And other examples of absurdist circularity range from Genet's *The Blacks* to Maruxa Villalta's *Esta noche juntos, amandonos tanto* (1970). Furthermore, a number of Latin American playwrights have also produced absurdist plays with a circular structure. These include the Cuban Virgilio Piñera's *El flaco y el gordo* (1959) and *La niña querida* (1966), Antón Arrufat's *La repetición* (1963), José Triana's *La noche de los asesinos* (1965), the Argentinian Jorge Diaz's *El cepillo de dientes* (1961) and the Nicaraguan Alberto Ycaza's *Asesinato Frustrado* (1968).

* * *

The narratives examined in this chapter are some of the most radical examples of circular structures in twentieth-century European literature. Many of them represent an outright defiance to linearity, a conscious rejection of the world view underlying such a structure. While the way in which they configure their circularity varies from text to text, in all cases they depict a literary cosmos that re-enacts Nietzsche's idea of eternal recurrence, albeit in different ways. Joyce's *Finnegans Wake* is perhaps the ultimate example of a circular narrative. By making the final sentence circle back to the book's opening, he produces a work that is truly endless. In it, story and discourse, like content and form, are inseparable, so that the entire narrative is subjected to a circular movement. It is a pure literary rendering of the idea of eternal recurrence that expresses Nietzsche's greatest thought in its language, plot and structure. Joyce's text is a celebration of the idea, a complete affirmation of life (as a cycle of birth, maturity, corruption and generation).

Borges, on the other hand, uses the notion within a fantastical frame in 'The Circular Ruins' as a way to reflect upon various aspects: the process of writing (and reading), the configuration of our identity, the deterministic nature of our subjectivity and perhaps even as a tacit anti-theological critique. While his circularity exists purely at the level of the story (since the text's discourse is linear), the implication is that the omniscient narrator is also contained within the circular structure(s) revealed in the story's denouement. In contrast, the various absurdist circular plays discussed in this chapter present life as a pointless ritual, in some cases a dreadful one (*The Lesson, All Against All*), since the desire for power sets in motion a vicious cycle of violence, with the implication that such cycles can never end.

Yet, if Joyce's novel is the epitome of circularity in prose, then Beckett is perhaps his correspondent in the theatre. With *Godot*, Beckett achieves a mise en scène of Sisyphus' bleak world. The movement underlying the play is an eternal recurrence of the similar, though one where the differences that set the repetitions apart carry no real weight (due to the protagonists' uncertainty), so that its centrifugal force is epitomized, becoming unbearable and drawing together the two kinds of eternal return (of the same and of the different). Whether or not yesterday was different from today does not matter because every moment is the same: 'one day we were born, one day we shall die, the same day, the same second' (Beckett 1966: 89).

6

Circular echoes

Robbe-Grillet, Calvino, Cortázar and Blanchot

The second half of the twentieth century sees an intensification of many of the practices in vogue in the literature of its first half. Modernism had accomplished a revolution in narrative that despite going into abeyance somewhat during the Second World War continued its course after the conflict. While the first half of the century was marked by a spirit of innovation, free from the burden of ethics and morality (Dada and Surrealism), the threat of an impending war encouraged many writers to leave aside their aestheticist projects to focus on warning against the rise of fascism and its threat to the peace of Europe. The interwar period hence sees the emergence of a copious amount of political literature, a phenomenon that continues even after the conflict's resolution. Nevertheless, the dissatisfaction left by the war led to a growing ambivalence regarding politics, which meant that many European writers decided to shift their focus, responding to the humiliation suffered during the conflict by questioning the radical ideologies of leading intellectuals such as Jean-Paul Sartre and Simone de Beauvoir. Focusing instead on creating a disengaged literature, autonomous and phenomenological, authors such as Alain Robbe-Grillet sought to give a voice to this disillusion by casting doubt on traditional notions and values, such as truth, order or meaning.

Despite the controversy surrounding the term 'postmodernism', it is hard to argue against the fact that many literary works of the second half of the twentieth century arise out of or respond to what Jean-François Lyotard identified as the postmodern condition.[1] This 'incredulity towards metanarratives [. . .] the obsolescence of the metanarrative apparatus of legitimation' finds its direct ancestor in Nietzsche, since it corresponds to 'the crisis of metaphysical

---

[1] Lyotard defines the postmodern condition as a period characterized by a crisis in 'the condition of knowledge in the most highly developed societies', a 'crisis of narratives' (1984: xxiii).

philosophy' inaugurated by his proclamation of the 'death of God' (Lyotard 1984: xxiii). Responding to this crisis in an attempt to shake off the remaining vestiges of the Enlightenment by doing away with mimetic representations of the world and intricate depictions of the human psyche in favour of self-reflexive or reader-oriented narratives that draw attention to the processes of subjective perception, literary writing and reading, many post-war European writers reappraise the circular form, albeit in ways that differ from their predecessors.

The works examined in this chapter range from more 'conventional' examples of circularity to structures that are paradoxically both linear *and* circular, or neither strictly one nor the other. Their effort is, as we shall see, directly concordant with the widespread rejection of grand narratives and the overcoming of structuralism. The awareness that the structuralist effort is ultimately totalitarian (see Derrida's essay 'Form and Signification', in *Writing and Difference* (1967)) exposes once and for all the vested nature of form, its inevitable ideological backdrop.

Alain Robbe-Grillet and the *nouveau roman*

Alain Robbe-Grillet was an author obsessed with form. Indeed, when discussing his work, a common starting point for many scholars is to highlight this aspect as the cornerstone of his writing.[2] This is no doubt because Robbe-Grillet himself avowed that what he found 'most important' in the novel is its 'structure, or form' (cited in Szanto 2014: 95). He even went as far as to assert controversially that 'the project of writing is always more or less a project of form', that his novels are 'devoid of meaning' and that they 'have nothing to say' (Robbe-Grillet 1989: 373). This has led critics such as Peter Bürger to align his work with the Flaubertian aim to write a book about nothing.[3] Certainly, if Robbe-Grillet's texts exhibit a 'formalist poetics', it is precisely because, as Hanna Meretoja observes, his 'aesthetics displays aspects of self-referential formal aestheticism' (2014: 51), whereby the literary work undermines its connections to the outside world, seeking to become an autonomous object instead of a signifier of an ulterior reality.

---

[2] See, for instance, Morrissette (1965: 5); Szanto (2014: 149); and Meretoja (2014: 54).
[3] See *Telos: Special Issue on Debates in Popular Culture*. 1985. New York: Telos Press

Robbe-Grillet's obsession with form lies at the heart of his attempt to create a 'new novel' (*nouveau roman*). In the series of essays written following the publication of *The Erasers* (1953) and *The Voyeur* (1955), and collected in *For a New Novel* (1963), Robbe-Grillet proclaims the need for formal innovation, arguing that 'the novel's forms must evolve in order to remain alive' (1989: 8). Prompted by the generally unfavourable reception of these first works but more specifically by the fact that they were criticized for diverging from 'the great novels of the past [. . .] always held up as the model', Robbe-Grillet directed his criticism towards a specific novelistic stance: psychological realism. He complained that 'the only conception of the novel to have currency' in his day was the bourgeois novel of authors such as Balzac, whose fundamental basis was character and plot (1989: 7–8). Robbe-Grillet rejects the view that a 'good' novel has to inherit a pre-established form, arguing that such a stance leads to 'a state of stagnation – a lassitude' that threatens to result in the death of the novel (1989: 17).[4] However, like his first works, these critical articles were also met negatively: allegedly deemed 'simplistic and silly' (Robbe-Grillet 1989: 8) and perceived as a manifesto, they established their author as the leader of a new and notorious novelistic school, despite his voiced reservations about considering him as such. Instead, Robbe-Grillet claimed that the term 'new novel' aimed to address 'all those seeking new forms for the novel, forms capable of expressing (or of creating) new relations between man and the world' (1989: 9). It was, then, not so much a concrete movement as an attempt to shift the focus from content to form, from psychology and metaphysics to technical virtuosity.

Like Zarathustra's call to 'write new values on new tables' (Nietzsche 1965: 16), Robbe-Grillet's essays bade writers to create their own novelistic values. Instead of identifying certain parameters that the 'new novelist' should follow, he stressed that 'Each novelist, each novel must invent its own form', arguing that 'No recipe can replace this continual reflection' (Robbe-Grillet 1989: 12). In overthrowing the conventions of realist writing, the *nouveau roman* subordinated plot and the psychological portrayal of the protagonists to the depiction of the remaining (formal) components of the story. Such a reversal of the traditional narrative hierarchy was necessary because this disposition implies a specific world view: one where the universe is not only intelligible but meaningful. As Robbe-Grillet writes: 'We had thought to control [the world] by assigning it a meaning, and the

---

[4] This recalled Raymond Queneau's fears decades earlier. In fact, Robbe-Grillet deemed *The Bark Tree* to be the first *nouveau roman*.

entire art of the novel, in particular, seemed dedicated to this enterprise, But this was merely an illusory simplification' (1989: 23). It is the collapse of this illusion that demands a new novel.

The *nouveau roman* bears a remarkable affinity with Nietzsche's philosophical project, not only in its desire to break with 'every pre-established order' (1989: 73) – strongly reminiscent of Nietzsche's transvaluation of the highest values – but because, as Robbe-Grillet avers, the *nouveau roman* is based in a shift away from perceiving the world as being 'designed according to our needs and readily domesticated', and a disbelief in the idea of 'depth' (1989: 24). This devaluation of depth was anticipated by Nietzsche almost a century earlier but made irrefutable by the horrors of the Holocaust:

> While essentialist conceptions of man met their destruction, the notion of 'condition' henceforth replacing that of 'nature', the *surface* of things has ceased to be for us the mask of their heart, a sentiment that had led to every kind of metaphysical transcendence. (Robbe-Grillet 1989: 24)

Robbe-Grillet's rejection of 'depth' parallels Zarathustra's pre-convalescent realization ('Joy to me! you come, – I hear you! My abyss speaks, my lowest depth have I turned over into the light!' (Nietzsche 1965: 167)). It is therefore hard to dismiss the Nietzschean aura that runs through Robbe-Grillet's narrative project, even if Robbe-Grillet was a trained scientist living in the age of Einstein's theory of relativity and Heisenberg's uncertainty principle (see Smith 2000: 169). Robbe-Grillet was certainly familiar with Nietzsche's work. He admitted reading *Zarathustra*, even if he claims it was 'the only book by Nietzsche that [he] read during [his] youth' (Robbe-Grillet in Smith 2000: 169).

Several critics have picked up on this affinity. Rob C. Smith argues that Robbe-Grillet 'sees himself as a bridge between past and future', recalling 'the depiction by Zarathustra of man as a rope suspended over a chasm' (2000: 128); and Jennifer Anna Gosetti-Ferencei deems the descriptions in his novels to be 'a Nietzschean festival of surfaces' (2010: 109). Smith also identifies a connection between the 'death of God' and the *nouveau roman*, noting that if Malraux reappraised Nietzsche's proclamation for a new generation by declaring '*man is dead*, after God', Robbe-Grillet repeated Nietzsche's warning, observing that 'since the death of God, it is being itself whose crumbling and dissolution endlessly go on' (cited in Smith 2000: 145). Furthermore, the *nouveau roman* sought to achieve a revaluation of narrative's highest values – an affirmation of form, beyond the 'old value' of content. So, while there are doubtless significant discrepancies between the two writers, in many ways Robbe-Grillet sets off from a very similar philosophical position to Nietzsche.

The *nouveau roman* sought to counteract the past reliance on intelligibility by attaining what Robbe-Grillet called '*freedom* of observation', not a naïve aspiration for objectivity but an attempt to rid narrative of the 'continuous fringe of culture (psychology, ethics, metaphysics, etc.)' that is added to all things, making them familiar:

> what is *literary* [. . .] functions like a grid or screen set with bits of different colored glass that fracture our field of vision into tiny assimilable facets [. . .] if an element of the world breaks the glass, without finding any place in the interpretative screen, we can always make use of our convenient category of 'the absurd' in order to absorb this awkward residue. But the world is neither significant nor absurd. It *is*, quite simply. (1989: 19)[5]

This desire to achieve observational freedom hence follows from the aim to represent reality unmediated by the literary, untransformed by ideology: a rendering of the universe seeking to be as faithful to the perceived world as possible, a pure phenomenological description. This kind of writing is fuelled by, but also underlines, the idea that human existence lacks significance, leading to the crumbling of 'the whole splendid construction' of our metanarratives (Robbe-Grillet 1989: 19). The disintegration of all meta-discourses of legitimization throws into question the validity of prior representations of the world, forcing the post-war writer to experience the 'shock' of the 'stubborn reality' that the Enlightened man thought (or perhaps only pretended) to have 'mastered', realizing instead that 'defying the noisy pack of our animistic or protective adjectives, things *are there*' (Robbe-Grillet 1989: 19). This disinterested or unbiased presence is what the new novelist seeks to render.

Robbe-Grillet's works represent the deliquescence of certainty through a twofold process. First, there is a hyperbolic focus on the (disinterested) description of objects or events. Second, there is a conscious undermining of the reader's expectations about narrative (specifically about its plot). This process accentuates Robbe-Grillet's belief that 'art cannot be reduced to the status of a means in the service of a cause which transcends it' – that is, 'the expression

---

[5] The disintegration of certainty, now seen as an illusion, and of meaning, seen as a simplification, also accentuates literature's autonomy. The events of the story do not exist outside of the text because narrative literalizes reality and in so doing transforms what it narrates. The *nouveau roman* thus positions itself in diametrical opposition to those works that find their value in the expression of a certain idea, teaching, moral or truth – the different forms of realism.

of a social, political, economic, or moral content' (1989: 37–8). If the realist novel, in accordance with the rational world upon which it relied, subordinated all formal constituents to plot because its meaning and value were derived from its teleological significance, the new novel should instead, like cinema, offer both the signification and the raw image (the former even becoming a surplus). If cinema is able to replace the virtual web of significations by a more immediate and real world of presence, then literature should strive to do the same. Consequently, Robbe-Grillet's response to the post-war crisis of meta-discourses is a predilection for 'presence' over 'signification (psychological, social, functional)' (1989: 21), as of form over content. Referentiality, meaning and purpose are undermined so that the narrative's different components accept 'the tyranny of signification only in appearance' (1989: 22). The new novel thus attempts to achieve precisely what Beckett praised in *Finnegans Wake*: rather than *meaning* something, his writing tries to *be* that something or in Robbe-Grillet's own words: 'the genuine writer has nothing to say [. . .] only a way of speaking' (1989: 45).

Circular structures, both internal (as a theme or motif) and overarching, play a definitive role in undermining the idea of causality, plot, teleology and the prioritizing of presence over signification in Robbe-Grillet's work. The circular form is used to undermine the semblance of a linear development that inevitably derives from describing objects in a sequence. The plot advances, though very slowly (in some texts painstakingly), but then folds back on itself, dissolving the little solidity it had seemed to acquire and leaving behind it the mere shadow of its purposeless unfolding. Barthes argues that Robbe-Grillet maintains 'the negation at the level of novelistic technique', because his visual rigour 'institutes nothing, or rather it institutes precisely the human nothing of the object' by rejecting (albeit sometimes only momentarily) 'the story, the anecdote, the psychology of motivations' through 'quasi-geometric' descriptions that shift the focus from sense to sign or stimulus (1972: 92). Thus, form is important for Robbe-Grillet, because it is one and the same thing as his negation of significance.

Nevertheless, Robbe-Grillet was very much aware of the difficulty of achieving such aims, not only because the novels of the past set the standard by which new novels are measured or because the contemporary writer is inevitably a product of tradition – requiring knowledge of the past to break away from it – but also because such a break is perhaps not completely possible (or even desirable). It is not hard to find predecessors to Robbe-Grillet's endeavour. David Weisberg notes that Robbe-Grillet looked towards 'Beckett's writing in support of his own vision of literary renewal' (2000: 138), and Kirk H. Beetz points out that 'Despite his lack of formal training in literature, Robbe-Grillet's work did not emerge out of nowhere, as he himself realized', noting that he 'enjoyed novels with circular plot structures', such as James M. Cain's *The Postman Always Rings Twice* (1934) and Kafka's *The Castle* (1926) (1996: xx). During a television interview, Robbe-Grillet was asked whether his critical and novelistic aspirations were revolutionary, to which he responded that he felt uneasy about using that term because although the *nouveau roman* sought to bring about a rebirth of the novel, it was also a repetition or continuation of the efforts of prior avant-garde movements.[6] Hence, while Robbe-Grillet rejects the Balzacian tradition, he nevertheless links his work to Flaubert and Kafka, claiming that the *nouveau roman* followed the same path as these and other predecessors.

It is perhaps as a result of this twofold movement (at the same time continuing and breaking away from tradition) that, while circular, the structures of Robbe-Grillet's texts differ from previous circularities. Szanto points out that the specific forms of his novels are 'more elusive, at least at first glance' than those of his predecessors (2014: 149), referring specifically to Beckett and Kafka. Accordingly, even if Szanto avows that 'a number of readers have concluded that his forms are essentially circular' (referring specifically to Bruce Morrissette's analysis of *The Erasers*), he argues that 'to assume circularity merely because the novel begins and ends in the same place – the first four novels retain this characteristic – is a critical superimposition that explains little about structure' (2014: 151). However, the tension between linearity and circularity in his novels is certainly telling. In many cases Robbe-Grillet produces what we may call a pseudo-circularity, since, although apparently linear, these texts lead nowhere, leaving us almost in exactly the same situation as we were at its opening. Thus, if, as Smith remarks, the new novel displays a tension between 'order and freedom', 'control and creativity', 'detailed description and fragmentation, between the language of ideology and the subversive word' (2000: 145), the same is true about their structures, which often lie between causality and arbitrariness, resolution and repetition, linearity and circularity.

This is already apparent in Robbe-Grillet's first published novel, *The Erasers*. There is considerable scholarly disagreement regarding the nature of its form (see Szanto 2014: 149). Although Barthes identifies its temporality as circular, he also characterizes it as an 'unfamiliar time, a time for nothing',

---

[6] Available online at: https://www.youtube.com/watch?v=NraQDi3nNX4.

since Robbe-Grillet allegedly restores 'time to the object [. . .] a litotic time; or, more paradoxically but still more accurately: movement minus time' (1989: 22). Barthes further describes it as 'the story of a circular time which in a sense annihilates itself after having involved men and objects in an itinerary at whose end they are left *almost the same* as the start', adding that the text's form transfigures the story as if it were 'reflected in a mirror' through the reduplication of the 'point of departure' (1972: 22). Robbe-Grillet's choice of the detective novel genre to begin his quest towards a literature of surface and form is in itself a clear statement against meaning, since while in conventional detective novels even insubstantial objects may acquire an ulterior significance as evidence of a crime, in *The Erasers* the detective's quest is transformed into an enigma that is devoid of solution and whose process therefore becomes more important than its outcome. Although the reader is encouraged to solve the mystery, the truth is that the only crime to be found in the novel is against narrative: causality, order, teleology and signification. The succession of points of views and shifting perspectives becomes the text's only secret, a facet radically undermining its genre. In this process, the various circular structures become crucial.

The novel achieves its circularity both through the inclusion of minor or internal circular devices and through an overarching circular return. The text is divided into seven parts: a prologue, five chapters and a brief epilogue – each of which consists of six sections, excluding the epilogue. The overarching circular structure is constructed through the symmetry of the prologue and epilogue. The novel's opening statement is reduplicated in the epilogue, bringing us back to the café where, once again, the waiter is engaged perfunctorily in the tasks of his daily routine as a barely awake automaton. The descriptions in the prologue and epilogue draw the reader's attention to the mechanical nature of the characters' actions – determined by habit, the monotony of the everyday. The bar owner's monotonous routine also establishes an underlying sense of circularity, setting a mechanical pace to the narrative: his actions appear automatic, driven by the inexorable unfolding of time, yet not a causally connected linear sequence of events but a relentless circular repetition of the similar. The epilogue also contributes to this sense of circularity through the reduplication of the crime (when the detective unintentionally kills Dupont).

Within the linear course of events that constitutes the detective's attempt to solve the mystery, there are also circular echoes or allusions. These include the name of the *boulevard circulaire*, the narrator's repetitive descriptions and certain inexplicable acts by the protagonist (such as his repeated mysterious visits to the stationery shop in search of an eraser). However, while the circularity generated by these tropes undermines the (expected) linear development of the plot and thus the underlying meaning or significance of the events, the circular structure destabilizing this development is undermined in turn both by the reader's assumptions that the crime can (and will) be solved and by the logical explanation that we can finally give to the unfolding of the events.

The main effect of Robbe-Grillet's pseudo-circularity is thus the foregrounding of the narrative's trajectory over its outcome or resolution. The subversion of the detective genre throws into question the certainty and order of the world, its causal structuration and presumed significance. Furthermore this pseudo-circularity also encourages a reader baffled by the lack of a tightly knit resolution to return to the beginning in an attempt to find some additional evidence that might shed more light on the nature of the events. However, instead of an explanation, the only thing to be found is, as Smith points out, 'the seed that will develop into the ensuing narrative' – that is, the numerous questions without answer: 'the establishing of the frame of reference' and setting up of a 'story' that will forever 'remain indeterminate' (2000: 23).

Further examples of pseudo-circular structures can be found in Robbe-Grillet's ensuing novels, much to the same effect. *The Voyeur*, for instance, enacts a variation of the circular form in the shape of a figure of eight, since the narrative follows the protagonist's double journey around the island. Like in *The Erasers*, many elements also foreshadow this structure of double return: objects taking its form and examples of doubling appear throughout the text. These include the sailor's tale about the discovery of the body, the reduplication of Mathias' room as a child on the island, the presence of doppelgangers (e.g. Jacqueline-Violette) or the reproduction of the crime committed against Jacqueline in Mathias' newspaper clipping and in the island's local legend. Besides, the novel also includes several *mises en abyme* that allude to its circular nature: the film showing at the cinema, *Mr X on the Double Circuit*, is a clear reference to the novel, as are the two sailors' lengthy and detailed explanations filled with redundant and contradictory details (see Smith 2000: 39).

An additional pseudo-circular structure appears in Robbe-Grillet's third published novel, *In the Labyrinth* (1959), a text that Meretoja describes as 'a form-oriented project of writing a novel in the form of a labyrinth' – both the description of a 'soldier's labyrinthine experience of disorientation' and a 'textual labyrinth' in itself (2014: 51). Even more than its predecessors, this novel fuses form and content to a point where they become indistinguishable. While a number of critics have argued that it alludes to a feeling of disorientation characteristic of the post-war period, the narrative rejects all meanings that may be superimposed upon it, particularly through the circular trajectory of its discourse. Robbe-Grillet emphasizes this rejection in an introductory note where he insists on the novel's fictive nature, stressing that the reader should 'see only the things, gestures, words, events that are reported without attempting to give them either more or less meaning than in his own life' (2012: 3). This lack of an ulterior significance is also stressed throughout the narrative, for example by the protagonist's ignorance about what he is doing, where he is going or why. For this reason, Szegedy-Maszák draws an analogy between *In the Labyrinth* and Queneau's *The Bark Tree*, since the soldier's box, like Père Taupe's door in Queneau's novel, establishes an expectation of 'some hidden meaning' which is finally undermined, since 'the goal towards which the whole sequence of events is directed' is 'invalidated at the end of both novels' (1997: 276).

In the Labyrinth achieves its circularity through repeated regressions which return the narrative to its point of departure time and again or shift the focus back to the disinterested description of objects whenever the faint plot seems to emerge. Thus, the recurrent descriptions of the soldier standing in the cold street with the package under his arm, of the raindrops and snowflakes, and of the deserted streets made up of rows of identical houses generate a circular movement that reverts the narrative reiteratively to square one. This is also the effect of the appearance and disappearance of the boy(s) leading the soldier through the streets, seemingly driving the narration towards a new determination but actually highlighting its indeterminacy over and over. Like the repeated descriptions of the soldier's footsteps, gradually covered up by the falling snowflakes, the text's regressions cover up the narrative's feeble plot as it begins to emerge from within this labyrinth of visual descriptions. Moreover, the repetition of the novel's opening passage in its ending ('Outside it is raining, outside you walk through the rain with your head down [. . .]') undermines the totality of the events, bringing into focus their pure presence, wholly devoid of purpose or meaning. The narrative's overall structure hence takes the shape of one of the descriptions found within the novel, if we interpret the third dimension mentioned in the description as the text's underlying significance: 'these concentric lines, instead of according the object a third dimension, seem to make it turn around itself' (2012: 96).

Circular forms are also apparent in some of Robbe-Grillet's other novels. In *Jealousy* (1957), for instance, it is hard to speak of a past, present and future, since the circular structure or time underlying the text would perhaps even allow us to start reading from almost any point of the narrative and conclude it at that same point without changing the whole drastically. This is because, as in most of Robbe-Grillet's novels, rather than being determined by the plot's logic, the structure of the protagonist's quest, the narrative's form is, as Szanto argues, determined by a mood or feeling (in this case, jealousy) (see 2014: 150). The same is true of the film *The Immortal* (1963), which acquires a circular structure by ending 'with the smiling face of a woman whose death seemed to give a tragic turn to the story' (Szegedy-Maszák 1997: 276), as well as his later novel *The House of Assignation* (1965), which Morrissette links to *Jealousy* owing to its narrative mode (it also starts and ends in the same place, a warehouse) as well as the numerous 'circular eddies' of its plot (1966: 821–2).

Overall, then, Robbe-Grillet's texts invite us to reflect on the ideological backdrop of form. By deviating from novelistic tradition and striving to create unconventional structures, he exposes linearity's bias, revealing that signification is not a given, that we impose it on the world and that form plays a significant role in this process; that objects and events can be structured in different ways, and that order is not intrinsic to reality but something we create or inscribe upon it. Robbe-Grillet's *nouveau roman* is an attempt to investigate form with the purpose of elucidating its key role in ascribing significance to reality. Although his narratives do not do away with plot completely, they include it merely to destabilize it. In this way, signification is mocked, its value is thrown into question and the idea that objects or events hold a single, exclusive meaning is subverted. The myriad circular returns that flood Robbe-Grillet's texts (both micro- and macro-circular structures) instil a subliminal polysemy upon every scene, event or object described, since they appear to gain a new significance (and to lose their previously accepted one) with each new description.

Italo Calvino's *If on a Winter's Night a Traveller* (1979)

Although Calvino began his career writing about his experiences as an anti-fascist partisan, thereby becoming aligned with the Italian neo-realist movement, he soon set these interests aside and turned to fiction. From the 1950s, Calvino's focus became fantasy, even if at times there was still a political concern, expressed allegorically, motivating this choice. However, after leaving the Communist Party in 1957 his belief that artists should not be driven by a political agenda becomes increasingly apparent. Calvino further explains this shift in an interview, claiming that even though 'the first things [he] wrote were realistic', his 'natural tendency would be toward fantasy and invention' (cited in Weiss 1993: 9). Indeed, it is in his later works that Calvino displays the greatest ingenuity in his choice of themes and formal structures. Beginning in the 1960s, we find an increasing propensity to do away with plot and psychological analysis in order to focus on the exploration of eccentric themes (scientific laws, paradoxical concepts, etc.) and, later, an attempt to shift the attention from the writer to the process of reading.

The short stories in *Cosmicomics* (1965) and *t zero* (1967) are particularly emblematic of this transition. These texts combined Calvino's interest in fantasy and science in an effort to render reality in new and eclectic ways. Yet, even if these works explore new themes and on occasion experiment with fragmentation, their form remains for the most part conventional, at times matching that of his neo-realist texts. They are generally first-person narratives following a traditional linear structure. Notwithstanding this formal conventionalism, inventiveness or play (thematic) was Calvino's new aim, an interest which prompted his association with Queneau's OULIPO group.

In one of his essays on Queneau, Calvino writes that the dominant concern for OULIPO was 'the acrobatics of the intellect and the imagination' (cited in Weiss 1993: 93), admitting that this became his central interest, too, from the late 1960s onwards. Although he drew inspiration from predecessors such as Edward Lear, Lewis Carroll or Jarry, he was particularly influenced by Queneau, specifically in his views on science, which had crucial consequences for his understanding of literature. Calvino felt that these disciplines faced similar problems, since they both construct 'models of the world which are continually being challenged', noting that science, which alternates between the 'inductive and the deductive method [...] has always to take care not to mistake its own linguistic conventions for objective laws' (cited in Weiss 1993: 95). Furthermore, he insisted on the fact that a 'culture' will be 'equal to the situation' only when 'the problems of science, those of philosophy, and those of literature are continually challenging each other' (Calvino in Weiss 1993: 95). It is this new-found conceptualization of literature, inherited from OULIPO, which encourages him to leave realism aside to focus on fantasy.

The first work to emerge from this affiliation was *The Castle of Crossed Destinies* (1969), which uses tarot cards as the structuring principle of the narrative.[7]

---

[7] Calvino's *The Castle of Crossed Destinies* and *The Tavern of Crossed Destinies* to some extent reappraise the procedure of relating an episode in different ways, deployed by Queneau in *Exercises*

Although this text is not linear, it is, as Robert Rushing notes, not precisely circular either, since even if the final words are 'ricominciano da capo', they do not promise 'a re-telling, but a new game' as the cards are shuffled, randomizing the order of the fragments (1998: 142). Moreover, when the narration does recommence, it does so with *The Tavern of Crossed Destinies* (1969). Be that as it may, the novel is clearly representative of an increasing attentiveness to structure which takes the shape of an attempt to rework conventional forms into new ones. Texts such as *The Castle* or *The Tavern* reveal an 'interdisciplinary command of literature' that allows Calvino to 'inventively use such literary structures as fable, story, plot, novel, and narration', reconfiguring them to produce what Wladimir Krysinski calls a 'philosophy of metafiction', a writing characterized primarily by its 'semiotic consciousness' (2002: 196). Calvino's metafiction reappraises and plays with conventional forms or patterns to express new preoccupations and realities through a fresh narrative language.

And so, if during the late 1950s Calvino's shift is chiefly thematic (from realism to fantasy), a decade later his desire for innovation is reflected in the structure of his works too. This decision to abandon psychology and introspection in order to focus on formal experimentation stems directly from the influence of Barthes' notion of *écriture*. Calvino had lectured on Barthes and the structuralist phenomenon,[8] discussing the problematic nature of language's referentiality, the arbitrariness of referential relationships and the way in which meaning depends on these. He also dwelled extensively on the role of the author and reader in interpreting a text, and the extent to which a narrative can incorporate diverse interpretations. His conclusion (like Barthes') was that writing should 'no longer' be 'narrating but saying that one is narrating', so that 'what one says becomes identified with the very act of saying' (Calvino in Weiss 1993: 130). Calvino sought to produce a kind of literature that would secure Barthes' approval as an author, rather than as a mere writer, drawing the reader's attention to the activity of writing (and reading) itself, rather than aiming to communicate something beyond the writing. In this way, both Barthes and Calvino (like Robbe-Grillet) struggle to make writing the 'end in itself', proclaiming the age of the reader and the death of the author. Calvino writes that in the future, the 'decisive moment of literary life will be that of reading', because the 'anachronistic' figure of the writer will 'vanish' (cited in Weiss 1993: 131). His own *écriture* clearly follows on from

---

in Style (1947).
[8] See 'Cybernetics and Ghosts' (1967).

Barthes' proclamation of 'the death of the author', a manifestation of the 'death of God' in literature.

In an oblique way, Calvino was thus responding to Nietzsche's philosophy in his desire to become an *écrivant* and produce reader-oriented narratives. However, other parallelisms draw these two writers together. Calvino appears to engage at a theoretical level with Nietzsche's philosophy in his opposition of *pathos* and *logos*, which bears a certain similarity to the opposition of Dionysus and Apollo. Some critics have also suggested that *Mr Palomar* (1983) responds to a crucial debate in philosophy, the opposition between systematization and objectivity (the Enlightenment, Hegelian idealism, dialectical materialism, analytical philosophy), and subjectivity and fragmentation (Nietzsche, Heidegger et al.), siding with the latter and therefore implying that 'he believed that in a postmodern age of uncertainty there are inevitably a lack of cohesive ideologies and an absence of decisive experience of life' (Simon 1986: 28). Moreover, Calvino famously discusses lightness in the first of his *Six Memos for the Next Millennium* (1988), reversing Nietzsche's notion of the eternal recurrence (in a manner similar to Milan Kundera's *The Unbearable Lightness of Being*) yet developing these views by analysing its presence in literature as a reaction to oppression. Although Nietzsche is absent from this memo, his influence in this respect is hard to deny since Calvino was familiar with the philosopher's work. Moreover, Leland Durantaye claims that Calvino discussed the idea of eternal recurrence with Giorgio Agamben, a topic to which the latter dedicated considerable attention, pointing out that in 'his last conversation with *Calvino*, Agamben recounts that they spoke not of the greatest weight but of the greatest lightness' (2009: 318).

Nietzschean tropes also appear in a number of the stories of *Cosmicomics*. In 'A Sign in Space', for instance, there is an analysis of language that is clearly reminiscent of Nietzsche's critique (notably in 'On Truth and Lies in a Nonmoral Sense'); and in 'Death' there is an allusion to the idea of eternal recurrence, or at least to the circularity of time and space, since Calvino describes the narrator's encounters with his beloved as 'a ritualistic repetition of an endless cosmic charade' (2018: 64). Although these stories are not themselves circular, there is a sense of circularity at the level of the collection as a whole (rather than within the stories' individual structures), since, as Weiss points out, 'the primordial experiences of the timeless Qfwfq [. . .] bring about a constant perspective, a continuous circularity and perpetual regression' (1993: 92).[9] Nevertheless,

---

[9] This effect is also present in Queneau's *Les fleurs bleues*, which Calvino translated into Italian.

this kind of circularity is not an absurd one (unlike Beckett's or Ionesco's). It is (somewhat like Borges') the outcome of the fusion of fantasy and reason, or as Geno Pampaloni puts it, of a 'poetic world' that, although it may cross 'over to the ineffable, or the metaphysical', nevertheless 'never disregards the rules of reason' (1988: 20).

Calvino also refers to Nietzsche's notion of the eternal return in his short story 't-zero', where he writes that 'the universe does nothing but pulsate between two extreme moments, forced to repeat itself forever – just as it has already repeated itself infinite times' (2012: 100). However, from his ideas on lightness we may gather that he did not take this notion seriously, either as a cosmological principle or as a psychological thought experiment. In fact, Calvino's texts are not circular because they reflect the idea of the eternal recurrence. His circularity is a subtle and playful one, achieved through faint allusions to the nature of time (as in 't-zero') or implicitly through the mediation of the narrator's consciousness, as in *Cosmicomics*. However, in what is perhaps Calvino's most original text, at least in terms of structure, *If on a Winter's Night a Traveller* (1979), the notion of circularity is of a very different nature and function.

Calvino described *If on a Winter's Night a Traveller* as a 'hypernovel', explaining that his aim was 'to give the essence of what a novel is by providing it in a concentrated form, in ten beginnings; each beginning develops in very different ways from a common nucleus, and each acts within a framework that both determines and is determined' (cited in Krysinski 2002: 197). The text is thus at the same time one novel and numerous stories: the ten individual uncompleted novels, the story of the reader(s) and the (implicit) overarching story of our reading the protagonist/reader's story. Owing to its nature as a complex patchwork of different narratives which the reader has to piece together, Gabriel Cram deems the text an '(almost detective) novel', stressing that it portrays 'a looped cycle of identity's confusion which describes an (endless) journey of self-referential nature, functioning as a metaphor for an act of reading itself, a permanent continuous discovery of the *plot*, the author and the creation system' (2008: 41). Above all, the text is a metanarrative, since its aim is not so much to tell a story as to explore the processes of literature and, more specifically, of reading, a feature that also becomes the underlying structuring principle of the work.

The novel is a clear example of the way in which Calvino reconfigured traditional forms in order to produce an experimental structure that addresses contemporary issues. In this case, he reappraises the frame-narrative device, refashioning it to create a new kind of narrative-within-a-narrative. While this technique has been used extensively throughout literary history (notably in texts like the *Arabian Nights* or *The Canterbury Tales*), unlike in conventional frame-narratives, it is not the act of storytelling or the voice of the author that prompts the different sub-stories but the act of reading. If in conventional narratives-within-a-narrative such as the *Arabian Nights*, it is figure of the narrator, that is, Shaharazad, who gives rise to and organizes the different sub-narratives, Calvino's novel is instead structured around the reader's experience: initially 'You'. As well as revealing Calvino's originality and exhibiting the influence of Barthes' ideas, this shift shows that Calvino was not only a writer, he was above all a reader, a viewpoint which he strived to impose on his writing, perhaps encouraged by his experiences as an editor.

Although several critics identify the novel as circular (and accordingly establish it as a postmodern text),[10] its circularity differs radically from that of the other circular narratives analysed in this book. In fact, the text's central story, the experiences of the couple of readers, follows a linear structure and has the conventional denouement of bourgeois marriage novels. Yet, this resolution is in actuality a subversion of the convention, since the protagonist's decision to marry is driven by his realization that in conventional narratives 'the hero and heroine married, or else they died' (Calvino 2010: 259), Moreover, this linear structure coexists with a number of circular ones. To begin with, the repeated inclusion of novels that start but never end brings the story reiteratively to a new beginning (albeit in each case a different one – an eternal recurrence of the similar). This constant intrusion of new unresolved texts creates a circular effect of return by continuously taking the narrative back to the point of departure. The repeated interruption of the succession of stories also undermines the idea and value of plot and of conventional narrative forms.

More importantly, however, the novel acquires a circular form at the level of the reading experience. The repeated references to its title, starting with its opening line, function as a token of the text's fictive status. These references remind the reader regularly that she/he is engaged in the process of reading a

---

[10] Jason P. Vest, for instance, remarks that owing to its 'circular plot', it 'becomes a postmodern narrative that threatens to endlessly repeat itself' (2009: 142), and Weiss claims that 'The text's circularity and reliance on repetition is paradigmatic of postmodernism' (1993: 183).

work of fiction (that work in particular). The narrative hence becomes circular by virtue of these constant reminders that bring the reader momentarily out of the work and then back into it. Thus, while the protagonist's story is linear, the act of reading becomes circular, both by virtue of the continuous inclusions of new beginnings (that bring the narrative back to the point of departure) and by the circular references that take the reader repeatedly out of the narrative, forcing us to reflect upon the reading experience. The recurrent references to the novel's title prompt the reader to become aware of the process of reading by reminding us that we are in fact engaged in such a process. The novel's auto-referentiality is therefore key in bringing about the circular effect that redirects the reader from story to discourse and, more specifically, to the process of narration, highlighting that its principal function is a metanarrative one.

Furthermore, the use of the second person imparts another circular effect on the narrative that also underscores this function. The repeated references to the reader accentuate its metanarrative status further since rather than encouraging a process of identification with the protagonist as in conventional narratives, they bring us out of the text (once again) through the paradoxical effect generated by the act of addressing us directly and telling us things about ourselves (the reader) that conflict with what we know or who we are.[11] As well as highlighting the fictive nature of the addressee (who we soon find out is not us but a fictional reader[12]), these appellations (like the references to the novel's title) take us, at the same time, through and *out* of the narrative because they invite us to freeze the story in order to compare ourselves to the hypothetical reader and hence to reconsider our reading experience in relation to his. So, while these self-references do not bring us back to the point of departure in a circular fashion, they nevertheless take us repeatedly out of the story into a non-temporal, purely discursive space of reflection.

The narrative's opening and ending also configure additional circular effects. As Marie-Laure Ryan observes, Calvino achieves 'The only way to generate infinite recursion in a closed and finite text' (2002: 381), through the self-referential

---

[11] This differs from the situation when the narrator of a first-person narrative speaks: we are encouraged to believe that narrator, since we know nothing about him/her.

[12] The author is also fictionalized in this process, since the narrator and author do not correspond (Calvino is referred to in the third person: 'You are about to read Italo Calvino's new novel').

opening statement ('You are about to read [. . .]'). This self-reference suggests a fractal infinite recursion, since if we were to include the whole novel within the reference, the text would contain itself and refer to itself infinitely, in the manner which Ryan outlines:

> the text expands logically into
>
>> You are about to read Italo Calvino's new novel, 'You are about to read Italo Calvino's new novel, *If on a Winter's Night a Traveler*'
>
> which in turn expands into
>
>> You are about to read Italo Calvino's new novel, 'You are about to read Italo Calvino's new novel, "You are about to read Italo Calvino's new novel, *If on a Winter's Night a Traveler*"'
>
> And so on ad infinitum.
>
> (cited in Richardson 2002: 381–2)

An equivalent ending also returns the reader to the novel's opening. This final self-reference entails a circular return through its allusion to the novel's opening, but also because, as Jason P. Vest argues, it underscores that the narrative's 'textual ambiguities may never cease' (2009: 142). This circular return allows the text to transcend all 'strict generic, thematic, and symbolic boundaries', both because it 'call[s] its own premise into doubt' and because the 'textual game' in which the reader is implicated 'never resolves itself into a firm denouement' (Vest 2009: 142). Moreover, as in the case of other circular narratives, its circular nature is augured through the inclusion of minor devices, such as the *mise en abyme* of Flannery's diary in chapter eight.

All things considered, Calvino's metanarrative achieves a reconfiguration of the circular form that differs radically from other examples of narrative circularity, through the symbiosis of an overarching linear development (undermined by the arbitrary conditions leading to it) and internal circular structures. In this way, Calvino shows that reading is not a linear process, that such a notion (implicit in conventional narratives) is a farce and that texts hold infinite interpretative possibilities. The novel's linear story is undermined through the constant digressions that break up its development, so that its discourse overpowers its plot. This discourse becomes circular through various self-references and appellations rather than through the repetition of a passage, forcing the reader to reflect repeatedly upon the roles and experiences of writer and reader.

Julio Cortázar's 'The Continuity of Parks' (1964)

Even more than Borges, Julio Cortázar was an author divided between Latin America and Europe, Buenos Aires and Paris. Born in Brussels, bearing European ancestors (Basque, French and German), spending his early life in Argentina, yet moving to Paris at the age of thirty-seven (where he was to reside for the remainder of his life, at first voluntarily but of necessity from 1977), he was irremediably torn between both continents. Thus, despite the fact that he wrote in a markedly Argentine Spanish, his European heritage cannot be overlooked. Leading Cortázar scholars such as Peter Sandish stress that it is of 'crucial importance' to keep in mind that Cortázar 'began and ended his life in Europe [. . .] if one is to understand his literature and the attitudes of some of his critics' (2001: 1). Cortázar was raised in French and did not speak any Spanish when he arrived in Argentina, making him an outsider both abroad and in his motherland from early childhood.[13] He famously commented on the fact that the inability to pronounce the Spanish 'r' further ostracized him from his classmates as a schoolboy, a division that he suffered throughout his lifetime. While he was criticized for being an ex-patriot by fellow Argentine writers, it was Borges who published his first story, 'House Taken Over', in 1946. Cortázar also stressed his compatriot's influence, avowing that he had a profound impact on his work, encouraging him to leave aside the rather romantic, realist popular literature that was typical at the time, by showing him (and his whole generation) 'the unprecedented possibilities of the fantastic' (cited in Alazraki 1999: 57; my translation).

Cortázar had a passion for reading so extreme that he was taken to hospital as a child for fear that it was having a detrimental effect upon his health, and, like Borges, displayed a vivid philosophical interest from a very young age, claiming that even as a child he had been 'a tiny metaphysical animal' (cited in Standish 2001: 2). Yet if his passion for reading, his interest in metaphysics and Borges' influence were decisive factors in his development as a writer, even more so was his move to Paris in the 1950s. It was in Paris that Cortázar published his first collection of stories, *Bestiary* (1951), found his own literary style and became widely recognized as a writer. In the same decade, two other collections followed: *End of the Game* (1956) and *The Secret Weapons* (1959). The second

---

[13] As we shall see, it is precisely the idea of alterity that encouraged Cortázar to write his first circular narratives.

of these collections, in particular, displays a growing interest in the notion of identity, the nature of existence and the process of fiction, subjects that would become crucial throughout his later work.

Although, as we shall see, there are hints of circular structures in some of Cortázar's early texts, including 'House Taken Over', his first stories display, in most cases, a rather conventional narrative form. Gradually, however, his works come to exhibit an increasing complexity, both thematic and structural, a development culminating in what has repeatedly been characterized as his magnum opus, *Hopscotch* (1963). Prior to the writing of this seminal text, Cortázar experimented with increasingly eclectic forms in the unclassifiable micro-narratives of *Cronopios and Famas* (1962). These texts, which range from outlines of stories to deep meditations, sometimes pages long and others of no more than a couple paragraphs, are irreverent towards traditional narrative conventions and display a growing attentiveness to form. They have such structural heterogeneity that some possess essayistic features, even if, as Martin S. Stabb points out, 'few critics would accept [them] as essays without serious reservations' (1995: 58). Peter Standish identifies Cortázar's increasing formal inventiveness as one of three fundamental features of his work, explaining that given 'the variety of [his] output', a great part of his oeuvre 'cannot easily be described in terms of traditional literary genres' (2001: xi).

While it may be hard to classify many of Cortázar's stories, this does not mean that they are chaotic or unorganized. On the contrary, Cortázar was particularly skilful in producing 'defined, precise, and clear-cut' texts that, as Calvino recognizes, are extremely effective in allowing 'images to crystallize into a well-defined, memorable, and self-sufficient *form*, the icastic *form*', so necessary in a society flooded by 'prefabricated and homogeneous images' (1988: 92). Candid about this preoccupation, as early as 1947 he had already written a text that, although was only published in 1994, details his major concerns as a writer, particularly in relation to the structure of the novel: 'The Tunnel Theory'. Aware of the effort of authors such as Robbe-Grillet, Cortázar begins by highlighting the 'splintering of structures considered as normative by scholarship' that had been taking place since the beginning of the century (2003: 69; my translation), referring specifically to the Balzacian model (like Robbe-Grillet). He argues that although such writing was satisfactory to its time and ambition, the contemporary author needs to create a new literature according to 'the problematics imposed by his own time', namely, the belief that 'the human condition is not aesthetically reducible' and that literature falsifies the human being when it tries to capture him in his essence or totality (2003: 69).

So, unlike Robbe-Grillet, Cortázar did not seek a destructive movement but a constructive one. He explains that the writer who transgresses the literary norms is aggressive only because he understands that any mode of literary expression is particular to its time and not because he believes that he is incapable of expressing himself effectively. Cortázar thus urges the 'contemporary' writer to be aggressive towards tradition in order to find freedom, which 'is not a free gift but an existential conquest' (2003: 70). He calls this a tunnel-like aggression, since it only destroys in order to build. He also insists that this is the common movement of philosophy, poetry and mysticism, three similar responses to one and the same ontological anxiety. Similar to Robbe-Grillet's subsequent call for a new novel and Calvino's insistence upon the infinite interpretative possibilities in reader-oriented texts, Cortázar's views are clearly reminiscent of Nietzsche's perspectivism and 'death of God' logic, since they reject a traditional idea of literature, based on the belief that reality is graspable and representable, essentially organized and whole, rather than plural and chaotic.

A man of his time, Cortázar was evidently familiar with Nietzsche's writings. There is an explicit reference to the philosopher in *Hopscotch* (see 2004: 118), and again in *From the Observatory* (1972) (see 1972: 31), as well as evidence of various parallelisms with Nietzsche's philosophy in several of his other works. In attempting to outline what he broadly identifies as Cortázar's conception of literature, Roberto González Echevarría points out that his 'mythology of writing' bears 'a Nietzschean imprint', signalling that Nietzsche's Dionysian-Apollonian dichotomy is embodied in the struggle between Theseus and Apollo in the early play, *The Kings* (1949), as well as between Johnny and Bruno in 'The Pursuer' (1959) (see 2010: 108). Likewise, Gustavo Pellón argues that the 'paradigm of ancient Greek culture' that operates in one of the poems included in *Around the Day in Eighty Worlds* (1967), 'Greece 59', is also 'Nietzschean' (see 1998). Furthermore, several scholars have identified the influence of the notion of the eternal recurrence on Cortázar, although they mostly refer to Heraclitus' discussions of the concept rather than to Nietzsche's.[14] Even the famous 'rallying cry of "hombre nuevo"', supposedly borrowed from Che, may be linked to Nietzsche's *Übermensch* since, as Domenic Moran points out, Cortázar 'always seemed to employ the term as if, in the last instance, it were apolitical' (2000: 20).

---

[14] See, for instance, Praet and Monballieu (2011: 27).

Moreover, Jaime Alazraki's characterization of Cortázar's work as exemplary of a neo-fantastic poetics clearly aligns him with Nietzsche's philosophy, since the Argentine writer's efforts were motivated by a desire to find an alternative to 'that false realism' that implies 'that everything can be neatly described as was upheld by the philosophic and scientific optimism of the eighteenth century' (Cortázar in Alazraki 1999: 11). In rejecting the idealist belief that the universe is governed by 'a system of laws, of principles, of causal relations, of well-defined psychologies, of well mapped geographies' (1991: 11), Cortázar shares Nietzsche's view of the world as 'an invention, a meagre sum of observations' (2018: 203), his rejection of metaphysics, particularly the Judaeo-Christian tradition, and his critique of language and the scientific or philosophical categorization of the world into binary oppositions. Like Calvino, Cortázar pushes reason to the irrational and strives to find new ways in which to describe or represent reality. Fantasy and formal experimentation are pitted against Platonism, positivism or Western thought more broadly, through the creation of narratives that depict the world beyond the conventional concepts and categories that frame it, aiming to render reality free from the filter of theology or systematization.

Cortázar sets out to dig his (formal) tunnel by experimenting with circularity in order to depict the relationship between identity and alterity in several of his short stories. Although the rough outline of a conventional linear narrative is in some ways preserved, the notion of circularity becomes crucial in these fictions. His first published text already contains circular undertones that subvert the reader's expectations of a neat resolution and set the story's movement. Written from the perspective of a plural first-person narrator, the action in 'House Taken Over' follows a circular trajectory whereby the protagonists, initially defined by their status as the inhabitants of an old mansion, gradually lose their identity in order to become the very entities to which they are initially opposed – an opposition upon which their very character relies. Although the text has been read as an allegory of Peronism, Cortázar denied this political focus, stressing that his stories should not be restricted by a particular interpretation. The narrative allows a broader range of allegorical significance, accommodating a variety of contrasting meanings. Standish argues that its central quality is precisely this ambiguity, owing to which the protagonists and their antagonists (the usurpers) may stand symbolically for a range of entities. Abstruseness aside, what remains clear is the movement underlying the development of the story, the gradual loss of stability and the protagonists' inability to overcome their tribulations, leading to a reversal of the initial situation. This circular movement, as well as representing the unfolding of a defeat, helps to elucidate the frail nature of their condition, the perpetual threat of incessant change and the latent 'otherness' in the depths of the protagonists.

Even more explicitly, Cortázar's short story 'Axolotl' (1956) displays a similar kind of circularity resulting from the protagonist's gradual transformation into the very otherness that (by opposition) initially seems to define him. Cortázar supposedly wrote the story in response to the idea that it is impossible for us to project ourselves 'for even a second into the structure of animals in order to get an idea, from their side, of the reality they perceive' (in Standish 2001: 53). It is this opposition of two irreconcilable perspectives that constitutes the narrative's key theme and structuring principle. Although it is related in a conventional manner, as a first-person narrative that develops chronologically, the text becomes circular through the narrator's final metamorphosis into an axolotl: from subject to object of the narration. Moreover, the story's linear development is undermined by the synopsis of the entire narrative included in the first paragraph, which contains its totality within three sentences. 'Axolotl' also includes various internal devices that anticipate or mirror the final circular twist (the first paragraph being one of them). There is a kind of *mise en abyme* or, rather, a 'self-referential twist' (a device which Cortázar reappraised in a number of subsequent texts) in the denouement, as the narrator confesses that he finds 'consolation in thinking that perhaps he [a new narrator] is going to write about us, believing he is imagining a story, he is going to write about axolotls' (1995: 385). Rather than providing us with a resolution, the denouement's circular movement opens the narrative: it appears to constitute its beginning, or at least a new starting point – that of a future narration and transformation. Consequently, stories such as 'House Taken Over' and 'Axolotl' display an underlying circularity that serves to allegorize the nature of identity. Their circular movement describes the way in which the protagonists' character, initially constructed in opposition to an unknown or alien 'other', develops and eventually collapses, leaving them at the opposite end of the spectrum that defined them at the outset.[15]

A different and more complex kind of circular structure can be found in Cortázar's major work, *Hopscotch*. The novel famously offers the reader two possible ways of reading it, a choice that subjects the narrative to two alternative

---

[15] The same structure is apparent in two of Camus' short stories included in *Exile and the Kingdom* (1957): 'The Renegade or a Confused Spirit' and 'The Guest', the second of which even alludes to the circular transformation of the protagonist (who becomes his 'other') in the original title ('L'Hôte'), since the French word means both host and guest, and that is precisely what the reader is left wondering at the end of the story: Who is who?

forms. If we follow the first choice, the overarching structure of the fragments is quasi-linear, beginning in Paris and ending in Buenos Aires, although with flashbacks and passages that are hard to locate. However, the second choice results in a more intricate structure: it is non-chronological and thus undermines the unity and importance of its plot, reinforcing the fragmented nature of the text instead. Additionally, the second choice also entails an infinite recursion. In this way, *Hopscotch* has the potential to become either a fragmented quasi-linear narrative or a circular one, yet one that diverges from other circular forms studied in this book since instead of achieving an endless regression by forcing the reader to return to the first chapter and reread the entire text, it is only the two final fragments whose eternal repetition is implied. Emily Hicks also reminds us that throughout the narrative Cortázar 'throws into question the unity of personal consciousness' by making the narrator a heterogeneous voice that shifts perspective, 'slips, and dissolves into a random order of bits of information' repeatedly, making the story 'one of eternally recurring fragments' (1991: 37). In both formal choices many of the descriptions and situations reappear elsewhere in the novel, undermining further the unidirectionality of the narrative and instilling a subtle sense of circularity.

Hicks links the effect of *Hopscotch*'s fragmented narrative voice and recurring structure to several passages where Nietzsche discusses the eternal recurrence (see 1991: 37), although she stresses that the text's poignancy lays precisely in Cortázar's decision to provide two formal alternatives rather than imposing one, leaving the matter of the text's structure an open question. Hicks also argues that despite certain echoes of previous moments, in the first formal choice 'the structures do not repeat themselves', emphasizing that by opting for this 'kind of undecidability', Cortázar is in fact distilling Nietzsche's notion of time in accordance with the crisis of values of the post-war period (1991: 38–9). As a result, *Hopscotch* achieves a plural structuration that contains various possibilities: on the one hand, a fragmented structure emphasizing a sort of discontinuous continuity through its faint linear development, and, on the other, an equally fragmented narrative which is non-linear and implies the infinite recursiveness of its two final fragments, submerging the reader in a whirlpool of dialogues that suggestively bestow an eternal quality upon the final moment of the narration.

Nevertheless, perhaps the best example of a circular narrative by Cortázar is his 1964 short story 'Continuity of Parks', a piece that blurs the boundaries between fiction and reality. Dulce María Zúiga characterizes it as a circular text that has the structure of the alchemic image of the Ouroboros (see 2006: 93), while Olive Classe describes it as a 'textual puzzle' playing 'on the idea of the intermingling of reality and fiction, literature and fact, author and reader' (2000: 313). Froilán Fernández goes as far as to claim that the story is Cortázar's test piece of a circular narrative, linking its author to Borges on account of their status as innovators of non-linear literature (see 2008: xx). To be sure, instead of providing the reader with various choices determining the kind of form that the narrative will follow (as in *Hopscotch*), in this story Cortázar deploys an explicitly circular structure which problematizes the text's referentiality, inviting us to reflect upon the process of reading and the nature of literature.

As in Cortázar's earlier 'pseudo-circular texts', in 'Continuity of Parks' circularity is achieved by means of a final revelation. Yet, this time it is not a change in the protagonist's identity that brings about the circular twist, but rather, the disclosure that the protagonist of the narration is also the protagonist of the book he is reading. In this way, the narrative fuses what the reader perceives as two different spaces (initial and final) into one in the text's denouement. The ending produces a kind of reversal that has a shocking effect, which Sara Castro-Klaren describes as a slap to the reader's face that forces us 'to follow and accept the inexorable denouement of the story as demanded by the obsessive game played by the writing subject' (cited in Chávez-Silverman and Hernández 2000: 241). The outcome is an undermining of the reader's expectations about the logical development of the text (which, as a detective story of some sort, implies causal connections and a clear resolution) and the problematization of its referentiality. The protagonist's double nature, at once an external entity in relation to the text he is reading and a character within it, destabilizes the implicit system of references intrinsic to narrative – it no longer refers to a world of fantasy but fails through its dual referentiality. In this way, the assumed relationship between literature and reality collapses, recalling Todorov's structuralist mantra that literature 'is created from literature, not from reality' (1975: 10).

The story's circular form thus challenges our assumptions about the relationship between narrative and the world, and between reader and narrative. The protagonist's transformation from a passive reader to one of the characters in the book mirrors the way in which we, as readers, embody (and, in so doing, complete) the characters of a narrative. By fusing reader and protagonist, the story also reveals the incompleteness of a subject's identity and the importance of another person's perspective in completing it. If the circular structures of Calvino's *If on a Winter Night* problematize our identification with the protagonist, Cortázar's circular twist instead seems to mimic the way in which we identify with the characters of the texts we read, indicating that this process of identification is fundamental in completing their characterization. The reader finishes writing the text by way of superimposing his personae on the narrative's protagonists and, in doing so, to some extent becomes (through his reading experience) the characters he embodies.

Cortázar's circular structures hence serve various overarching purposes. The subtle circular forms of his earlier texts represent the frail nature of identity and the key role of alterity in its configuration. The protagonists' very character arises from an opposition to an alien 'other' that gradually collapses – the unbridgeable abyss separating them from their antagonists breaking down in the text's denouement. This gradual deterioration of the opposition displays an inherent 'sameness', which is initially imperceptible. While some of his works are not circular at the level of the story or discourse, Cortázar achieves an undermining of linearity through circular twists. Sometimes the circular form is merely suggested, on other occasions it is presented as a choice (as in *Hopscotch*), yet in every case it elucidates the unstable nature of an apparent or assumed stability. Rather than constructing his circular structures through the repetition of a final passage, Cortázar reverses the initial state of affairs, shocking the reader with such reversals. His circular forms thus aim to encourage reflection upon different aspects of the process of reading, the nature of narrative and identity: the way in which we construct reality inadvertently, often losing sight of how our representations make up our world.

Maurice Blanchot's 'The Madness of the Day' (1949/1973)

A French writer and literary theorist, Maurice Blanchot became a student of philosophy at the University of Strasbourg in the late 1920s, where he received a formal education that shines forth unequivocally throughout his oeuvre. Blanchot spent the decade prior to the outbreak of the Second World War criticizing the French government from a right-wing nationalist position, while also warning against the threat of Nazi Germany in several articles published in various nationalist journals, including *Le Rempart*, *Aux écoutes* and *L'Insurgé*. Yet, following the outbreak of the war, he turned his focus almost exclusively to the literary world, dedicating his time to writing works of literary criticism and fiction, reflecting on the nature of language and its relationship to truth, and setting the scene for much of the ensuing continental philosophy in France. Blanchot's work displays a persistent struggle to overcome the limitations of genre, making many of his texts hard to categorize as either strictly literary, critical or philosophical. However, his break with tradition and his interest in exploring the limits of narrative form are not so much a consequence of a desire to innovate as of his philosophical outlook. For Blanchot's focus was chiefly philosophical, which is why Emmanuel Levinas famously described his writing as 'language of pure transcendence, without correlative' (1996: 41).

More specifically, Blanchot's central concern was the question 'What is literature?', which he believed had received 'only meaningless answers' in the past (2003: 294). Traditionally literature was mostly understood as *poiesis*, a notion that Blanchot countered with the idea of writing as a negative force: a '*force caustique*'. Beginning with his 1943 collection of almost sixty essays, *Faux Pas*, and his 1949 collection *The Work of Fire*, Blanchot plays out this meditation on the nature of literature and writing, discussing a heterogeneous array of authors (particularly of the nineteenth and twentieth centuries), at times fusing critical and fictional discourses. As John Gregg observes, these texts show 'the emergence of a kind of literary pantheon' to which Blanchot would return throughout his career 'in his future discussions of what he calls the approach to the space of literature: Mallarmé, Kafka, Char, Hölderlin and Nietzsche' (1994: 3).

Although Blanchot did not engage explicitly with Nietzsche's work in depth until the late 1950s, his relationship with the philosopher was significant throughout his life. Joseph D. Kuzma points out that in 1946 Blanchot was living in Eze (the village in the south of France where Nietzsche wrote some of the most important parts of *Zarathustra*), a conscious choice of setting representative of the importance of the philosopher for him, even before his move to Paris. Blanchot would go on to write about Nietzsche repeatedly, and Gregg has demonstrated that his work owes much to 'Nietzsche's call to overthrow Platonism' (1994: 6). Blanchot published several texts on Nietzsche after the war, reappraising his work in later years in essays such as 'Nietzsche, Today' (1958) and in longer narratives like *The Infinite Conversation* (1969). Nietzsche was particularly influential in Blanchot's thinking about form, specifically on the notion of the fragmentary:[16]

> Fragmentary: meaning neither the fragment, as part of a whole, nor the fragmentary in itself. Aphorisms, sayings, maxims, quotations, proverbs,

---

[16] See, in particular, Blanchot's 'Nietzsche and Fragmentary Writing' (1969).

themes, set phrases, are perhaps all further removed from it than that infinitely continuous discourse whose only content is 'its own continuity', a continuity that is only sure of itself when it supposes itself to be circular and, in that circuit, accepts the precondition of a return whose law is outside [*au-dehors*] and where the outside is outside the law [*hors-loi*]. (Blanchot in Hill 2012: 31)

For Blanchot, fragmentary writing avoids or precludes closure, achieving instead a discourse without end: fragmented yet infinitely continuous, transgressing all laws and led by a radical scepticism. Leslie Hill observes that when 'writing about Nietzsche, Blanchot was fond of citing Jaspers's remark that every proposition in the thinker's work is echoed elsewhere by another that contradicts it', not to highlight inconsistencies in his thought but to show that Nietzsche's philosophy is fragmentary because it exposes the irregularities of concepts, the 'otherness that escapes conceptual explication and can only be inscribed by way of a logic of supplementarity' (2012: 36). Blanchot argued that Nietzsche's aphorisms are underpinned by a 'fragmentary demand' because they at once reject systematization and tend towards it.

His desire to create a fragmentary language that could 'simultaneously name the possible and respond to the impossible' (Hill 2012: 37) brought Blanchot face to face with the question of nihilism. In an essay called 'The Limits of Experience: Nihilism', he examines Nietzsche's discussion of the concept, defining it paradoxically as both 'an extreme that cannot be gotten beyond' and 'the only true path of going beyond', noting that these 'oscillations' should not be 'attributed to Nietzsche's unstable genius or character' or 'to his own "shortcomings"', since 'They are the very sense of his thought' (1977: 121). Blanchot also discusses Nietzsche's idea of eternal recurrence as the culmination of this 'logic of terror', a paradoxical outcome of the willing of absolute nihilism, a reversal of absolute negation into an absolute, eternal affirmation. Blanchot warned against the theodicy of the Hegelian dialectic, which posits the end of history and the synthesis of all conflict as absolute knowledge (indeed, his oeuvre persistently rejects Hegelian idealism). He draws attention to the fact that philosophical discourse presupposes this 'Aristotelian/Hegelian temporality', namely 'a logical time or narrative with plot and hero (the concept) who achieves self-identity by overcoming (*Aufhebung*) the random and contingent, subsuming them into his destiny as purposeful and justified after all' (Bruns 1997: 191). While he countered this notion with the idea of the eternal return, he did not choose one temporality over the other (or mean this as 'Nietzsche overcoming Hegel'), but, as Gerald Bruns stresses, emphasized both as 'multiple dimensions' allowing us 'to "live" each of the events that is ours by way of a double relation' (1997: 192). As we shall see, it is this double relation that is exposed through the use of the circular form in some of his narratives.

Gregg sketches a rough outline of Blanchot's narrative oeuvre consisting of three stages: 'the novels of the 1940s, the *récits* of the 1950s, and the fragmentary books (unclassifiable as purely narrative works) of the 1960s and 1970s' (1994: 3–4). These late texts in particular display what Blanchot calls the 'bizarre dialogue' between the words 'critique' and 'creative', as well as his belief that the aim of the writer is to dwell upon the question of the origin and nature of literature. According to Blanchot, critics should not impose value judgements on a work but explore its range of possibilities and seek to elucidate the conditions that make it possible. He links this process to the Kantian critique of pure reason, noting that if Kant's work 'is the interrogation of the conditions of possibility of scientific experience', criticism should likewise be 'tied to the search for the possibility of literary experience', understanding this search here as an 'action within and in view of the creative space' (Blanchot in Allen 2016: 284).

Blanchot's two first novels, *Thomas the Obscure* (1941) and *Aminadab* (1942), are clearly representative of this preoccupation. These works raise his central question of the nature of literature by overthrowing many of the core values of conventional narratives, such as cohesion, coherence or verisimilitude. Like the earlier short stories 'The Last Word' (1935) and 'The Idyll' (1936), his two first novels present an initial stability that is shattered violently in the course of the story. The texts are 'anti-realistic'. They have abrupt beginnings, where almost no pre-contextual information is given to situate the characters or state of affairs and sudden endings where the story precipitously breaks down for no apparent reason. In particular, *Thomas L'Obscur* throws the reader into an uncanny narrative world, whose heterogeneity problematizes many of the distinctions upon which we categorize and explain conventional novels. Hill identifies this work as 'Part philosophical inquiry, part *Bildungsroman*, part inner experience, part self-reflective *mise en abyme*, part Pentecostal fable, part apocalyptic rhapsody, part ironic romance, part stylistic *tour de force*' (2002: 54), a description that clearly underscores its complexity, multiplicity and unconventionality. Aside from the difficulty in defining the text thematically and stylistically, it is also formally ambiguous. As Hill argues, the novel retains a 'residual narrative structure that follows a vaguely circular pattern' (2002: 54), since it both begins and ends with the protagonist by the sea, throwing himself into 'the currents, which quickly immersed him' at the novel's opening and again into 'the flood of crude images' at its closing (Blanchot 1988: 7, 108). However, this circular structure is downplayed by a coexistent linear development of sorts that also disintegrates at the cost of the protagonists' reflections, which occupy the narrative's limelight.

In any case, the importance of circularity for Blanchot is evident throughout his oeuvre, from his early discussions of Nietzsche to his late dialogues with Klossowksi (author of *Nietzsche and the Vicious Circle* (1969)). In discussing Mallarmé's *Igitur* (published posthumously in 1925) in *The Space of Literature* (1955), Blanchot dwells upon the concept of circularity, symbolically represented in the moment of midnight, describing it as a 'pure presence where nothing but the subsistence of nothing subsists':

> Midnight is precisely the hour that does not strike until after the dice are thrown, the hour which has never yet come, which never comes, the pure, ungraspable future, the hour eternally past. (1989: 116)

Midnight represents the circularity of time, the being of becoming, Nietzsche's 'Moment portal'. For Blanchot, circularity also represents the crucial movement of thought, which whenever it is 'caught in a circle [. . .] has touched upon something original, its point of departure beyond which it cannot move except to return' (1982: 93). Thought's movement is circular because it does not seek definite answers but perpetual reflection, in the same way that the Aristotelian/Hegelian requires the eternal return as its counterpart if one is to experience reality fully (and not merely as a means towards a specific end). Circularity is thus vital for Blanchot because it represents the focal point of fragmentary writing, the eternal renewal of thought, the moment of pure affirmation.

First published in 1949 in the literary review *Empédocle* under the dual title 'Récit?/Récit' and republished in book form as *The Madness of the Day* in 1973, Blanchot's abstruse first-person narrative brings together many of the issues which lie at the heart of his preoccupation with fragmentary writing, the nature of thought and literature. As Derrida points out, the dual title (it appears with a question mark on the cover of the review and without it elsewhere) is already representative of this fixation, inviting us to reflect upon a text's different versions – 'what is a version? what is a title?' (2004: 73). The first title frames the text within ambiguity in various respects: it offers no clues as to what the *récit* is about and problematizes its status as a *récit* through its initial question mark. In spite of its subsequent disappearance, this ambiguity remains (if only in the work's claim to the status of a *récit*). With the amended title of the second version, however, the text loses some of that ambiguity, and there is an intensification of the thematic focus by foregrounding the notions of light,[17] time and madness. The various titles suggest a hesitancy and a questioning of the work's nature as narrative. Moreover, they also allude to its circular form, since they are all in fact quotations from the text, suggesting a sort of *mise en abyme*.

While the term is absent in the original title, the idea of madness (*folie*) is clearly central to the work in an abstruse manner. As Derrida observes, it is unclear whether the madness to which the work refers is that of the 'impossible narrator', of an object of the narration ('the madness of a "character" following the narrator on the street'), of the reader, who becomes mad by reading the text, or of 'the day itself', this last notion reflecting another ambiguity (2004: 74). Is the madness of the day a madness of the times, as Levinas claims – the 'Madness of now, madness of the day. Madness of Auschwitz which has not been able to pass' (1996: 159); the madness of the light of Enlightenment or a more perplexingly abstract madness? According to Derrida, the madness here is the one that

> consists in seeing the light, vision or visibility, from an experience of blindness. If from 'life' we appeal to 'light', from *vie* to *vision*, we can speak here of sur-vie, of living on in a life-after-life or a life-after-death, as sur-vision, 'seeing on' in a vision-beyond-vision. To see sight or vision or visibility, to see beyond what is visible, is not merely 'to have a vision' in the usual sense of the word, but to see-beyond-sight, to see-sight-beyond-sight. (Derrida 2004: 91)

This madness is thus the result of an extreme lucidity, an ability to see beyond the structures that condition sight, the experience of seeing itself. It is, as Bruns claims, far from a 'delusion or bewilderment, not incoherent but merely open (neutral or cool) with respect to the rule of noncontradiction or the internal logic of propositions, narratives and systems' (1997: 148). In trying to describe this madness – to express the inexpressible, write the unwritable or put into a system of words what is unsystematic – the narrative's circular form becomes crucial. The narrator falls into an endless regression, his tale becomes an eternal circle because only through an infinite circular fragmentary sequence can this 'madness of the day' be expressed.

Derrida links this moment of 'vision-beyond-vision' (2004: 75) to Nietzsche's observation in *Ecce Homo* that he is located at the middle point between life and

---

[17] The word 'jour' is translated as both 'day' and 'light'.

death, past and future, recalling (once again) Zarathustra's 'Moment portal'. The experience of the madness of the day corresponds to the realization of the idea of eternal recurrence – the sight of the eternal present around which everything revolves in a continuous flux. This experience is rendered through fragmentary writing: an intermittent sequence of passages combining the discontinuous description of scenes and of the experience of the madness of the day, of pure thought. Structuring this relentless succession of images is the circular twist, which also unveils the narrative's origin: 'I had been asked: Tell us "*just* exactly" what happened. A story? I began: I am not learned, I am not ignorant' (Blanchot 1981: 18). This return to the opening lines causes a fissure in the text, generating what Derrida calls a 'double cross-invagination structure' within which the whole text threatens to repeat itself endlessly:

> The beginning of the end describes in an abyss-structure [i.e. in an inserted miniature representing the whole] the structure of the 'narrative', the 'recit' (?) entitled *La folie du jour*. This 'narrative' *seems* indeed to *begin* with a certain sentence that will subsequently be quoted towards the end as part of the narrative, unless the first sentence quotes in advance the one that comes at the end and that relates the first words of a narrative. [. . .] this structure [. . .] deprives the text of any beginning and of any decidable edge or border, of any heading or letterhead. (2004: 92–3)

The moment of return represents the focal point of the abyss within which the madness of the day strives to come to light. The narrator's circular tale attempts to render the madness, to explain it to his addressees, but it cannot conform to the structure of conventional narratives. It requires an endless regression that strives to cast new light on the nature of the madness, forever circumscribing a nucleus that remains inexpressible.

By unveiling the origin of the story, the circular denouement also brings into focus once again Blanchot's fundamental question regarding the nature of literature:

> I told them the whole story and they listened, it seems to me, with interest, at least in the beginning. But the end was a surprise to all of us. 'That was the beginning,' they said. 'Now get down to the facts.' How so? The story was over. (1981: 18)

The narrator's acknowledgement that he is 'not capable of forming a story', and his describing the issue as an 'illness', casts further light on the nature of the madness (Blanchot 1981: 18). While the circular return represents the narrator's struggle to speak the unspeakable thought, his inability to produce a meaningful story that satisfies his listeners (doctors) places the idea of narrative in diametrical opposition to the madness of the day: as a dark or nocturnal sanity perhaps (the Platonic, Aristotelian, Hegelian description of life as plot). Narrative is equated to the causal structuration of reality – of a significant sequence of 'facts' as reality, the imposition of teleology upon existence, the logical explanation and connection of phenomena. The process of creating stories, antithetical to the narrator's chaotic experience of illumination, is rejected on account of its incapacity to render the experience of madness or to describe his life subsequent to the transformation. Consequently, the narrator rejects the process of storytelling not because of a personal incompetence but because of the narrative's inherent inability to render reality.

The fissure caused by the circular form also suggests additional ideas about the nature and origin of literature. As Christophe Bident observes, the resolution does not bring us to a last event but to 'the narrative word itself' (1998: 283). Rather than referring to an external reality, the *récit* describes the process of storytelling. This is why Michael Newman argues that the text 'is impossible in so far as the event that is to be described or narrated was never present' (cited in Gill 2005: 164),[18] this event being the *récit* itself. Accordingly, the narrator's tale is rejected by its listeners and then by its narrator, not because of its lack of causal connections and circular structure but because of its problematic referential status (implicitly identifying linearity and referentiality as prerequisites of narrative). Furthermore, the circular twist unveils the practical reasons motivating the tale (the doctors' interrogation), establishing narrative as the response to a demand for answers. However, instead of an explanation (given the impossibility of one), the circular form transforms the text into 'a *representation*, a *mise en scène*' of the 'demand for narrative' (Derrida 2004: 94).

Although the *récit* is forced out of its circular movement, halted by the addressee's rejection of it, the unrelenting spectre of the circular form remains. While the narrator's final words attempt to put an end to the story (indeed, to all stories), they fail to do so, referring back as they do to the original title of the work (and thus suggesting a spectral circularity). The promise to have done with all stories only suggests a refusal to conform to the addressee's requests and expectations. Hence, such a promise does not so much imply the end of the

---

[18] For this reason, the ending has been interpreted by Michael Newman as re-enacting Nietzsche's thought of eternal recurrence, since the anti-referential nature of the story is indicative of the idea that 'there simply is no present' (see Gill 2005: 164).

narrator's voice or text, as the end of rationality, causality and teleology; the end of the conventional story: *of the linear form*. The narrator will not write another *récit* because (if any) his subsequent narratives will not abide by the addressee's rational demand for a logical sequence; they will be fragmentary narratives of pure, perpetual madness. Thus, the story does not collapse because it would recur endlessly if the narrator were not stopped by his addresses, but because the narrator realizes that the idea of narrative cannot do justice to his experience of madness – because the narrative itself has failed him.

So it is not that the story ends but that its status as a story is thrown into question, even rejected. The final avowal that the narrative is not a *récit* should be read as an attack not on this particular tale but on the idea of narrative itself. The story challenges the idea of narrative because it is not a story about something but about stories as such. If the madness of the day is the seeing of visibility, Blanchot's *récit* is the never-ending story of its own telling. This is why the account fails as a *récit*; it transcends it. The circular sequence of discontinuous passages defies the logic of conventional narrative order, creating a *récit* that is not the disintegration of thought but thought's self-awareness of its own limits. The circular structure subjects the whole to a part that contains it and repeats it endlessly. It also subordinates the faintly discernible vestiges of a story to the attempt to render the process of telling and the moment of seeing visibility, of thinking thought. It is therefore, also, a mise en scène of the experiencing of the limit. Blanchot writes in order to show that writing betrays, because incapable of rendering reality, it transforms it. The narrator's refusal to comply with the narrative's standards makes explicit its inevitable failure. The story collapses – or, rather, the notion of story collapses – as it turns back upon itself. The coherence demanded by the narrator's interlocutor(s) breaks the circular inclination of the *récit*, forcing it towards a halt that shatters once and for all his belief in the narrative.

* * *

The texts examined in this chapter arise out of a conscious effort to reroute narrative, following the crisis of meta-discourses that followed the Second World War. Instead of merely focusing on the critique of certain values, on exposing the limitations of the linear model or on the portrayal of a post-death-of-God world, the works considered in this chapter use circular forms in order to reflect upon the basis and function of narrative and language, the processes of writing and reading, and the nature of perception. In most cases, these narratives conflate linearity and circularity or blur the margins between the two forms, sometimes by providing the reader with a choice between both (as in *Hopscotch*) and on other occasions by allowing various structures to coexist in unison. Alain Robbe-Grillet uses circular forms as a way to destabilize the linear progression of the events he describes and above all to subvert their signification. The plot's development and its teleological value are repetitively undermined through the inclusion of myriad details that are hard to locate temporally, continuous regressions in the discourse that bestow it a circular character, by having it return to the moment of departure in his novels' endings. In this way, he throws into question the certainty and order of the world, revealing that signification is not inherent to reality: that we impose it upon reality and that form is crucial in this process.

In contrast, Calvino produces a multi-structural narrative (*If on a Winter's Night a Traveller*), where linearity concurs with several circular forms. Alongside the ostensibly linear development of its discourse, there is a reiterative circular motion arising from the succession of novels that fail to conclude, and beyond that, the reading experience also becomes a circular process through the repeated direct appellations to the reader, which inevitably force us out of the story, making us self-conscious about the reading process. Furthermore, the text bears yet another kind of circularity, a fractal one, through its numerous self-references. Cortázar, on the other hand, uses circular forms to excavate his formal tunnel in an effort to reflect upon the concept of identity and explore its relationship to alterity. However, like Calvino (albeit in a wholly distinct manner), he also presents us with a meditation on the process of reading and the nature of literature by problematizing his text's referentiality, so that we are forced to reflect upon the relationship between a text's characters, its narrator and ourselves as readers.

Finally, Blanchot presents us with what is perhaps the most complex circular form analysed in this chapter. Its return ab initio creates a fissure in the text, representing the abyss of the limits of thought, language and narrative. Rather than referring to an external reality, Blanchot's *récit* describes the process of storytelling itself, its origins, function and especially its limitations, and in so doing allows the reader to experience those limits. He portrays the failure of narrative: the death of the (linear) story.

7

Conclusion

Circular narratives in modern European literature

The preceding analysis has shown how a preoccupation with narrative form encouraged many twentieth-century European writers to experiment with circularity in a variety of ways and with various aims. As we saw in the Introduction, linearity was gradually conceptualized and established as the ideal structure for narrative in the course of literary history, mainly as the result of a series of teleological determinations and valuations of literature. These determinations were for the most part *didactic* (in mythology and Platonism) – ranging from the extremism of Plato's devaluation of literature to a more aestheticized didacticism following the Horatian maxim 'delight and instruct' – and *mimetic* (Aristotelian), but also on occasion *expressionistic* (as in Romanticism).

In the face of these teleological valuations, the idea of linear form is retained up until the late nineteenth century, often through the very question of narrative form not being considered. However, with Kant's definition of art as a disinterested aesthetic experience and Schiller's poetics, literature came to be revalorized for its own sake, even to the extent of the Flaubertian aspiration to write a book of pure form (a book about nothing). Yet, if Kant's concept of disinterestedness gradually leads to a focus on form, it is Nietzsche's critiques of truth and teleology that problematize the very notions underpinning linearity's conceptualization and prevalence as a narrative model. By arguing that art is always interested, Nietzsche established it as a physiological process: an outcome of an interpretative will to power, a way of imposing a perspectival order upon an intrinsically chaotic world. Nietzsche's critique is therefore one that subliminally highlights the importance of the way in which we structure reality (and so also narrative), by uncovering its inherent ideological roots.

Nietzsche, then, exposed linearity as a false abstraction of reality and in concordance with this revelation gradually emerged a tendency to reject linearity in favour of circular narrative structures. Although not a conscious, homogeneous or organized movement, various features (aside from the use of circular forms) link those works in which circularity prevails. The first circular texts, emerging at the turn of the twentieth century, produce ferocious critiques of many of the bourgeois values that had been taken for granted for much of the nineteenth century but which began to be problematized as a result of the growing ideological crisis in Europe at that time. Many of these critiques parallel Nietzsche's: they reflect upon ideas such as the nature of consciousness, identity and subjectivity, presenting them as fluctuating constructs shaped by external forces (social, cultural, political, etc.).

As we have seen, several of these circular narratives depict their protagonists as performative figures devoid of essential attributes, rejecting the stability of prior models (identity as a soul). They also explore the dynamics of psychological change, the configuration of our identity in relation to alterity, the deterministic nature of our subjectivity and the way in which consciousness is affected by language. Thus, language itself also became suspect at that time, and some of these texts paraphrase Nietzsche's critique in 'On Truth and Lies in a Nonmoral Sense'. They also present meditations on the nature of time, in some cases by suspending its course and in others by bestowing an atemporal character to the narrative that annuls the distinction between past, present and future through the peculiar temporality of the eternal recurrence. Moreover, the most radical examples of circularity are 'infinite' works where story and discourse, and content and form, are inseparable. Literalizing the idea of eternal recurrence in their language, 'plots' and structures, these works produce tacit anti-theological critiques or mises en scène of Sisyphus' world. They depict life as a pointless ritual, in some cases a dreadful one, where the desire for power sets in motion a vicious cycle of eternally recurring violence.

Most importantly, these circular forms subvert the function and value of plot by destabilizing the linear progression of their stories, ridiculing the idea of a narrative *telos* and hence notions such as meaning or signification. In so doing, they throw into question the idea that there is inherent certainty and order in the world, exposing the arbitrary (or rather perspectivist) nature of systematization. Furthermore, by overthrowing our expectations of a conventional resolution they challenge our assumptions about the nature and function of narrative. Rather than referring mimetically to an external reality, these texts are allegorical critiques, aestheticist renderings of an absurd world or auto-referential objects, 'anti-narratives' that depict the processes of narrative itself (reading and writing), its origins (or cause), purpose and limits (on occasion allowing us, as readers, to experience these limits too). At times, they force us out of the story-world, making us self-conscious about the reading experience and confronting us with questions such as whether and how a text can be interpreted or what the relationship between its characters, its narrator and ourselves as readers is. At others, they invite us to reconsider the end or aims of writing, what a story (or literature) actually is and what relationship it has to experience, thought, language, meaning, structure and reality.

The commitment to circular narrative forms seems to undergo several stages in the course of the twentieth century, which although neither clear-cut nor representing a smooth linear development help us to draw a general picture of the phenomenon. At first, the break with convention is in many cases neither conscious nor recognized by the work's critics because the use of circularity arises from an aspiration to hasten the effort of these same conventions by representing reality in a more realistic manner. Yet, this leads to an ever more explicit underscoring of the problems of mimesis, linearity and an eschatological-teleological *Weltanschauung*. If Nietzsche identifies linearity as Christianity's (or Platonism's) 'master plot', the various circular narratives examined in this book both arise out of this awareness (the crisis of values precipitated by the 'death of God') and further expose the delusions leading to it. As well as revealing their distrust of the traditional ways in which reality had been conceptualized, systematized and structured, and throwing into question the validity and value of such efforts to explain and systematize reality, the circular form represents the materialization of Nietzsche's epistemological scepticism in literature, a tendency that becomes increasingly patent, achieving its epitome as an 'anti-conventional convention' towards mid-century, with works such as *Finnegans Wake* and *Waiting for Godot*. The most explicit examples of circularity are an outright defiance to the linear form, a conscious rejection of the world view underlying such a structure.

After the Second World War, the tendency to adopt circular forms continues in an attempt to reroute narrative by giving a voice to the disillusionment regarding 'the metanarrative apparatus of legitimation' brought about by that global conflict (Lyotard 1984: xxiii). In this stage, narratives conflate linearity and circularity or blur the margins between the two forms, rather than replacing one model (linear) with another (circular). These works appear to be driven by a metanarrative drive: to show the hidden implications of each structure and to give voice to a profound distrust of systematization as such.

The literary works considered in this book may therefore be called anti-didactic or at least representative of a sceptical didacticism. Sometimes they challenge traditional values and sometimes they problematize the very idea of valuation by accommodating various interpretations or resisting circumscription to a specific reading. However, in every case they force the reader to consider whether the structures they destabilize are truly representative of reality or rather motivated by a specific ideological interest. Accordingly, the texts studied in this book may be considered 'nihilistic' if we read them as rejections of the traditional conception of certain notions considered fundamental in Western thought (consciousness, identity, individuality, signification, communication, progress, truth, meaning, etc.) – a charge which many of them have had to endure. Yet, they could also be considered as 'anti-nihilistic', in their rejection of abstract values in favour of revealing and aestheticizing bare life: life as perpetual change devoid of meaning or end.

In consequence, beyond the question of whether these narratives are in fact nihilistic or anti-nihilistic, they indubitably arise out of and engage with that profound crisis of values from which the discourse on nihilism derives. The undermining of the causal development and teleological resolution prototypical of linear narratives allows these circular texts to force a question upon the reader, rather than an answer. Thus, while one may argue that like linear narratives, they also posit certain ideals (even if they tend to antagonize those posited by linear texts), the manner in which they do so is radically different: frequently by encouraging the reader to consider questions that they consciously leave unanswered, opening up the text precisely by precluding and mocking the prototypical closure demanded by the customary didacticism of linear narratives. Additionally, many of these circular works undermine the very notions of structurality and valuability or produce metatextual critiques through their subversion of the conventional plot structure: that of the hero's quest (the overcoming or failure to overcome a conflict, resulting in a recognition or reversal of the initial status quo), rejecting, in so doing, the idea of life as plot.

It is important to note that while this book has included reference to a fairly wide range of works that adopt circular narrative forms, it makes no claim to be exhaustive. Rather, the aim has been to identify some of the most radical examples of anti-teleological circularity, in order to examine the nature and effects of these structures. Nevertheless, perhaps one obvious omission of a twentieth-century European circular narrative on which some comment is warranted is Marcel Proust's *A la recherche du temps perdu* (1913–27). There are a number of justifications for this omission, aside from the fact that the form of this multi-part novel is extremely complex (since the same is true of *Finnegans Wake*, for instance), and a whole study could rightly be (and have been) dedicated to its discussion.[1] Although Proust himself defined his text as a circular narrative,[2] claiming that the 'last page of *Le Temps retrouvé* (written before the rest of the book) comes full circle to meet the first page of *Swann*' (1989: 292), and many critics have followed him in this classification (a description that has almost become a cliché when describing the text's form),[3] the fact is that defining this work's structure as circular is arguably an oversimplification. This is not only because its driving force is the chronological biography of its protagonist/narrator but also because, as Miguel de Beistegui claims, 'two different types of planes – a plane of organization and a plane of fragmentation – coexist and interact', so that 'the structure, outline, and organic unity of the work' provided by the circular form 'find themselves confronted with an excess they cannot integrate, a fracture they cannot reduce' (2012: 98).

Proust's novel is in fact both circular and non-circular, both arche-teleological and rhizomatic. On the one hand, it contains a unity that 'partakes of an ideal organicity, where beginning and end, however distant, finally meet up, where every piece fits in, every part refers to the whole' (Beistegui 2012: 98). This is the well-known premeditated structure that Proust refers to in his letter, where the 'end was planned from the beginning, with the beginning', meaning that 'from the arche-teleological point of view, the novel did not evolve much from the moment it was first conceived' (2012: 99). Yet this structure coexists with 'an infinitely elastic and uncanny duration', not that of 'a time that keeps pressing ahead along a straight line, but of a time that halts, moves downward, and drags us into unsuspected depths', so that the text becomes both 'a *roman fleuve*' and a '*roman marais*, or a *roman delta*' (Beistegui 2012: 100). Proust's paragraphs are a result of a repeated internal expansion achieved by 'inserting relative and

---

[1] Genette, for instance, drew his theory of temporality from the analysis of the novel.
[2] In one of his letters to Clément de Maugny.
[3] Steve Bachmann paraphrases Proust claiming that the work has a 'circular structure' since 'everything in Volume I (and all subsequent volumes) immediately follows the end of LTR'; Daniel Karlin writes that it has a 'circular form whose meaning can only be understood in an act of memory' (2005: 19); and William C. Carter provides a compositional justification to his choice of structure, claiming that since 'Proust never composed in a linear manner or according to an outline (...) the circular form suited his needs perfectly' given that 'the structure would expand while keeping its basic shape and relation among the parts' (in Carter 2002: 481).

conjunctive prepositions in between principal clauses', which is why Beistegui argues that his writing 'ceases to be a line, and becomes a rhizome', causing his book to grow 'anarchically, cancerously, like an organism gone mad, hovering between organization and disorganization, between order and chaos', reflecting the tension between 'the arche-teleo-logic (the structure and unity) of the novel' and an 'unmasterable logic of deformation' (2012: 100).

Furthermore, aside from being problematized by a rhizomatic fragmentation that transforms the linear continuum of the discourse with myriad digressions which fragment the narrative line time and again, Proust's circularity is intrinsically teleological. It is a kind of Hegelian circularity, or rather cyclicality. Instead of displaying a Nietzschean anti-teleological critique, it represents the very essence of both an interpretative and a compositional teleology:

> For Proust himself [. . .] the demands of structure were constant and conscious, manifesting themselves through marvels of (neither true nor false) symmetry, recurrence, circularity, light thrown backward, superimposition (without adequation) of the first and the last, etc. Teleology here is not a product of the critic's projection, but the author's own theme. The implication of the end in the beginning, the strange relationships between the subject who writes the book and the subject of this book, between the consciousness of the narrator and that of the hero – all this recalls the style of becoming and the dialectic of the 'we' in the *Phenomenology of the Mind*. We are indeed concerned with the phenomenology of a mind here. (Derrida 1978: 22)

The text's ending presents us with the unification of narrator and hero, a fulfilling of the latter's quest to become the former:

> after a long march during which each sought after the other, sometimes very close to each other, sometimes very far apart; they coincide at the moment of resolution, which is the instant when the hero becomes the narrator, that is, the author of his own history. The narrator is the hero revealed to himself, is the person that the hero, throughout his history, desires to be but never can be; he now takes the place of this hero and will be able to set himself to the task of edifying the work which has ended [. . .] The end of the book makes its existence possible and comprehensible. The novel is conceived such that its end engenders its beginning. (Quoted in Derrida 1978: 22)

The protagonist's identity is caught up in a continuous flux but one that is also a progression. Most importantly, time is consuming both itself and the narrator, passing relentlessly and running out, regained only in fleeting instances: a lost past a passing future, not an abysmal return or pervasiveness, only fleeting returns that appear and are lost. This is very different, for instance, to the way in which Azorín stops time with some of his descriptions or shows various (historical) temporalities existing within the same scene. It is also very different from the way in which Nabokov uses circularity to capture the relentless revisiting of a memory. The text's circular teleological logic is closer to that of Cortázar's pseudo-circular forms (where the narrator becomes the subject of the narration), and yet, rather than affirming such a structure, Cortázar undermines it through uncanny transformations or the explicit undermining of the initial status quo (as opposed to its assertion). While, in Proust's text, teleology is the very principle dictating the circular form, in the texts studied in this book it is an anti-teleological circularity that overpowers fragmentation and linearity, precluding unity (and its significance).

However, there are certainly many other examples of circularity in the European literature of the twentieth century that are absent from this analysis and may well be closely aligned to the works examined in this study, since they express similar ideas or construct their texts in analogous ways to the ones analysed here. Within European literature, examples include Flann O'Brien's *The Third Policeman* (1967), Quim Monzó's 'The Sleeping Beauty' (1975), José Luis Sampedro's *The Shadow of the Days* (1994) and those narratives referred to at the end of Chapter 3, which deploy circular forms to express feminist critical perspectives. Beyond Europe, and as mentioned in Chapter 5, there are also various Latin American absurdist authors who deploy circular forms in their plays, and in North American literature we find several other examples, in both drama and prose, notably in texts such as John Barth's 'Frame-Tale' (1968) and 'Bellerophoniad' (1972). However, as mentioned earlier, the aim of this study was not to be comprehensive but to analyse specific key instances, where the circular form is used to subvert teleology, the structure of the hero's quest and the idea of life as plot.

As for examples of works prior to the twentieth century, and prior to Nietzsche, where the linear model is challenged or subverted, perhaps the most obvious examples are Cervantes' *Don Quixote* and Laurence Sterne's *Tristram Shandy* (1759). However, these works stand out as significant exceptions to the general trend, and it is precisely for this reason that they were championed by theorists of narrative in the twentieth century – Sterne's novel attracting particular attention from the Russian Formalists.

In recent years, a number of narratologists have focused on discussing some of these alternatives to the linear form, defining them as 'unnatural narratives'.

These theorists aim to 'trace the history of unnatural narratives from antiquity to the present, to provide some analyses of unnatural texts, and to address a number of pressing theoretical questions' in order to 'provide a substantial adjustment to narrative theory [. . .] by adding a significantly new perspective to the basic model that is currently used' (Richardson 2002: xiii). Brian Richardson, for instance, proposes a typology consisting of six different kinds of 'unnatural' narrative forms: circular, contradictory, antonymic, differential, conflated and dual or multiple. Alongside these six 'antichronies', Richardson also identifies three 'metatemporal' structures: achronic, unknowable and self-negating temporalities (see Richardson 2000: 24). This classification attempts to fill in the gaps left by the standard analysis (i.e. Genette's model of narrative temporality). Richardson believes that 'narrative theory from Aristotle to cognitive narratology has had a pronounced mimetic bias, and thus, their theoretic models are necessarily inadequate' (2012: 95). His typology of narrative structures derives from a foundational division between mimetic and anti-mimetic narratives,[4] and takes the following overall shape:

Mimetic:

- Chronological narratives: pure linearity, fragmented linearity, etc.
- Non-chronological narratives: analepses, prolepses

Anti-mimetic:

- Antichronies: circular, contradictory, antonymic, differential, conflated, dual or multiple
- Metatemporal narratives: achronic, unknowable, self-negating temporalities

However, the referential or mimetic criterion dictating this classification is problematic, since the adherence to, or deviation from, mimesis implies that there is a 'natural' way in which narratives can depict reality. Moreover, if we focus instead on the ways in which narratives are structured in order to construct or express meaning, we find that many of the alternatives identified by Richardson are actually variations of the linear form, relying on the same basic framework. Given that the linearity of a text is essentially reducible to the opposition of its opening and its ending, most of these experimental narratives

---

[4] Anti-mimetic narratives bear a dialectical relationship with mimetic narratives, since 'it is only through that concept that we can understand its violation' (Richardson 2000: 25).

safeguard the possibility of a teleological (linear) significance, despite conscious efforts to distort its sequence. Even if some of these structures undermine linear progression by obscuring the plot's development or the idea of causality and of a clear resolution through ambiguous finales, their endings nevertheless point to a number of possible conclusions, allowing the reader to select one among them.

Many of these anti-mimetic narratives thus still allow a teleology of reading, since the implications that arise out of the antagonism between the initial and final states of affairs inevitably endow the sequence of events with an implicit meaning, regardless of how ambiguous or consciously obscure the progression that leads to it is constructed to be. In view of this, and while consciously defying mimetic representation, many of the alternatives to the conventional three-part Aristotelian linear structure proposed by the unnatural narratologists are themselves essentially linear, given that they are unable to rid themselves completely of the subliminal progression (and its derivative implications) that underlies the text. So, what Genette says of the last part of *A la recherche*, if reversed, is applicable to most of these supposedly non-linear 'unnatural' texts: the 'large-scale linearity does not exclude the presence of a great number of anachronisms in the details' (cited in Richardson 2002: 27).

Nietzsche's idea of eternal recurrence shows that the only possible way to escape from the implications of eschatology, to avoid the ending inscribing its meaning upon the text – and therefore to avoid the degradation of the text's trajectory as a means towards an end – is to reject the idea of a final state. Circularity is the only authentic way of destroying both the explicit and the inferred resolution of a text. Any other sort of deviation from the conventional narrative model, from the use of the traditional in medias res technique to the fragmented discourse of multi-perspectival narratives, necessarily entails a logical linear sequence underlying the story that can be recomposed from the text's denouement – even if it is blurred by avant-gardist techniques that seek to augment expectation, playing a game with the reader that has clear rules nonetheless. For when these deviations conclude, the narrative becomes a unified whole – and one that can be understood and interpreted within the traditional concept of narrative.

We will thus conclude by proposing an alternative typology of narrative structures, disregarding the mimetic/anti-mimetic opposition and building on the Formalist notions of story (*fabula*) and discourse (*sjuzhet*). Within this framework, narratives may fall into one of two broad categories, depending on the basic nature of their structure: discourses with story and discourses without a story.⁵ Each of these overarching categories can in turn be subdivided into linear, pseudo-linear (all of Richardson's antichronies except for the circular kind would fall in this category) and circular structures. However, this does not clarify the typology completely. In order to grasp the complexity of this ostensibly simple division, it is necessary to examine the specific ways in which linearity can be overcome – that is, the different kinds of circularity. These range from the devaluation of the story (in discourses with story) to the annihilation of the story (in discourses without story). In the former class, we find (1) 'cyclical texts', where the story has a circular structure (but the discourse is linear), and these would include texts such as Borges' 'The Circular Ruins' or Cortázar's 'The Continuity of Parks'; (2) 'circular texts', where there is one or various linear stories but the structure of the discourse is circular, as in Nabokov's 'The Circle'; and (3) 'hyper-circular texts', where both the story and the discourse have a circular structure, such as Queneau's *The Bark Tree* and Joyce's *Finnegans Wake*. In the second class, we find (1) 'meta-cyclical texts',⁶ where the discourse is linear yet characterized by circular returns, such as Azorín's *Doña Inés* and Stein's 'Melanctha' (although there the discourse is both linear and circular);⁷ and (2) 'meta-circular texts', which have no story and consist purely of a circular discourse: Blanchot's *The Madness of the Day* is to some extent representative of this category, although there the vestiges of a story remain, and Beckett's *Worstward Ho* (1983) also falls into this category.⁸

The circular forms studied in this book highlight that the only way to escape the ideological implications of progression is through infinite recurrence: no end, no escape, no external viewpoint from which to assess or construct value, life (or narrative) without additives, without an inherent meaning or aim. The puzzling effect caused by the undermining of the reader's expectations makes them 'anti-narratives', since it is the *shock* that the reader experiences through the final realization that the text does not conform to the assumed 'pure' form of narrative that constitutes their underlying purpose,

---

⁵ This second category coincides with Richardson's metatemporal narratives.
⁶ To preserve Richardson's prefix.
⁷ This category falls somewhere between linearity and circularity, since the absence of a story does not allow teleology to function properly: assuming that there are no determinate initial and final states of affairs from which significance can be drawn.
⁸ This typology also reveals a limitation of Richardson's categorization: its failure to account for the different types of circularity.

their 'anti-message': an anti-teleological *telos*. Furthermore, this subversion of progression and end is reflective of a specific world view:

> 'Mechanical necessity' is not a fact: it is we who first interpreted it into events. We have interpreted the formulatable character of events as the consequence of a necessity that rules over events. [. . .] Only because we have introduced subjects, 'doers', into things does it appear that all events are the consequences of compulsion exerted upon subjects – exerted by whom? again by a 'doer'. Cause and effect – a dangerous concept so long as one thinks of something that causes and something upon which an effect is produced. (Nietzsche 1968: 297)

These narratives are metaphorical embodiments of the values inherent in the phrase 'God is dead'. They invite constant reflection, given their failure to provide an absolute frame of reference with which to derive value or meaning from the story – such as teleology. So, in the same way as Nietzsche's *Circulus Vitiosus Deus* emerges as the sole antithesis to theology, the anti-teleological circular narrative structure is revealed as the only possible way to make a narrative work *truly writerly*. The disappointing of the reader's structural expectations being an indispensable step in this process.

The importance of Nietzsche's idea of eternal recurrence was not merely to encourage temporal or structural experimentation but to incite a formal revaluation of narrative. By turning writing on its head, by bringing the text's tale to the ouroboros' mouth, the circular texts examined in this book pose the question 'What is literature?' The problematizing of their status as supplements of an external reality undermines the very idea of supplementarity. If conventional narratives establish causal relationships between events, giving them (and thus reality) meaning through the systematic organization of certain units (events or concepts), the anti-teleological circular form destabilizes this logic, evincing its fictiveness. The circular form compels the reader to ask whether such a method of representation truly describes reality and whether the world is governed by the principles that narrative presupposes within it. The theological, mechanistic world view presumed by empiricism is subjected to a violent deconstruction. The upshot of this process is the narrativization of discourse. The critique of absolute truth and of systematization exposes all texts (historical, scientific, etc.) as narrative.

This book has also sought to show that the anti-teleological circular form appears to have been a phenomenon that arose at a specific historical moment. Not only does linearity continues to dominate narrative today, but Western society seems to have gone back to (or to have never really abandoned) an essentially theological and teleological way of thinking. And yet, God will inevitably die again, for nihilism itself is circular; it has become (or perhaps always was) the condition of our (eternal) present. The temporality of nihilism is the eternal recurrence: values collapsing cyclically. So there is no reason to think that circular forms will not re-emerge.

References

Abrams, M. H. and Geoffrey Galt Harpman. 2014. *A Glossary of Literary Terms*. Stanford, CA: Cengage Learning.
Adamov, Arthur. 1965. *Théâtre I: La parodie, L'Invasion, La grande et la petite manoeuvre, Le Professeur Taranne et Tous contre tous*. Paris: Gallimard.
Alazraki, Jaime. 1999. *Critical Essays on Julio Cortázar*. Boston, MA: G. K. Hall & Co.
Alexandrov, Vladimir E. 2014. *The Garland Companion to Vladimir Nabokov*. London: Routledge.
Allen, William S. 2016. *Aesthetics of Negativity: Blanchot, Adorno and Autonomy*. Berlin: De Gruyter.
Altizer, Thomas J. J. 1985. *History as Apocalypse*. New York: SUNY Press.
Altman, Rick. 2008. *A Theory of Narrative*. New York: Columbia University Press.
Antelme, Ruth Schumann and Stéphane Rossini. 1998. *Becoming Osiris: The Ancient Egyptian Death Experience*. Rochester, NY: Bear & Co.
Antliff, Mark. 2007. *Avant-Garde Fascism: The Mobilization of Myth, Art, and Culture in France, 1909–1939*. Durham, NC: Duke University Press.
Aristotle. 2004. *Rhetoric*, trans. W. Rhys Roberts. New York: Dover Publications.
Aristotle. 2018. *Poetics*, trans. Kenneth McLeish. London: Nick Hern Books.
Arrojo, Rosemary. 2017. *Fictional Translators: Rethinking Translation through Literature*. London: Routledge.
Attridge, Derek. 2004. *The Cambridge Companion to James Joyce*. Cambridge: Cambridge University Press.
Azorín. 1969. *Obras selectas*. Madrid: Biblioteca Nueva.
Barthes, Rolland. 1972. *Critical Essays*, trans. Richard Howard. Evanston, IL: Northwestern University Press.
Barthes, Rolland. 1988. *Image, Music, Text*, trans. Stephen Heath. London: Fontana Press.
Beckett, Samuel. 1966. *En attendant Godot*, ed. Colin Duckworth. Paris: Éditions de Minuit.
Beckett, S., Eliot, P., Brion, M., Budgen, F., Gilbert, S., Jolas, E., Llona, V., McAlmon, R., MacGreevy, T., Rodker, J., Sage, R. and Williams, W.C. 1974. *Our Exagmination Round His Factification for Incamination of Work in Progress*. London: Faber and Faber.
Beetz, Kirk H. 1996. *Beacham's Encyclopedia of Popular Fiction*, Vol. 13. Osprey: Beachham.
Behar, Lisa Block de. 2014. *Borges: The Passion of an Endless Quotation*. New York: SUNY Press.

Beistegui, Manuel de. 2012. *Proust as Philosopher: The Art of Metaphor*. New York: Routledge.
Benedict, Gerald. 2011. *The Maya: 2012*. London: Duncan Baird Publishers.
Bennett, Andrew and Nicholas Royle. 2016. *Introduction to Literature, Criticism and Theory*. New York: Routledge.
Bennett, Michael Y. 2011. *Reassessing the Theatre of the Absurd*. New York: Palgrave Macmillan.
Berghaus, Gunter. 1996. *Futurism and Politics: Between Anarchist Rebellion and Fascist Reaction, 1909–1944*. New York: Berghahn Books.
Berman, Jessica. 2001 *Modernist Fiction, Cosmopolitanism and the Politics of Community*. Cambridge: Cambridge University Press.
Berry, Ellen E. 1993. *Curved Thought and Textual Wandering: Gertrude Stein's Postmodernism*. Ann Arbor, MI: University of Michigan Press.
Bident, Christophe. 1998. *Maurice Blanchot: partenaire Invisible: essai biographique*. Paris: Champ Vallon.
Bixby, Patrick. 2017. 'Becoming "James Overman": Joyce, Nietzsche, and the Uncreated Conscience of the Irish', *Modernism – Modernity*, 24 (1), 45–66.
Blanchot, Maurice. 1981. *La Folie du jour*, trans. Lydia Davis. Barrytown: Station Hill Press.
Blanchot, Maurice. 1988. *Thomas the Obscure*, trans. Robert Lamberton. Barrytown: Station Hill Press.
Blanchot, Maurice. 1993. *The Infinite Conversation*, trans. Susan Hanson. Minneapolis: University of Minnesota Press.
Borges, Jorge Luis. 1962. *Ficciones*, trans. Anthony Kerrigan. New York: Grove Press.
Borges, Jorge Luis. 2004. *Selected Non-fictions*, Vol. 1, ed. Eliot Weinberger. New York: Viking.
Boyd, Brian. 2001. *Nabokov's Pale Fire: The Magic of Artistic Discovery*. Princeton, NJ: Princeton University Press.
Boyd, Brian. 2016. *Vladimir Nabokov: The Russian Years*. Princeton, NJ: Princeton University Press.
Bridgman, Richard. 1971. *Gertrude Stein in Pieces*. Oxford: Oxford University Press.
Brooks, Peter. 1984. *Reading for the Plot: Design and Intention in Narrative*. Cambridge: Harvard University Press.
Brunel, Pierre. 2015. *Companion to Literary Myths, Heroes and Archetypes*. New York: Routledge.
Bruns, Gerald L. 1997. *Maurice Blanchot: The Refusal of Philosophy*. Baltimore, MD: Johns Hopkins University Press.
Burt, John Foster Jr. 1993. *Heirs to Dionysus: A Nietzschean Current in Literary Modernism*. Princeton, NJ: Princeton University Press.
Buxton, Richard. 2001. *From Myth to Reason?: Studies in the Development of Greek Thought*. Oxford: Oxford University Press.

Cahill, Thomas. 2010. *The Gifts of the Jews: How a Tribe of Desert Nomads Changed the Way Everyone Thinks and Feels*. New York: Knopf Doubleday Publishing.

Calder, John. 2002. 'Martin Esslin: Illuminating Writer and Radio Drama Producer', *Guardian*, 27 February. http://www.theguardian.com/news/2002/feb/27/guardianobituaries.booksobituaries (accessed 21 June 2014).

Calvino, Italo. 1988. *Six Memos for the Next Millennium*, trans. Patrick Creagh. Cambridge, MA: Harvard University Press.

Calvino, Italo. 2010. *If on a Winter's Night a Traveller*. New York: Vintage.

Calvino, Italo. 2014. *Why Read the Classics?*, trans. Martin McLaughlin. Boston, MA: Houghton Mifflin Harcourt.

Campbell, James. 2003. *Exiled in Paris: Richard Wright, James Baldwin, Samuel Beckett, and Others on the Left Bank*. Berkeley: University of California Press.

Campbell, Joseph. 2008. *The Hero of a Thousand Faces*. Princeton, NJ: Princeton University Press.

Camus, Albert. 2012. *The Myth of Sisyphus: And Other Essays*, trans. Justin O'Brien. New York: Vintage International.

Carter, William C. 2002. *Marcel Proust: A Life*. New York: Penguin Books.

Carvalho, Paulo Eduardo and Rui Carvalho Homem. 2008. *Plural Beckett Pluriel*. Porto: Universidade do Porto.

Chakraborty, Thirthankar and Juan Luis Toribio Vazquez. 2020. *Samuel Beckett as World Literature*. New York: Bloomsbury Academic.

Chandler, Richard E. and Kessel Schwartz. 1991. *A New History of Spanish Literature*. Baton Rouge, LA: Louisiana State University Press.

Chávez-Silverman, Susana and Librada Hernández. 2000. *Reading and Writing the Ambiente: Queer Sexualities in Latino, Latin American, and Spanish Culture*. Madison: University of Wisconsin Press.

Cho, Stephen Wagner. 1995. 'Before Nietzsche: Nihilism as a Critique of German Idealism', *Graduate Faculty Philosophy Journal*, 18 (1), 205–33.

Christ, Ronald J. 1969. *The Narrow Act: Borges' Art of Allusion*. New York: New York University Press.

Clark, Maudemarie. 1990. *Nietzsche on Truth and Philosophy*. Cambridge: Cambridge University Press.

Classe, Olive. 2000. *Encyclopedia of Literary Translation into English: A-L*. Milton Park: Taylor & Francis.

Cornwell, Neil. 1991. *Daniil Kharms and the Poetics of the Absurd*. New York: Springer.

Cortázar, Julio. 1972. *Prosa del observatorio*. Barcelona: Lumen.

Cortázar, Julio. 2003. *Obra crítica*. Madrid: Galaxia Gutenberg.

Cortázar, Julio. 2004. *Rayuela*. Caracas: Fundacion Biblioteca Ayacuch.

Cortázar, Julio. 2014. *Blow-Up: And Other Stories*. New York: Knopf Doubleday Publishing Group.

Cram, Gabriel. 2008. *Other Than Yourself: An Investigation between Inner and Outer Space*. New York: Distributed Art Publishers.
Crawford, Claudia. 1988. *The Beginnings of Nietzsche's Theory of Language*. Berlin: Walter de Gruyter.
Critchley, Simon. 2009. *Very Little . . . Almost Nothing*. Abingdon: Routledge.
Culler, Johnathan. 1981. *The Pursuit of Signs: Semiotics, Literature, Deconstruction*. New York: Cornell University Press.
Culler, Jonathan. 2011. *Literary Theory: A Very Short Introduction*. Oxford: Oxford University Press.
Danto, Arthur C. 1965. *Nietzsche as Philosopher*. New York: Columbia University Press.
Dapía, Silvia G. 2015. *Jorge Luis Borges, Post-Analytic Philosophy, and Representation*. London: Routledge.
Davison, Neil R. 1998. *James Joyce, Ulysses, and the Construction of Jewish Identity: Culture, Biography, and 'the Jew' in Modernist Europe*. Cambridge: Cambridge University Press.
Deleuze, Gilles. 1983. *Nietzsche and Philosophy*, trans. Hugh Tomlinson. London: Athlone.
Deming, Robert H. 1970. *James Joyce, the Critical Heritage: 1928–1941*. New York: Barnes & Noble.
Derrida, Jacques. 1978. *Writing and Difference*, trans. Alan Bass. Chicago: University of Chicago Press.
Derrida, Jacques. 2004. 'Living On', in *Deconstruction and Criticism*, ed. Harold Bloom. London: A&C Black.
Diken, Bülent. 2009. *Nihilism*. Abingdon: Routledge.
Dragunoiu, Dana. 2011. *Vladimir Nabokov and the Poetics of Liberalism*. Evanston, IL: Northwestern University Press.
Drain, Richard. 2002. *Twentieth-Century Theatre: A Sourcebook*. New York: Routledge.
Durantaye, Leland de la. 2009. *Giorgio Agamben: A Critical Introduction*. Palo Alto, CA: Stanford University Press.
Echevarría, Roberto González. 2010. *The Voice of the Masters: Writing and Authority in Modern Latin American Literature*. Austin: University of Texas Press.
Epstein, Edward Jay. 2013. 'An A from Nabokov', in *The New York Review of Books*, Vol. 4. https://www.nybooks.com/articles/2013/04/04/a-from-nabokov/ (accessed 1 October 2020).
Esslin, Martin. 1968. *The Theatre of the Absurd*. London: Cox & Wyman Ltd.
Fargnoli, A. Nicholas and Michael Patrick Gillespie. 2014. *Critical Companion to James Joyce: A Literary Reference to His Life and Work*. New York: Infobase Publishing.
Farwell, Marilyn. 1996. *Heterosexual Plots and Lesbian Narratives*. New York: New York University Press.
Fernández, Froilán. 2008. 'Borges Binario', in *Mapocho, Issues 63–64*. Santiago de Chile: Dirección de Bibliotecas, Archivos y Museos.

Flaubert, Gustave. 1980. *The Letters of Gustave Flaubert: 1830–1857*. Cambridge, MA: Harvard University Press.

Flynn, Annette U. 2011. *The Quest for God in the Work of Borges*. London: Bloomsbury.

Ford, Sara J. 2012. *Gertrude Stein and Wallace Stevens: The Performance of Modern Consciousness*. New York: Psychology Press.

Förster-Nietzsche, Elizabeth. 1895. *Das Leben Nietzsches*. Leipzig: Verlag von C.G. Naumann.

Fox, E. Inman. 1898. *Ideología y Política en las letras de fin de Siglo*. Madrid: Espasa Calpe.

Genette, Gérard. 1983. *Narrative Discourse: An Essay in Method*. New York: Cornell University Press.

Gibian, George. 1997. *The Man with the Black Coat: Russia's Literature of the Absurd*. Evanston, IL: Northwestern University Press.

Gill, Carolyn Bailey. 2005. *Maurice Blanchot: The Demand of Writing*. London: Routledge.

Golomb, Jacob. 2004. *Nietzsche and Zion*. New York: Cornell University Press.

Gordon, Lois. 2008. *Reading Godot*. New Haven, CT: Yale University Press.

Gosetti-Ferencei, Jennifer Anna. 2010. *The Ecstatic Quotidian: Phenomenological Sightings in Modern Art and Literature*. University Park, PA: Penn State Press.

Graver, Lawrence. 2004. *Beckett: 'Waiting for Godot'*. Cambridge: Cambridge University Press.

Gray, Martin. 2007. *A Dictionary of Literary Terms*. London: Pearson Education.

Greene, Gayle. 1990. 'Feminist Fiction, Feminist Form', *Frontiers: A Journal of Women Studies*, 11 (2/3), Spirituality, Values, and Ethics, 82–8. Lincoln: University of Nebraska Press.

Gregg, John. 1994. *Maurice Blanchot and the Literature of Transgression*. Princeton, NJ: Princeton University Press.

Grethlein, Jonas and Antonios Rengakos. 2009. *Narratology and Interpretation: The Content of Narrative Form in Ancient Literature*. Berlin: Walter de Gruyter.

Hamburger, Michael. 1954. 'Art and Nihilism: The Poetry of Gottfried Benn', *Encounter*, 3 (4), 49–59.

Hatab, Lawrence. 2013. *Nietzsche's Life Sentence: Coming to Terms with Eternal Recurrence*. Milton Park: Routledge.

Hardison, O. B. 1997. *Poetics and Praxis, Understanding and Imagination*, ed. Arthur F. Kinney. London: University of Georgia Press.

Harty, John III. 2015. *James Joyce's 'Finnegans Wake': A Casebook*. London: Routledge.

Hassan, Ihab. 1975. 'Joyce, Beckett and the Postmodern Imagination', *Triquarterly*, 34, 179–200.

Hatab, Lawrence. 2013. *Nietzsche's Life Sentence: Coming to Terms with Eternal Recurrence*. New York: Routledge.

Heidegger, Martin. 1958. *The Question of Being*. Lanham, MD: Rowman & Littlefield.

Heidegger, Martin. 1984. *Nietzsche*, Vols. I–IV, trans. F. A. Capuzzi. San Francisco, CA: Harper & Row.
Heller, Vivian. 1995. *Joyce, Decadence, and Emancipation*. Champaign, IL: University of Illinois Press.
Herring, Phillip F. 2014. *Joyce's Uncertainty Principle*. Princeton, NJ: Princeton University Press.
Herrnstein Smith, Barbara. 1980. 'Narrative Versions, Narrative Theories', *Critical Inquiry*, 7 (1), On Narrative (Autumn, 1980), 213–36.
Heydt-Stevenson, Jillian and Charlotte Sussman. 2010. *Recognizing the Romantic Novel: New Histories of British Fiction, 1780–1830*. Liverpool: Liverpool University Press.
Hicks, D. Emily. 1991. *Border Writing: The Multidimensional Text*. Minneapolis, MN: University of Minnesota Press.
Hill, Leslie. 2012. *Maurice Blanchot and Fragmentary Writing: A Change of Epoch*. London: A&C Black.
Horace. 2001. 'Ars Poetica', in *The Norton Anthology of Theory and Criticism*, ed. Vincent B. Leitch, trans. D. A. Russell. New York: Norton.
Hühn, Peter, Jan Christoph Meister, John Pier, and Wolf Schmid. 2014. *Handbook of Narratology*. Berlin: Walter de Gruyter.
Hutchinson, Ben. 2011. *Modernism and Style*. Basingstoke: Palgrave Macmillan.
Ionesco, Eugène. 2013. *La Cantatrice chauve suivi de La Leçon*. Barcelona: Folio.
Ionesco, Eugène. 2015. *The Bald Soprano & Other Plays*. New York: Grove Atlantic.
Jakovljevic, Branislav. 2009. *Daniil Kharms: Writing and the Event*. Evanston, IL: Northwestern University Press.
Jurkevich, Gayana. 1999. *In Pursuit of the Natural Sign: Azorín and the Poetics of Ekphrasis*. Lewisburg, PA: Bucknell University Press.
Kant, Immanuel. 2007. *Critique of Judgement*, trans. James Creed Meredith. Oxford: Oxford University Press.
Karlin, Daniel. 2007. *Proust's English*. Oxford: Oxford University Press.
Kaufmann, Walter Arnold Kaufmann. 1956. *Nietzsche, Philosopher, Psychologist, Antichrist*. Princeton, NJ: Princeton University Press.
Kennedy, Andrew K. 1991. *Samuel Beckett*. Cambridge: Cambridge University Press.
King, Katherine Callen. 2012. *Ancient Epic*. Hoboken, NJ: Wiley.
Klarer, Mario. 2013. *An Introduction to Literary Studies*. New York: Routledge.
Kristeva, Julia. 1989. *The Kristeva Reader*. New York: Columbia University Press.
Krysinski, Wladimir. 2002. 'Borges, Calvino, Eco: The Philosophies of Metafiction', in *Literary Philosophers: Borges, Calvino, Eco*, ed. Jorge J. E. Gracia et al. London: Psychology Press.
Kujundzic, Dragan. 1997. 'A Knight's Move: Nietzsche and the Genealogy of Russian Formalism', in *The Returns of History: Russian Nietzscheans after Modernity*. New York: SUNY Press.

Leighton, Angela. 2007. *On Form: Poetry, Aestheticism, and the Legacy of a Word*. Oxford: Oxford University Press.
Levinas, Emmanuel. 1996. *Proper Names*. London: Athlone Press.
Lévi-Strauss, Claude. 1955. 'The Structural Study of Myth', *The Journal of American Folklore*, 68 (270) 'Myth: A Symposium' (October–December), 428–44.
Linett, Maren Tova. 2010. *The Cambridge Companion to Modernist Women Writers*. Cambridge: Cambridge University Press.
Lipner, Julius. 2012. *Hindus: Their Religious Beliefs and Practices*. London: Routledge.
Londré, Felicia H. 1999. *The History of World Theatre: From the English Restoration to the Present*. New York: The Continuum Publishing Company.
Löwith, Karl. 1995. *Martin Heidegger and European Nihilism*, New York: Columbia University Press.
Lutzkanova-Vassileva, Albena. 1999. 'Rethinking the Canon: *Ulysses*: Modernist – Postmodernist – Minor', *Journal X: Jx*, 3–4, 183–201. Department of English, University of Mississippi, 2000.
Lyotard, Jean-François. 1984. *The Postmodern Condition: A Report on Knowledge*. Minneapolis: University of Minnesota Press.
McQuillan, Martin. 2000. *The Narrative Reader*. London: Psychology Press.
Meretoja, H. 2014. *The Narrative Turn in Fiction and Theory: The Crisis and Return of Storytelling from Robbe-Grillet to Tournier*. Berlin: Springer.
Merrell, Floyd. 1991. *Unthinking Thinking: Jorge Luis Borges, Mathematics, and the New Physics*. West Lafayette, IN: Purdue University Press.
Mitchell, Andrew John. 2002. '"So It Appeals to All of Us": The Death of God, *Finnegans Wake*, and the Eternal Recurrence', *James Joyce Quarterly*, 39 (3, Spring), 419–33.
Moran, Domenic. 2017. *Questions of the Liminal in the Fiction of Julio Cortazar*. London: Routledge.
Morell, John Reynell. 1984. *A History of European Literature in the Middle Ages and Modern Times*. London: T. J. Alman.
Morris, Richard. 1986. *Time's Arrows: Scientific Attitudes toward Time*. New York: Simon and Schuster.
Morrissette, Bruce. 1965. *Alain Robbe-Grillet*. New York: Columbia University Press.
Morrissette, Bruce. 1966. 'Robbe-Grillet, Alain: La Maison de rendez-vous', *French Review*, 39, 5 (April), 821–2.
Moses, Omri. 2014. *Out of Character: Modernism, Vitalism, Psychic Life*. Palo Alto, CA: Stanford University Press.
Moss, Susan L. 1980. *Neurosis and Commitment in the Theatre of Arthur Adamov*, Durham, NC: Durham University Press.
Nabokov, Vladimir. *The Stories of Vladimir Nabokov*. New York: Knopf Doubleday Publishing.
Nakhimovsky, Alice S. 1982. *Laughter in the Void: An Introduction to the Writings of Daniil Kharms and Alexander Vvedenskii*. Viena: Institut für Slawistik der Universität Wien.

Nietzsche, Friedrich. 1965. *Thus Spoke Zarathustra: A Book for All and None*, ed. Adrian Del Caro and Robert B. Pippin, trans. Adrian Del Caro. Cambridge: Cambridge University Press.

Nietzsche, Friedrich. 1967. *The Birth of Tragedy and the Case of Wagner*, trans. Walter Kaufmann. New York: Vintage.

Nietzsche, Friedrich. 1968. *The Will to Power*, trans. W. Kaufmann and R. J. Hollingdale. New York: Vintage.

Nietzsche, Friedrich. 1974. *The Gay Science, with a Prelude in Rhymes and an Appendix of Songs*, trans. Walter Kaufmann. New York: Vintage.

Nietzsche, Friedrich. 1976. *The Portable Nietzsche*, trans. Walter Kaufmann. London: Penguin.

Nietzsche, Friedrich. 1989a. *Beyond Good and Evil: Prelude to a Philosophy of the Future*, ed. Rolf Peter Horstmann and Judith Norman, trans. Judith Norman. Cambridge: Cambridge University Press.

Nietzsche, Friedrich. 1989b. *Friedrich Nietzsche on Rhetoric and Language*, ed. Sander L. Gilman, Carole Blair, and David J. Parent. Oxford: Oxford University Press.

Nietzsche, Friedrich. 2005. *Human, All too Human*, ed. Richard Schacht, trans. R. J. Hollingdale. Cambridge: Cambridge University Press.

Nietzsche, Friedrich. 2007. *Untimely Meditations*, ed. Daniel Breazeale, trans. R. J. Hollingdale. Cambridge: Cambridge University Press.

Nietzsche, Friedrich. 2010. *On the Genealogy of Morals and Ecce Homo*, trans. W. Kaufmann. New York: Knopf Doubleday Publishing.

Norris, Margot. 1996. 'The Critical History of Finnegans Wake', in *Joyce and the Subject of History*. Ann Arbor: University of Michigan Press.

O'Neal, Robert. 1980. *Guide to World Literature*. New York: National Council of Teachers of English.

Ouspensky, P. D. 1997. *A New Model of the Universe*. Chelmsford: Courier Corporation.

Page, Norman. 2013. *Vladimir Nabokov*. New York: Routledge.

Pampaloni, Geno. 1988. 'Il lavoro dello scrittore', in *Italo Calvino: Atti del Convegno internazionale*, ed. Giovanni Falaschi. Milan: Garzanti.

Pasley, Malcolm. 2010. *Nietzsche: Imagery and Thought: A Collection of Essays*. Milton Park: Taylor & Francis.

Pellérdi, Márta. 2010. *Nabokov's Palace: The American Novels*. Newcastle upon Tyne: Cambridge Scholars Publishing.

Pellón, Carlos J. 1998. 'Cortázar and the Idolatry of Origins', in *Julio Cortázar: New Readings*. Cambridge: Cambridge University Press.

Pope, Alexander. 1841. *The Poetical Works of Alexander Pope*, ed. Rev. Henry Francis Cary. London: William Smith.

Praet, D. and A. Monballieu. 2011. 'Reversals of Fire. The Philosophy of Heraclitus as Thematic Subtext of Julio Cortázar's *All Fires the Fire*' *Bulletin of Hispanic Studies*, 88 (8), 945–63.

Preus, Anthony. 2015. *Historical Dictionary of Ancient Greek Philosophy*. Lanham, MD: Rowman & Littlefield.
Proust, Marcel. 1989. *Selected Letters*, Vol. 4., ed. Joanna Kilmartin. New York: HarperCollins.
Queneau, Raimond. 1971. *The Bark Tree (Le chiendent): A Novel*. New York: New Directions.
Queneau, Raimond. 2007. *Letters, Numbers, Forms: Essays, 1928–70*. Champaign: University of Illinois Press.
Ramos, Alice. 2000. *Beauty, Art, and the Polis*. New York: American Maritain Association.
Rampley, Matthew. 1993. 'Physiology as Art: Nietzsche on Form' *British Journal of Aesthetics* 33 (3), 271–82.
Ratcliffe, Stephen. 2000. *Listening to Reading*. New York: SUNY Press.
Restuccia, Frances L. 1985. 'Teller and Tale in Joyce's Fiction: Oscillating Perspectives', *Modern Philology*, 82 (4 (May)), 443–5.
Richardson, Brian. 2000. 'Narrative Poetics and Postmodern Transgression: Theorizing the Collapse of Time, Voice, and Frame', *Narrative*, 8 (1 (January)), 23–42.
Richardson, Brian. 2002. *Narrative Dynamics: Essays on Time, Plot, Closure, and Frames*. Columbus: Ohio State University Press.
Robbe-Grillet, Alain. 1989. *For a New Novel*. Evanston, IL: Northwestern University Press.
Robbe-Grillet, Alain. 2012. *In the Labyrinth*. London: Alma Classics.
Rosenthal, Bernice Glatzer. 1994. *Nietzsche and Soviet Culture*. Cambridge: Cambridge University Press.
Ruddick, Lisa. 1991. *Reading Gertrude Stein: Body, Text, Gnosis*. New York: Cornell University Press.
Rushing, Robert Allen. 1998. *Writing without End: Epistemology in Italo Calvino and Carlo Emilio Gadda*. Berkeley: University of California Press.
Ryding, William W. 1971. *Structure in Medieval Narrative*. The Hague: Mouton & Co.
Sagi, Avi. 2002. *Albert Camus and the Philosophy of the Absurd*. Amsterdam: Rodopi.
Sanders, Carol. 1994. *Raymond Queneau*. Amsterdam: Rodopi.
Schwartz, Sanford. 2014. *The Matrix of Modernism: Pound, Eliot, and Early Twentieth-Century Thought*. Princeton, NJ: Princeton University Press.
Seung, T. K. 2005. *Nietzsche's Epic of the Soul: Thus Spoke Zarathustra*. Lanham, MD: Lexington.
Shorley, Christopher. 1985. *Queneau's Fiction*. Cambridge: Cambridge University Press.
Sidney, Philip. 1860. *The Miscellaneous Works of Sir Philip Sidney: With a Life of the Author and Illustrative Notes*. Boston, MA: T. O. H. P. Burnham.
Simolke, Duane. 1999. *Stein, Gender, Isolation, and Industrialism: New Readings of 'Winesburg, Ohio'*. Lincoln: iUniverse.
Simon, Claude. 1986. 'Italo Calvino', *Graph*, 1 (1–5), 17–29.

Simplicius. 2014. *On Aristotle Physics 4.1–5 and 10–14*, trans. J. O. Urmson. London: Bloomsbury.
Slade, Andrew. 2007. *Lyotard, Beckett, Duras, and the Postmodern Sublime*. New York: Peter Lang.
Slote, Sam. 2004 'Apres mot, le deluge' 2: Literary and Theoretical Responses to Joyce in France', in *The Reception of James Joyce in Europe: Germany, Northern and East Central Europe*, Vol. 1. London: A&C Black.
Slote, Sam. 2013. *Joyce's Nietzschean Ethics*. Berlin: Springer.
Smith, Roch C. 2000. *Understanding Alain Robbe-Grillet*. Columbia, IN: University of South Carolina Press.
Stabb, Martin S. 2014. *The Dissenting Voice: The New Essay of Spanish America, 1960–1985*. Austin: University of Texas Press.
Standish, Peter. 2001. *Understanding Julio Cortázar*. Columbia, IN: University of South Carolina Press.
Stein, Gertrude. 1998. *Writings, 1932–1946*. New York: Library of America.
Stein, Gertrude. 2000. *Three Lives*, ed. Linda Wagner-Martin. Basingstoke: Palgrave Macmillan.
Sternlicht, Sanford V. 1998. *A Reader's Guide to Modern Irish Drama*. Syracuse, NY: Syracuse University Press.
Strindberg, August. 1997. *Seven Plays*. Bern: Peter Lang.
Strindberg, August. 2008. *Miss Julie and Other Plays*, trans. Michael Robinson. Oxford: Oxford University Press.
Stump, Jordan. 1998. *Naming and Unnaming*. Lincoln: University of Nebraska Press.
Sturrock, John. 1999. *The Word from Paris: Essays on Modern French Thinkers and Writers*. London: Verso.
Szalczer, Ezter. 2009. 'A Modernist Dramaturgy', in Michael Robinson (ed), *The Cambridge Companion to August Strindberg*. Cambridge: Cambridge University Press.
Szalczer, Ezter. 2011. *August Strindberg*. New York. Routledge.
Szanto, George H. 2014. *Narrative Consciousness: Structure and Perception in the Fiction of Kafka, Beckett, and Robbe-Grillet*. Austin: University of Texas Press.
Szegedy-Maszák, Mihály. 1997. 'Nonteleological Narration', in Matei Calinescu (ed), *Exploring Postmodernism. Douwe Wessel Fokkema*. Amsterdam: John Benjamins Publishing.
Tasso, Torquato. 1875. *Le prose diverse. Nuovaemente raccolte ed emendate da Cesare Guasti*, Vol. 1. Florence: Le Monnier.
Taylor, Karen L. 2006. *The Facts on File Companion to the French Novel*. New York: Infobase Publishing.
Todorov, Tzvetan. 1975. *The Fantastic: A Structural Approach to a Literary Genre*. New York: Cornell University Press.
Toker, Leona. 1989. *Nabokov: The Mystery of Literary Structures*. New York: Cornell University Press.

Toribio Vazquez, Juan Luis. 2019. 'On a Circular Road: Queneau, Beckett, Arrabal and Robbe-Grillet', in *W drodze/On the Road – Perspektywy badawcze*. Płock: Wydawnictwo Naukowe Mazowieckiej Uczelni Publicznej w Płocku.
Toribio Vazquez, Juan Luis. 2020. 'Nietzsche's Shadow: On the Origin and Development of the Term Nihilism', in *Philosophy & Social Criticism*. New York: SAGE Journals. https://doi.org/10.1177/0191453720975454.
Valente, Joseph. 1987. 'Beyond Truth and Freedom: The New Faith of Joyce and Nietzsche' *James Joyce Quarterly*, 25(1), Twenty-Fifth Anniversary Issue (Fall), 87–103. University of Tulsa.
Verene, Phillip Donald. 1994. 'Introductions, Vico and Nietzsche', in *The Personalist Forum*, Vols. 10–13. Greenville, SC: Furman University Press.
Vest, Jason P. 2009. *The Postmodern Humanism of Philip K. Dick*. Lanham, MD: Scarecrow Press.
Vesterman, William. 2014. *Dramatizing Time in Twentieth-Century Fiction*. New York: Routledge.
Villanueva, Darío. 1983. *La novela lírica*, 2 vols. Madrid: Taurus.
Watt, Ian. 2001. *The Rise of the Novel*. Berkeley: University of California Press.
Weisberg, David. 2000. *Chronicles of Disorder: Samuel Beckett and the Cultural Politics of the Modern Novel*. New York: SUNY Press.
Weiss, Beno. 1993. *Understanding Italo Calvino*. Columbia, IN: University of South Carolina Press.
Weller, Shane. 2005. *A Taste for the Negative: Beckett and Nihilism*. London: Routledge.
Weller, Shane. 2008. *Literature, Philosophy, Nihilism: The Uncanniest of Guests*. Basingstoke: Palgrave Macmillan.
West, M. L. 2003. *The East Face of Helicon: West Asiatic Elements in Greek Poetry and Myth: West Asiatic Elements in Greek Poetry and Myth*. Oxford: Clarendon Press.
Westerdale, Joel. 2013. *Nietzsche's Aphoristic Challenge*. Berlin: Walter De Gruyter.
White, Hayden. 1999. *The Content of the Form: Narrative Discourse and Historical Representation*. Baltimore, MD: Johns Hopkins University Press.
Williamson, Edwin. 2013. *The Cambridge Companion to Jorge Luis Borges*. Cambridge: Cambridge University Press.
Wishnia, Kenneth J. A. 1999. *Twentieth-Century Ecuadorian Narrative: New Readings in the Context of the Americas*. Danvers, MA: Bucknell University Press.
Wolfreys Julian. 2004. *Critical Keywords in Literary and Cultural Theory*. Basingstoke: Palgrave Macmillan.
Young, Julian. 2010. *Friedrich Nietzsche: A Philosophical Biography*. Cambridge: Cambridge Universtiy Press.
Zúiga, Dulce María. 2006. *El mundo Cortázar*. Guadalajara: Universidad de Guadalajara.

Index

absurdism/Theatre of the Absurd   34, 79, 126, 128–30, 132, 134, 136, 153–7, 159–60, 165, 171, 181, 205, 209
Act without Words II   156, 164
Adamov, Arthur   156, 159–61, 165
All Against All   156, 159, 161, 165
allegory/allegorical   60, 62, 65, 79–81, 126, 144, 151–2, 177, 188, 189, 204
alterity   160, 185 n.1, 188, 192, 201, 204
   the Other   152–3, 189
Altizer, Thomas J. J.   139, 143
America
   Latin America   146, 165, 185, 209
   Mesoamerica   47
   North America   83, 209
   Unites States of America   115
Apollo/Apollonian   41, 180, 187
Arabian Nights   149, 182
Aristotle   1, 14, 16–20, 23–6, 210
Arrabal, Fernando   156, 164
art   1, 15–16, 24, 30–2, 39, 41, 46, 76, 84, 100, 105–6, 115–16, 118, 125–7, 135, 170, 203
avant-garde/avant-gardist   79, 89, 125, 127, 135, 173, 211
Azorín/José Martinez Ruiz   93–101, 125, 209, 212

Babylonia   12 n.1, 47–8, 68
Balzac, Honoré de   169, 173, 186
Barthes, Rolland   4–5, 14–15, 16 n.1, 172–4, 179–80, 182
Beckett, Samuel   38–9, 117 n.1, 135–6, 141–2, 154, 156, 160–4, 166, 172–3, 181, 212
Bergson, Henri   3, 86, 120, 137
Beyond Good and Evil   41, 43, 70–1, 77
bildungsroman   30, 136, 195
bilingualism   146

The Birth of Tragedy   41–3, 45, 138
Blanchot, Maurice   192–201, 212
blind   106, 163, 197
Borges, Jorge Luis   145–53, 165, 181, 185, 191, 212
Brandes, Georg   77
Breton, André   104
Buddhism   41–3, 45, 47–9

Calvino, Italo   104–7, 177–88, 192, 201
Campbell, Joseph   2, 10–11
canon   19, 26, 89
Christianity   1, 6, 21–2, 33, 40–3, 45, 50–1, 57, 60, 73, 77, 138, 188, 205
chronological   1, 7–9, 12–13, 33–4, 73, 87, 95–8, 142, 189, 190, 207, 210
cinema   126, 172, 175
comedy   13–14, 18, 26–7, 106, 158
communism   53, 177
conventions   14, 18, 21, 24, 26–7, 36, 75, 77, 86, 88–9, 93, 103, 106, 111, 126, 135, 140, 154, 169, 178, 186, 205
Cortázar, Julio   185–92, 201, 209, 212
Cosmicomics   178, 180–1
cosmos/cosmic   22, 25, 48, 69, 105, 112, 124, 155, 165, 180
crime   131, 157–8, 174–5
Cuba   154, 165
Cubism   84, 89
culture   3, 5, 22, 38, 45, 54, 77, 105, 135, 138 n.2, 171, 178, 187
currency   10, 27, 31, 40, 169

Dadaism   122, 132 n.1, 167
dance/dancing   66, 80, 82, 124, 131, 145
Dante Alighieri   21, 139, 141
Darwin, Charles   55–6
Deleuze, Gilles   3 n.1, 44, 72 n.1, 128, 149–51, 158

Derrida, Jacques   168, 196–9, 208
Descartes, René   32, 107–8, 160
destabilization   46, 55, 100, 114, 131, 153, 175, 177, 191, 201, 204, 206, 213
didacticism/didactic   1, 5 n.2, 6, 9, 11, 15–16, 18–22, 28–30, 73, 114, 203, 206
discourse/*sjuzhet*/*récit*   8–9, 13–14, 16, 62, 68, 87–9, 92, 96–7, 101, 122–3, 133–4, 165, 171, 176, 183–4, 192, 194, 201, 204, 208, 211–13
displacement   18, 39, 115
domestication   170
Don Quijote de La Mancha/*Don Quixote*   26, 146, 209
drama   14, 20, 21, 25, 38, 78–9, 126, 129–31, 154, 160–1, 163, 209
dreams   64, 77, 97, 113, 131
   dreamer   151–3, 156
dualism/dualistic/duality   20 n.1, 50, 60, 85, 98–9, 106–8
Dublin   137, 143
Dubliners   136, 138
Duckworth, Colin   161, 164 n.1

Egypt/Egyptian   47–8
Eisenstein, Albert   137, 170
ekphrasis   94, 100, 125
Elizabeth Bam   125, 128, 130–1
Empiricism/empirical   6, 32, 74 n.1, 84, 139, 213
Endgame   156, 164
England   115
English (also British, Anglophone)   8, 22, 116, 125, 137, 138 n.1, 141, 146
Enlightenment   53, 55–6, 168, 171, 180, 197
Esslin, Martin   79, 106, 154–6, 158–9
eternal return/eternal recurrence   3–4, 33–5, 39–43, 46–52, 56–73, 92, 95–101, 121, 124, 134, 139, 142–5, 147–50, 153, 156, 158, 165–6, 180–2, 187, 190, 194, 196–8, 204, 211, 213–14
ethics   167, 171
Europe   27, 43, 52–4, 56, 76, 93 n.1, 146, 185, 204

existential/existentialist
   conflict, predicament   79, 90
   conquest   187
   features   104, 160
   nihilism   128 n.1
   teachings   12
   views   33

failure   29–30, 52–3, 79, 88, 90–1, 101, 158, 200–1, 206, 213
field (literary)   75
   (grammatical)   109
   (of vision)   171
film   175, 177
Finnegans Wake   122 n.1, 136–44, 165, 172, 205, 207, 212
Formalism   8, 125, 168, 209, 211
France   22, 24, 26, 53–4, 115, 193
Freud, Sigmund   137

The Gay Science   39–44, 57–8, 61, 65, 72, 138, 144–5
Genette, Gérard   4, 207 n.1, 210–11
German   22, 31, 34, 52–4, 77, 83, 125, 128, 146, 185
Germany   54, 192
God/gods   48–50, 60, 66, 70, 151–2, 156
   'death of God'   34–5, 38, 42–3, 45–6, 55, 57–8, 103, 106, 115, 119, 138 n.1, 140, 143–5, 152, 155, 168, 170, 180, 187, 200, 205, 213–14
Goethe, Johann Wolfgang von   29, 147 n.1
Gorgias of Leonium   15–16
Greece/Greek   6, 12–14, 18–19, 21, 23, 49, 51–2, 57, 148, 187

Hegel, Georg Wilhelm Friedrich   53–6, 72, 104, 120, 159, 180, 194, 196, 199, 208
Hindu/Hinduism   45, 47, 49
history/historical   1–2, 4, 6, 7 n.2, 10, 16, 23, 29, 31–2, 37–9, 41, 45, 51, 53–7, 69, 76, 93 n.1, 97–8, 101, 105, 109, 118, 130, 139–42, 145, 149, 152, 155, 159, 182, 194, 203, 208, 210, 213
Holocaust   3, 170

Homer/*The Odyssey*/*The Iliad*   11 n.2, 12–14, 16–20, 107, 136
Horace   19–21, 26
horror   3, 56, 170
Human, All too Human   39, 41–2, 65

If on a Winter's Night a Traveller   177–81, 184, 201
Ionesco, Eugene   136, 153–4, 156–62, 165, 181
Ireland, Irish   137–8
Italy/Italian   21 n.1, 23, 25, 28, 53–4, 177

Jarry, Alfred   154, 178
journey   1, 12 n.1, 13, 48, 175, 181
joy   60, 69, 70, 170
Joyce, James   84, 107, 110, 112, 122 n.1, 136–45, 149, 151, 165, 212
Judaeo-Christian   1 n.1, 50, 57, 188

Kant, Immanuel   1, 30–1, 35–6, 195, 203
Kharms, Daniil   103, 125–34, 151
knowledge   4 n.1, 6, 7 n.2, 8, 10, 16, 37, 46, 60, 65–7, 105, 109, 115, 120, 158, 172, 194

language   1–2, 8, 11, 17, 19, 21, 31, 35–6, 40, 52, 59–60, 78, 84–91, 94, 100–1, 105–10, 127–8, 132–4, 136, 140, 143–4, 147, 152, 157–8, 160, 165, 173, 179–80, 188, 193–4, 200–1, 204–5
Latin   5, 21 n.1, 23, 146
Latin America   146, 165, 185, 209
linearity/linear   1–2, 4, 6, 8–15, 17–20, 22, 24–35, 38, 40, 47–51, 56–7, 59, 73–6, 78–9, 86–94, 96–101, 104, 110, 114, 120, 123, 131, 134–6, 139, 150, 158, 161, 163–5, 172–5, 179, 184, 188–92, 196, 199–201, 203–13
logos   6, 8–9, 16, 20–1, 180

mechanical/mechanism/mechanistic   44, 57, 119, 152, 174, 213
medieval   21–6, 28, 78–9, 129
metaphor/metaphorical   15, 25, 58, 78–9, 111, 124, 141 n.1, 181, 213
metaphysics/metaphysical   2, 35–6, 42, 44, 55, 57, 72 n.1, 146–7, 155, 167, 169–71, 181, 185, 188, 213

mimesis   1, 8, 17–18, 20, 26, 30 n.1, 78, 94, 126–7, 205, 210
mind   85, 119, 120, 122, 125, 208
modernism/modernist   8, 32–3, 76, 79, 84–6, 89, 92, 121, 135–7, 152, 167, 182
monomyth   2, 10–11
morality/moral   1, 11, 15, 18–19, 25, 28, 36, 40–3, 45, 54–5, 72, 77, 79, 87, 90, 95, 115, 147, 160, 167, 172
music/musical   14 n.2, 57–8, 80–1, 126–7
The Myth of Sisyphus   155–6, 160, 166, 204
mythos/myth/mythical/mythology   6, 8–11, 14 n.2, 16, 20, 47, 49, 51, 95, 97, 114, 121, 156, 161, 187, 203

Nabokov, Vladimir   115–25, 134, 209, 212
narratology   7–8, 21, 209–10
national/nationalism/nationality   22, 53–4, 56, 121, 138, 192
naturalism   2, 74 n.1, 75–9, 81, 88, 89, 103 n.1, 115, 136
Nazism   3, 71 n.2, 147, 192
Nietzsche, Friedrich   2–4, 8–9, 25, 32–47, 49–52, 54–73, 77–8, 81, 83–6, 92, 95, 98, 100, 104–5, 107–8, 115, 119–21, 125, 127–8, 137–40, 142–51, 153, 155–6, 158, 163, 165, 167, 169–71, 180–1, 187–8, 190, 193–4, 196–7, 199, 203–5, 208–9, 211, 213
nihilism   2–4, 33–5, 40–7, 51–2, 55, 68–9, 71 n.2, 72–3, 103, 128, 143, 155–6, 194, 206, 214
novel   28–31, 34, 38, 55, 67, 76, 93–100, 106–16, 121–2, 138–41, 189–90, 195–6, 201, 207–9
   antinovel   106
   new novel/*nouveau roman*   104, 168–73, 177, 183–4, 187

On the Genealogy of Morals   41–2, 77

pain   60, 67, 69
painting/painter   30, 84, 89, 91, 97, 100, 138

Index

Paris/Parisian 83–4, 86, 104, 108, 138, 153–4, 185, 190, 193
philology 35, 158
philosophy/philosopher/philosophical 2–3, 16, 19, 24, 30–6, 39, 41, 43–6, 51–2, 55–7, 59, 61, 71–2, 77–8, 83–4, 86, 89–90, 95, 101, 104–7, 109, 114–15, 118, 128, 138, 144, 146–9, 155–6, 160, 168, 170–1, 178–80, 185, 187–8, 192–5
Pinter, Harold 156, 164
Plato/Platonic/Platonism 8–9, 15–16, 19–21, 26, 43–5, 55, 64, 71, 73, 81, 107 n.1, 109, 128, 146–7, 149, 188, 193, 199, 203, 205
plot 8–9, 12–13, 17–18, 20–2, 27, 30, 32, 64, 73, 74 n.1, 78–83, 87, 89, 91, 94–6, 101, 106, 112, 114, 116–18, 125–7, 129–31, 133–4, 136, 140–1, 143–4, 150, 157, 159–65, 169, 171–3, 175–9, 181–2, 184, 190, 194, 199, 201, 204–6, 209, 211
poetry/poet/poetic 1 n.2, 3, 13–27, 31, 43, 47, 58–9, 61–2, 79, 96, 104, 111, 113–14, 125–6, 128, 130, 139, 148, 163, 168, 181, 187–8, 203
politics/political 3, 32, 53–7, 76, 106, 130, 138, 147, 159, 160, 167, 172, 177, 187–8, 204
postmodern/postmodernism 5, 7 n.2, 135–6, 167, 180, 182
prose 14–15, 17, 22, 27, 29, 31, 93, 95, 128–9, 132, 136, 140, 148, 150, 165, 209
Proust, Marcel 120, 207–9

Queneau, Raymond 103–15, 122, 134, 169 n.1, 176, 178, 180 n.1, 212

reading 3, 21, 34–5, 51, 61, 84, 104, 115, 118, 122–3, 141, 145, 147, 151, 165, 168, 170, 177–9, 181–5, 189, 191–2, 197, 201, 205–6, 211
realism 29, 31–2, 55, 75–81, 83, 88–90, 139–40, 154, 156, 169, 171 n.1, 172, 177–9, 185, 188, 195
reason 6, 42, 44, 55–6, 65, 85 n.1, 108, 131, 158, 181, 188, 195
reception 75, 154, 169

religion 37–8, 45–51, 54–5, 70, 73, 79, 142
representation/representational 16, 30 n.1, 36, 50, 75, 77, 86, 124, 127, 147–8, 152–4, 157, 159, 161, 168, 171, 192, 199, 211, 213
revolution 3, 53–4, 56, 115, 140
rhetoric/rhetorical 1 n.2, 14–17, 19–21, 31, 36, 139
river 143–4
Robbe-Grillet, Alain 94, 167–77, 179, 186–7, 201
romanticism 1, 20, 27, 29–32, 128, 139, 203
Rome/Roman 13, 18–21, 23
Rusia/Russian 3, 8, 56, 115–16, 116 n.1, 121, 128, 209

Schiller, Johann Christoph Friedrich 31, 147 n.2, 203
Scott, Walter 29
setting 25–7, 62–3, 74 n.1, 78–80, 82, 89, 95, 98–9, 112, 116, 131, 140, 151, 155, 163–4, 174–5, 193
Sidney, Philip 25–6
Socrates 15, 16 n.2, 44–5, 61, 65, 72
Spain/Spanish 21 n.1, 22, 56, 94, 146, 157, 185
Spinoza, Baruch 40, 146
Stein, Gertrude 75, 83–93, 96, 101, 109, 139, 212
story/*sjuzhet* 1, 5 n.2, 6–13, 21, 23–4, 29, 81–2, 87–9, 91–2, 94–8, 101, 111–14, 117, 120–5, 129–34, 149–53, 156–7, 165, 169, 172, 174–5, 177, 179, 181–5, 188–92, 195, 198–201, 204–5, 211–13
Strindberg, August 75–83, 85, 87, 101, 139, 154, 157, 162
structuralism/structuralist 4, 168, 179, 191
  poststructuralism 4, 9
Surrealism 104, 109, 135, 167
synchrony/synchronic 94, 100

teleology 1–2, 8–9, 11, 14, 16–17, 20, 25–6, 32–40, 46, 51, 73, 74 n.1, 75, 79, 86, 93 n.1, 101, 110–11, 114, 129, 136, 139, 144, 157, 161, 163, 172, 174, 199–201, 203, 205–9, 211, 213–14

theatre   76, 78–9, 126–7, 129–30, 136, 153–4, 156, 161, 164–5
Théâtre de Babylone   154
Thus Spoke Zarathustra   2 n.2, 40, 42 n.1, 43, 47, 61–70, 72, 138, 147, 149, 151, 169–70, 193, 198
time   1, 3 n.1, 7, 13, 16 n.3, 25–7, 36–7, 40, 43, 45–52, 59, 63–4, 69, 73, 87, 91–2, 94–5, 97–101, 107, 112–13, 119–22, 124, 137, 142, 147–8, 158–9, 163–4, 173–4, 180–1, 190, 194, 197, 204, 207–9
  circular time   47–52, 56, 63–4, 93, 149–50, 161, 196
totalitarianism   3, 158–9, 168
tradition/traditional   1, 5, 8, 9, 16, 21, 24, 26–8, 45, 47–50, 55–6, 77, 79, 93, 106, 117–18, 126, 129–30, 137, 139–40, 163–4, 167, 169, 172–3, 177–8, 181, 186–8, 193, 205–6, 211
translation/translator   11, 23, 59, 83 n.1, 107, 113, 116 n.1, 128, 138, 147, 180 n.1
travel   62, 177–84
truth   2, 6, 8, 15–16, 18, 21, 30, 32, 35–6, 38, 44–5, 55, 63, 74 n.1, 77, 105, 108, 115, 119, 128, 147, 167, 171 n.1, 193, 203, 206, 213

Ulysses   107, 136–40, 141 n.1
unity   13, 17–19, 21–7, 38, 45, 98–9, 155, 190, 207–9

universal   32, 49, 96, 105, 149
Untimely Meditations   37, 39, 41–2, 52, 57

Vico, Giambattista   51, 141–3, 145, 149
violence   3, 85, 93, 101, 158–9, 165, 195, 204

waiting   151, 160–2
Waiting for Godot   117 n.1, 136, 154, 156, 160–6, 205
Weller, Shane   41, 43, 45–6, 163 n.2
west/western   1 n.1, 2, 4, 10, 43, 53, 55, 57, 188, 206, 213
The Will to Power   2 n.2, 52, 71
will to power (concept)   32, 46, 159, 203
World War
  First World War   3, 56, 135
  Second World War   3, 56, 71 n.2, 135, 154, 167, 192, 200, 205
Worstward Ho   212
writing   9, 15, 21 n.1, 28–9, 58, 76–7, 89, 93–5, 100, 106, 109–10, 116, 118, 120, 122, 125, 128–9, 139–41, 145, 165, 168–9, 171–2, 175, 177, 179, 182, 186–7, 192–4, 196, 200, 205, 213
  academic writing   14
  fragmentary writing   196, 198
  re-writing   107

Zeitgeist   27, 84
Zoroastranism   51, 57

www.ingramcontent.com/pod-product-compliance
Lightning Source LLC
Chambersburg PA
CBHW062148300426
44115CB00012BA/2050